Academic Listening

Research perspectives

Edited by

John Flowerdew

City University of Hong Kong

CAMBRIDGE
UNIVERSITY PRESS

Published by the Press Syndicate of the University of Cambridge
The Pitt Building, Trumpington Street, Cambridge CB2 1RP
40 West 20th Street, New York, NY 10011–4211, USA
10 Stamford Road, Oakleigh, Melbourne 3166, Australia

10046926 2 ×

First published 1994
First printing 1994

A catalogue record for this book is available from the British Library.

Library of Congress cataloging in publication data applied for.

ISBN 0 521 45544 8 hardback
ISBN 0 521 45551 0 paperback

Transferred to digital printing 2004

Contents

Contributors

Desmond Allison, University of Hong Kong
Malcolm J. Benson, Hiroshima Shudo University, Japan
Janice Cook, Kapi'olani Community College, Honolulu
Craig Chaudron, University of Hawaii
James N. Davis, University of Arkansas
Tony Dudley-Evans, University of Birmingham
Patricia A. Dunkel, Georgia State University
Christa Hansen, University of Kansas
Christine Jensen, University of Kansas
Philip King, University of Birmingham
Lester Loschky, Nanzan University, Japan
Tony Lynch, University of Edinburgh
Abelle Mason, Georgetown University
Lynne Young, Carlton University, Canada
Michael Rost, Temple University, Japan
Steve Tauroza, City University of Hong Kong

Series Editors' Preface

English is one of the major languages of tertiary education and academic discourse, both in English-speaking and non-English-speaking countries. It is the language of university lectures as well as the commonest language used in international conferences and seminars worldwide. Comprehension of spoken academic discourse by non-native speakers of English is, therefore, an important issue in the acquisition and dissemination of scholarly knowledge and the promotion of academic exchange.

The nature of listening comprehension in such settings, however, has received relatively little attention among researchers, compared to the large amount of research that has been directed at the nature of written and spoken discourse and second language reading comprehension. The present volume is, therefore, a welcome addition to our understanding of the nature of academic listening in a second or foreign language. It contains a valuable series of original papers which illustrate both research findings in lecture comprehension, and a variety of research approaches which can be used in the study of academic listening. Issues covered include quantitative and qualitative approaches to the investigation of academic listening, processes employed by listeners in understanding academic discourse, the discourse structure of lectures, and the testing and teaching of academic listening skills.

The present book will, therefore, be of great interest to teachers, applied linguists, curriculum and materials developers, researchers, and all those interested in the nature and comprehension of spoken discourse. It provides an invaluable source of theory, research fundings, and pedagogical approaches that can be used both in investigating and teaching academic listening in a second or foreign language.

Michael H. Long
Jack C. Richards

Acknowledgments

I should like to thank the following: Jack Richards, series editor, for his encouragement and support in this project; three anonymous referees, who reviewed the original manuscript and provided invaluable feedback; Eva Cheung Lai Fong, here in Hong Kong, for her patient help with correspondence; Alison Sharpe, at Cambridge, for her moral support; Helena Gomm, for her meticulous work on the manuscript; and, finally, the contributors, for their extreme patience during what has been a much more lengthy gestation period for this book than anyone expected.

I should like to dedicate this book to my family.

Introduction

This book presents a state-of-the-art collection of original research papers in the field of academic listening in a second language. The papers represent a variety of approaches to the empirical study of academic listening and present a wide range of research findings, together with implications and suggestions for pedagogy.

English is now well-established as the language of international academic exchange. It is being increasingly employed as the second language medium of instruction at tertiary level. As such, it is being used in three main contexts. First, it is being used as a second language by students studying overseas in English-speaking countries such as the United States, Canada, Great Britain and Australia. Second, it is being used by students studying in their own countries where for historical reasons English is the second language, for example, Sri Lanka, Malaysia, Singapore, many of the Arab states and the Philippines. Third, and perhaps more unexpectedly, English is also being used as the language of instruction in countries like Japan, Germany and the newly independent Eastern European states, countries where there is no *prima facie* internal need for the language, but where English is being adopted as part of the internationalization of academic studies.

Within the field of academic study, from among the many instructional media at the disposal of teachers – reading assignments, writing assignments, seminars, tutorials, project work, field work, video, various types of self-access learning, etc. – the lecture remains the central instructional activity, achieving what Waggoner (1984, cited in Benson, this volume) refers to as "paradigmatic stature", or what Benson (this volume) calls "the central ritual of the culture of learning".

In spite of the growing importance of academic study in a second language and the important place of lectures within this context, while a number of collections of papers have been published on research into academic reading and academic writing, there has been no collection of papers, to date, on the theme of research into second language academic listening. The purpose of the present collection, in presenting a state-of-the-art set of research findings concerning the comprehension of aural discourse in a second language, is to fill this gap.

1

The book is organized into five main sections, together with a concluding chapter. Each section of the book is preceded by a short introductory overview of the issues addressed by the chapters in the section.

Part I, *Background*, consists of a single chapter which is an overview by the editor of research to date of relevance to the comprehension of lectures in a second language. The purpose of this chapter is to provide a framework within which to situate the research papers presented in the rest of the volume.

The remaining four sections of the book are organized according to the research perspective adopted in that section: psychometric approaches to the investigation of the academic listening process, discourse analysis of lectures, ethnography (i.e., the direct observation and description of the lecture event), and the application of theoretical findings to pedagogic issues.

Part II, *The Second Language Academic Listening Process*, contains four chapters which consider different aspects of how listeners go about processing the information presented to them in a lecture: the relation between discourse structure and comprehension (Tauroza and Allison), the effects of rhetorical signalling devices on comprehension and recall of information (Dunkel and Davis), the effect of note-keeping on lecture recall (Chaudron, Loschky and Cook), and the way comprehension processes can be reflected in listener summaries (Rost).

Part III, *Discourse of Academic Lectures*, consists of three chapters which each examine different features of lecture discourse: discourse topics (Hansen), variation in discourse structure across subject areas (Dudley-Evans), and macro-structure and micro-features (Young).

Part IV, *Ethnography of Second Language Lectures*, presents three chapters which investigate how lecturers and listeners view the L2 academic listening process within the context of the learning process as a whole: Benson employs ethnographic description to investigate various features of L2 academic listening and to place them within the much broader framework of the "culture of learning"; Mason employs interviews with lecturers and students to build up a picture of the problems and strategies which occur in L2 lectures; while King investigates student listening processes and strategies by means of lecture observation and the examination of students' notes.

Part V, *Pedagogic Applications*, has two chapters which relate research findings in L2 academic listening to particular pedagogic situations; the first of these focusses on the testing of academic listening comprehension (Hansen and Jensen) and the second considers the training of content lecturers who lecture to non-native speakers of English (Lynch).

The conclusion draws together the findings of the collection, both in terms of research and of potential pedagogical application. In addition, key areas for future research are highlighted.

This book thus provides a broad range of perspectives on the question of academic listening, starting with analyses of aspects of the cognitive processes which are involved (Part II, *The L2 Academic Listening Process*), moving on to an examination of the object of the comprehension process (Part III, *Discourse of Academic Lectures*), broadening out the concept of listening comprehension to situate it within the wider context of the "culture of learning" (Part IV, *Ethnography of Second Language Lectures*), and relating the theory of L2 listening comprehension to specific pedagogic problems (Part V, *Pedagogic Applications*).

This book will be of interest to teachers of English for Academic Purposes, lecturers in the content areas to non-native speakers of English, researchers in second language comprehension and discourse analysis, and students on post-graduate courses in TESOL.

PART I:
BACKGROUND

Editor's introduction to Part I

The single chapter in this section presents an overview of research to date of relevance to L2 academic lecture comprehension. The first section of the chapter outlines the distinctive features of L2 lecture comprehension as they fit into current models of comprehension in general, and listening comprehension in particular. The next section reviews the research on lecture discourse. The third and final section focusses on modifications which can be made to language with a view to enhancing the lecture comprehension process. The chapter concludes by noting that although there is a not inconsiderable body of research findings of relevance to L2 lecture comprehension, a lot more research is needed before meaningful statements can confidently be made about many areas of pedagogy. While a lot of the research reviewed has not been targeted specifically at L2 lectures, the research base would develop more quickly if a research agenda specifically targeted at L2 lectures were to be drawn up.

1 Research of relevance to second language lecture comprehension – an overview

John Flowerdew

Abstract

This chapter presents an overview of research to date of relevance to L2 lecture comprehension. After a general introduction to the topic, the first main section of the paper considers the lecture comprehension process. Theoretical conceptions of the process are dealt with under three headings: comprehension in general, distinctive features of listening comprehension, and distinctive features of lecture comprehension. The literature on lecture comprehension micro-skills and note-taking is also considered in this first main section. The second main section of the paper deals with the literature on lecture discourse. This work is divided up into a number of areas: lecturing styles, discourse structure, meta-pragmatic signalling, interpersonal features and lexico-grammatical features. The third and final main section of the paper discusses work on lecture input variables. Under this heading are grouped input studies, speech rate research and work on accent.

Introduction

As pointed out in the introduction to this volume, the spread of English as a world language has been accompanied by ever-growing numbers of people studying at university level through the medium of English as a second language, whether in their own country or in English-speaking countries as overseas students. A major part of university study remains the lecture (e.g., Johns 1981; Richards 1983; Benson 1989). Academic listening skills are thus an essential component of communicative competence in a university setting. And yet, although, as Richards (1983) has pointed out, "academic listening" (in contrast to "conversational listening") has its own distinctive features, there has been relatively little research in this specific area.

The purpose of this chapter is to provide an overview of the research which has been done in this area and of related research in other areas which is of relevance to second language lecture comprehension. For reasons of space, a decision has been made not to include the

7

considerable amount of literature on first language lectures, although this is, of course, relevant to those interested in second language lecture comprehension. However, some of this research is reviewed by some of the other contributors to this book (see chapters by Chaudron, Dunkel and Davis, and King, in particular).

The lecture comprehension process

Research into the lecture comprehension process is of value in applied linguistics because an understanding of how lectures are comprehended can suggest appropriate ways to encourage second language learners to listen to lectures. It can thus feed into ESL teaching methodology, on the one hand, and learner strategy training, on the other. In addition, information about the lecture comprehension process can guide content lecturers in how to present their lectures to ensure optimal comprehension.

Comprehension in general

Even though listening comprehension has held an important place in language teaching ever since the days of audio-lingualism, most second language research into comprehension has been concerned with reading (Lund 1991). The same emphasis on reading holds true for research into first language comprehension. However, it has generally been assumed that comprehension is a general construct and that the principles of reading comprehension also apply to listening (Anderson 1983, 1985; O'Malley, Chamot, and Kupper 1989; Lund 1991). The following outline of the comprehension process is, therefore, derived mainly from research into reading (although, of course, references to the phono-logical dimension of comprehension apply solely to listening).

Linguistic theory tells us that there are at least five types of knowledge which will be called upon in the comprehension process as it relates to listening: pragmatic, semantic, syntactic, lexical, and phonological. Psycholinguistic theory (or cognitive science, as this area of enquiry is usually referred to nowadays) posits that these areas of knowledge interact (Anderson 1983, 1985), with the different processes facilitating each other (see Figure 1 in the chapter by Lynch in this volume for a schematic representation of a similar model of the listening process; also Rost, this volume).

To take an example, pragmatic knowledge, in the form of world knowledge and knowledge of the linguistic context up to the point of the utterance being processed, can interact with phonological processing. Thus, at the beginning of a lecture, our knowledge of the schematic structure of this genre allows us to make predictions about what is likely to be said, as the lecture progresses. We can predict, therefore, that the utterance fragment, "Today, I am going to be . . . ", is quite likely to be followed by the phrase "talking about". However, processing at the phonological level is required to confirm whether the predicted continuation of, "Today, I'm going to be . . . " occurs or not.

There has been a tendency on the part of comprehension theorists to see the different processes involved in comprehension as being in a hierarchical relationship. Thus, for a considerable time, scholars conceived of comprehension as a "bottom-up" process, starting with the "lower level" decoding of the language system, and the representation in working memory of this decoding then being interpreted in relation to "higher level" knowledge of context and the world (e.g., Liberman, Cooper, Shankweiler, and Studdert-Kennedy 1967). Later, scholars working with "top-down" models posited the "higher level" pragmatic, inferential processes as the starting point, with linguistic data at the "lower levels" being processed only if required by comprehenders' expectations and goals (e.g., Sperber and Wilson 1986).

However, metaphors of the comprehension process in terms of "top-down" and "bottom-up" processing are perhaps misleading, as it is far from clear what exactly is meant by "higher" and "lower" levels; in what dimension are they higher or lower? Most scholars now accept the view that comprehension involves a variety of processes, all of which interact, but in what way it is not possible to say (e.g., Clark and Clark 1977; Anderson 1983, 1985). This is the consensus adopted by the leading writers of textbooks on L2 listening comprehension (Ur 1984; Anderson and Lynch 1988; Brown 1990; Rost 1990), (see also Rost; Hansen and Jensen; and Lynch, this volume).

Although the empirical validity of distinguishing between higher and lower level skills must be questioned, one conceptualization along these lines which has been adopted by many second language learning theorists (see Buck 1991, 1992 for references) is worthy of note. This conceptualization sees comprehension as a two-stage process, the first stage consisting of purely linguistic processing and the second of application of the results of this linguistic processing to background knowledge and context. This is an important distinction for those concerned with L2 lecture comprehension because those non-native speakers involved in L2 lecture listening are often considered to have already acquired to a considerable degree the skills involved in the first stage of the process, and any training in lecture comprehension they are offered tends to emphasize the "higher level" skills of the second stage.

Finally, in this brief overview of the comprehension process in general, some reference should be made to schema theory. Schemata are posited as the underlying structures which account for the organization of text in memory and which allow for hypotheses to be generated regarding the possible interpretation of texts (Anderson 1983, 1985). They are thus a key element in top-down text processing. Although most work on the role of schemata in comprehension has been done in the field of reading (see, e.g., Carrell, Devine, and Eskey 1988), as Buck (1992) points out, there is every reason to suggest that they play just as important a role in listening (see also Long 1989). A number of papers make reference to schema theory in this collection (e.g., Tauroza and Allison; Young; Hansen and Jensen).

Distinctive features of listening comprehension

Although there is an overall high correlation between reading and listening comprehension abilities, the last decade has shown an increasing awareness that listening in a second language involves a set of skills in its own right (Long 1989). The distinctive features of listening comprehension can be grouped under two main headings (see Rost 1990; Lund 1991; Buck 1991, 1992): real-time processing and phonological and lexico-grammatical features.

Real-time processing

A listening text exists in time rather than space; it is ephemeral and must be perceived as it is uttered. Although there is redundancy in spoken, as there is in written, text (often more, indeed), and listeners' understanding (or lack of understanding) of a segment of text may be revised in the light of new material (Brown and Yule 1983; Buck 1991, 1992), listeners do not have the same degree of control over the text as do readers, who can dwell on parts of the text, skip over other parts, backtrack, etc. (Rost 1990; Buck 1991, 1992).

Phonological and lexico-grammatical features

Problems are posed by the sound system: cognates in print may differ phonetically in ways which are hard to perceive aurally; the listener must recognize unit boundaries phonologically which would be marked visually in a written text; she or he must also recognize irregular pausing, false starts, hesitations, stress and intonation patterns. As Brown (1990) points out, these features present particular challenges to those non-native speakers who have learned English in an idealized, perhaps written, form and have thus not been exposed to the characteristics of rapid colloquial speech. In addition to these phonological features, spoken text has its own particular lexico-grammatical features which require the application of particular sets of knowledge on the part of listeners (Biber 1988).

Distinctive features of lecture comprehension

Just as listening comprehension has its own distinctive features, with regard to reading, so lecture comprehension has its own distinctive features, with regard to listening in general. Richards (1983) was the first to distinguish between listening skills required for conversation and skills required for academic listening. Some of the differences between conversational listening and academic listening are differences in degree, whilst others are differences in kind.

One difference that is a matter of degree is the type of background knowledge required. In a lecture, listeners are likely to require a knowledge of the specialist subject matter, while in conversation, necessary background knowledge will be more general. Another difference in degree is the ability to distinguish between what is relevant and what is not relevant. While in all comprehension there is a need to be able to understand what is relevant (Grice 1975; Sperber and Wilson 1986), the ability to distinguish between what is relevant to the main purpose and what is less relevant (digressions, asides, jokes, etc.) is paramount in lectures, though perhaps less important in conversation. A third difference of degree between academic and conversational listening is in the application of the turn-taking conventions. In conversation, turn-taking is obviously essential, while in lectures turn-taking conventions will only be required if questions are allowed from the audience or come from the lecturer. A fourth difference of degree between academic and conversational listening is in the amount of implied meaning or indirect speech acts. The emphasis in lectures is generally assumed to be on the information to be conveyed, on propositional meaning, while in conversation interpersonal, or illocutionary meaning is more important (Brown and Yule 1983). (Although see below under the heading "interpersonal meaning" for a different perspective on this question.)

Turning now to differences that are a matter of kind, a number of particular skills are associated with lectures. The first of these is the requirement to be able to concentrate on and understand long stretches of talk without the opportunity of engaging in the facilitating functions of interactive discourse, such as asking for repetition, negotiating meaning, using repair strategies, etc. A second difference of kind is note-taking. James (1977) sees lecture comprehension as a five-stage process which culminates in the note-taking process: decode, comprehend, identify main points, decide when to record these, write quickly and clearly. Chaudron, Hansen, and King (this volume) also emphasize the importance of note-taking in the lecture comprehension process. Another skill related to the lecture comprehension process and not found in conversation is the ability to integrate the incoming message with information derived from other media. These other media may take the form of handouts given out at the start of the lecture, the textbook which forms the basic reading for the course, or visually displayed materials presented on a blackboard, overhead projector or by some other means.

Lecture comprehension micro-skills

A number of researchers into L2 lecture comprehension have investigated the specific skills, or micro-skills, which are necessary for or facilitate effective comprehension. Although the extent to which micro-skills can be empirically identified and separated is controversial, the micro-skills approach has been influential in the field of second language curriculum development (e.g., Munby 1978; Weir 1990). Micro-skills categories have been derived from three sources: information from comprehension theory, information from lecturers and information from students.

Information from comprehension theory

Starting from what is known about the listening process, a number of writers on L2 comprehension have extrapolated sets of micro-skills which they assume to be necessary for the comprehension of lectures in a second language. The first such list is incorporated in Munby's well-known micro-skills taxonomy, designed as a tool in overall needs analysis and course design (Munby 1978). Richards (1983) contains the first taxonomy for listening *per se* and also the first for academic listening, as opposed to conversational listening. Richards's list of 18 skills for lecture comprehension includes the following:

– ability to identify purpose and scope of lecture
– ability to identify topic of lecture and follow topic development
– ability to recognize role of discourse markers of signaling structure of lecture
– ability to recognize key lexical items related to subject/topic
– ability to deduce meanings of words from context
– ability to recognize function of intonation to signal information structure (e.g., pitch, volume, pace, key)

Weir (1990) makes use of a similar list of micro-skills to that of Munby and Richards in devising a model for L2 testing

Information from lecturers

Powers (1986) surveyed 144 faculty members in the United States, to find out their views on the relative importance of 21 lecture-related micro-skills, as they relate to academic performance. Nine skills were rated as most important:

- identifying major themes or ideas
- identifying relationships among major ideas
- identifying the topic of a lecture
- retaining information through note-taking
- retrieving information from notes
- inferring relationships between information
- comprehending key vocabulary
- following the spoken mode of lectures
- identifying supporting ideas and examples.

Of course, as Powers points out, such a rating has two major inherent limitations: faculty members who are not involved in language instruction may not be competent to analyze listening activities of non-native students, and faculty perceptions are only one of many sources of information (students and ESL instructors being two obvious others) that must be considered in assessing necessary listening skills.

Information from learners

Another source of information on skills necessary for lecture comprehension is the non-native listeners themselves. Flowerdew and Miller (1992) conducted a study in which they administered questionnaires, supervised diary studies and conducted interviews to find out the problems and strategies of a group of first year Hong Kong Chinese undergraduates attending a lecture course in ESL methods. Problems encountered by the students were speed of delivery, excessive load of new terminology and concepts, and difficulties in concentrating. Strategies used to help comprehension were pre- and post-reading of the set text, peer help, lecturer/tutor help, highlighting relevant sections of the set text during the lecture, note-taking, and efforts to concentrate harder.

Benson (1989) used an ethnographic approach to investigate in depth the listening activities of one overseas student at a university in the United States. He found that his subject, "rather than being preoccupied with the acquisition of new facts, was engaged in a variety of processes relating both to the material and to the teacher" (p. 421) and that "[t]hese processes involved the reduction of incoming linguistic data, the making of new connections within already familiar concepts, and an identification with the teacher's viewpoints." (p. 421)

Note-taking

Note-taking was referred to above as an important micro-skill in the lecture listening comprehension process, although it is worth pointing out that the extent to which note-taking is employed may depend on the amount of support material available to students in the form of hand-outs, or students' use of highlighting techniques on their set texts. Flowerdew and Miller (1992), for example, found the students they observed in a series of lectures which used a set text relied heavily on marking the text, rather than taking notes.

Rost (1990) provides a chart of types of notes classified into "topic-relation notes" (e.g., writing down a word or phrase, copying, translating, diagramming), "concept-ordering notes" (e.g., listing topics in order, labelling notes as main points, indenting), "focussing notes" (e.g., highlighting, parenthesizing), and "revising notes" (e.g., inserting, deleting). King (this volume) investigates the relationship between students' notes and the structure of the lectures on which they were based, noting the importance of incorporating visual information from the lecture into the notes.

A number of researchers have studied students' notes as a means of gaining insights into the comprehension process itself (Dunkel 1988; Chaudron, Loschky, and Cook, this volume). As Rost (1990) points out (supported by Chaudron, Loschky, and Cook, this volume), however, there is no direct correlation between quantity or quality of notes and level of understanding. The literature on note-taking is reviewed much more extensively in the chapters in this book by King and by Chaudron, Loschky, and Cook.

Lecture discourse

If research into the lecture comprehension process can provide infor-mation of relevance to the *how* of teaching and learning in relation to lectures and can thus feed into teaching and learning methodology, research into lecture discourse can provide information of relevance to the *what* of teaching and learning, i.e., it can indicate to teachers and course designers what linguistic and discoursal features learners need to be familiar with in order to understand a lecture and what, therefore, should be incorporated into ESL courses. In addition, a knowledge of the linguistic/discoursal structure of lectures will be of value to content lecturers in potentially enabling them to structure their own lectures in an optimally effective way.

Lecturing styles

A number of different styles have been identified for delivering lectures. Morrison (1974, reported in Jordan 1989: 153) divided science lectures into two kinds: formal ("close to spoken prose") and informal ("high informational content, but not necessarily in highly formal register").

Dudley-Evans and Johns (1981) (also Dudley-Evans, this volume) distinguish three styles of lecturing: "reading style", where the speaker reads or speaks as if reading from notes; "conversational style", where the speaker speaks informally, with or without notes; and "rhetorical style", where the speaker presents herself or himself as a "performer", using a wide intonational range and making frequent digressions, marked by shifts of key and tempo. Goffman (1981) recognizes three modes of lecture: "memorization", "aloud reading" and "fresh talk". In keeping with modern trends in teaching and a greater encouragement of student participation, Frederick (1986, cited in Benson 1989) refers also to the "participatory lecture", which is closer to discussion. In their contributions to this volume, both Benson and Mason detect a move towards the more interactive style of lecturing.

Extrapolating from these various approaches, the key parameters in characterizing lecture styles would seem to be whether the lecture is processed by the speaker in real time or is read and whether it allows for any spoken interaction with the audience or is pure monologue. Although there is no published survey of the relative frequency of types of lecture style, the general consensus is that the informal, conversational style, based on notes or handouts, is probably the predominant mode of lecture presentation, to both native and non-native-speaker audiences (McDonough 1978; DeCarrico and Nattinger 1988; Dudley-Evans, personal communication; a number of contributors to this volume). Concerning levels of interactivity in lectures, Hansen and Jensen (this volume), based on a survey of introductory lecture classes in their university in the United States, found the level of interactivity to vary according to class size: the larger the groups, the less the interaction.

The move towards greater informality in lectures, at least in the United States, it is worth pointing out, could cause problems for non-native speakers from backgrounds where lecturing is carried out on more traditional lines. These problems might be of a cultural nature, relating to the role and status of university lecturers and the degree of deference accorded to them; or they might be related to content, interactive lecturers blurring the more clear-cut structure of the traditional lecture monologue.

Discourse structure

Surprisingly little work has been done on analyzing the discourse structure of academic lectures, when compared with other academic genres such as the research article (Swales 1990). Much of the research that has been done was carried out in the 1970s (e.g., Cook 1975; Montgomery 1977; Murphy and Candlin 1979; Coulthard and

Montgomery 1981) and is developed out of the Sinclair and Coulthard (1975) model of primary school classroom discourse.

Murphy and Candlin note the similarity between lectures and the sort of settings Sinclair and Coulthard had in mind for their analysis of classroom discourse:

... fairly formal situations [where] one participant has the floor whenever he wants it (Coulthard 1975, cited in Murphy and Candlin 1979: 13).

Although lectures are basically monologue, unlike school lessons, which are dialogue, Murphy and Candlin (1979) are able to provide a range of examples to show how a number of the interactive acts from the Sinclair and Coulthard model occur also in lectures:

marker:	*Well.* Obviously . . .
	Right. Everybody . . .
	Now. Let me . . .
starter:	Well now. *Let's get on with the engineering.*
informative:	for the three forces to be in equilibrium their vectors must form a closed triangle
aside:	running out of blackboard here
metastatement:	let me sound reveille, *I want to mention two types of generator.*
conclusion:	So there you've got three forces which are in equilibrium.

Another feature in common with classroom discourse is the rank scale of discourse units. Cook (1975), for example, adapted Sinclair and Coulthard's rank scale for primary classroom discourse of Lesson, Transaction, Exchange, Move, and Act to propose for lectures the following ranks: Lecture, Exposition, Episode, Move and Act. Starting at the top of the hierarchy, each level is made up of elements at the rank below. Thus a "lecture" is made up of various classes of "exposition", an "exposition" is made up of different classes of "episode", etc. However, Cook is only able to describe the boundaries of these units and is unable to say much about their internal structure (there is the same problem in Sinclair and Coulthard 1975).

Coulthard and Montgomery (1981), in their application of the Sinclair and Coulthard model to lectures, offer a framework consisting of just four ranks – Lecture, Transaction, Sequence, Member – where Transaction is characterized by its focussing boundaries, Sequence by phonological means (the use of high pitch), and Member syntactically (it consists of a free clause). Coulthard and Montgomery distinguish two types of Member: those Members whose activity functions on a "main discourse" (informative) level and those which function on a "subsidiary discourse" (metapragmatic) level.

An inability to recognize macro-structure is seen by a number of applied linguists as an important problem of non-native speakers in understanding lectures (Wijasuriya 1971; Lebauer 1984; Chaudron and Richards 1986, Tauroza and Allison, this volume; Young, this volume). In a study of comprehension of engineering lectures by non-native speakers, Olsen and Huckin (1990) claim that although students may understand all the words of a lecture, they may still fail to understand the main points and logical argument. This lack of understanding Olsen and Huckin attribute to a failure to employ knowledge of the overall discourse structure (as well as background knowledge). Similar conclusions are drawn from a follow-up study, reported in this volume by Tauroza and Allison.

Dudley-Evans (this volume) is in broad agreement that a knowledge of macro-structure is likely to aid comprehension. However, he notes that, based on contrasts between Olsen and Huckin's findings for engineering lectures and his own for plant biology and highway engineering, frameworks will vary according to discipline. This variation across disciplines is also pointed to by Strodt-Lopez (1991), who found that her corpus of humanities and social science lectures did not exhibit the hierarchical structuring identified by Olsen and Huckin for engineering:

> The work on discourse structures and interpretive frames suggests that a professor should adhere to a conventional lecture structure, thereby maintaining topicality and evoking in students at least a partially pre-existing frame to reinforce the intended interpretation. This is not, however, what professors do. Rather, they develop topics from many angles and evoke numerous interpretive frames. (Strodt-Lopez 1991: 118)

This view of macro-structure outlined by Strodt-Lopez accords with the rather different approach to lecture discourse of Young (this volume), based on the analytical unit of the strand, or "phase". Young identifies six phases, which reoccur in a discontinuous manner, interspersed with each other in any lecture. What is interesting about this approach is that it allows different types of lecture to be analyzed using the same system of analysis. Thus certain phases might be more prominent in engineering lectures, say, while other phases would be more prominent in, say, humanities lectures.

Metapragmatic signalling

Reference was made in the previous section to Coulthard and Montgomery's distinction between the "main discourse", or informative level, and the "subsidiary discourse", or metapragmatic level in lectures. The importance of metapragmatic signalling devices in facilitating comprehension has been recognized by a number of researchers (Chaudron and Richards 1986; DeCarrico and Nattinger 1988; Rounds

1987; Tyler, Jefferies, and Davies 1988) and writers of ESL texts (Dunkel and Pialorsi 1982; Mason 1983; Ruetten 1986). Coulthard and Montgomery (1981) make the interesting speculation that what makes "reading style" lectures difficult to follow is the very lack of such devices.

DeCarrico and Nattinger (1988) analyzed "macro-organizers" occurring in lectures from a variety of disciplines. They set up eight main categories of "lexical phrase", as they refer to these devices, according to their various functions (e.g., "lemme start with . . . " (topic marker), "so let's turn to . . . " (topic shifter), "to tie this up . . . " (summarizer). The assumption is that these markers will aid comprehension. Empirical testing of the hypothesis that metapragmatic signals aid comprehension is reviewed later in this chapter in the section on lecture input variables.

Interpersonal features

Increasingly, researchers are becoming aware that a lecture is not merely a medium for conveying information, but also for relating to the audience and conveying attitudes and opinions. A number of studies have alerted applied linguists to this dimension of lectures. In a series of papers analyzing definitions in science lectures, Flowerdew (1991, 1992a, 1992b) showed how definitions, which might be thought of as an informative speech act *par excellence*, are hedged with all sorts of pragmatic features to do with how the speaker relates to the audience, how the definitions fit into the overall discourse, the attitude of the speaker to the definition, the amount of emphasis to be put on the definition, and so on. Strodt-Lopez (1987, 1991) analyzed two interpersonal features of lectures – anecdotes and asides – showing how both contribute to the global coherence of lectures in conveying speakers' attitudes and opinions.

Working within a broader framework – that of providing non-native-speaker teaching assistants with a characterization of what constitutes communicatively competent teaching discourse – Rounds (1987) has provided a description of a number of interpersonal features of mathematics lectures. Of particular interest in Rounds's analysis is the emphasis put on the ability of competent lecturers to develop "an atmosphere of cooperative interaction and consensus – a sense of working together to achieve a common goal" (p. 666). Rounds calls this "elaboration", as opposed to the mere transmission of information. "Elaborative" features of discourse identified by Rounds include the following:

1 naming processes
2 overtly marking major points, both to evaluate and reinforce student achievement

3 developing cohesion and continuity within and between lectures by
  repetition and "linking talk"
4 explicitly organizing topics and marking topic change
5 stating the scope of the students' responsibility
6 using questions in a timely fashion
7 using persuasive techniques.

To date, unfortunately, little attention has been paid to interpersonal
features such as these, in L2 academic listening texts.

Lexico-grammatical features

Reference was made earlier in this chapter to the distinction between two
phases in listening comprehension – a linguistic decoding phase and an
application of the results of this decoding to background knowledge and
context phase – and the emphasis on the part of some of those concerned
with academic listening on the second of these two phases. However, as
a number of writers who emphasize the importance of the role of lexis
and syntax in listening comprehension suggest, this emphasis on the
second of the two stages needs to be treated with caution. Not only may
linguistic decoding be a problem in itself, especially with more limited
proficiency listeners, but, as McLaughlin (1987, cited in Rost, this
volume) has pointed out, problems in linguistic decoding on the part
of L2 listeners can distract cognitive resources away from the second-
stage processes which native listeners are able to focus on more
fully.

Kelly (1991), based on an empirical study of learners' lexical errors,
or "misperceptions", has argued that lexical ignorance is the main
obstacle to listening comprehension with advanced learners. Rost (this
volume) also singles out lexis as a key problem shared by the subjects
involved in the lecture comprehension experiment he reports. The
students in Flowerdew and Miller's (1992) study, as mentioned earlier,
also reported lexis to be one of their main problems in lecture
comprehension.

Only a few studies have been published on the lexis of academic
lectures. Johns and Dudley-Evans (1980) analyzed the lexis of lectures in
the two very different areas of transportation and plant biology into
three categories: technical, semi-technical and colloquial, identifying the
particular problems encountered by students with each type. In a
computerized analysis of a corpus of biology lectures given to non-native
speakers, Flowerdew (1993) noted the very restricted lexical range of
these lectures, arguing that teaching materials derived from such a
corpus would have a very manageable set of lexis.

Turning now to syntax, lectures, as a type of spoken text, might be
thought to be characterized by those syntactic features which are typical

of spoken, as opposed to written, language (Tannen 1982; Halliday 1985/89; Horowitz and Samuels 1987). However, as Biber (1988) points out, there is no single parameter of linguistic variation that distinguishes spoken and written texts. Instead, there are what he refers to as dimensions, i.e., clusterings of features which work together to fulfil some underlying function within the various spoken and written genres, e.g., formal/informal, restricted/elaborated, contextualized/ decontextualized, involved/detached. On these parameters spoken text will, in general, tend to be informal, restricted, contextualized and involved. However, different types of spoken texts may vary in their characteristics. Thus, lectures, as relatively literate, planned artefacts, are likely to share many of the features of written texts, although the extent to which they manifest this trait will again be subject to variation. A read lecture, for example, is likely to be more formal, elaborated, decontextualized and detached than a more spontaneously produced one.

In general, spoken text is characterized by a high incidence of the following linguistic features:

"that" clauses, subordinate cause clauses, subordinate conditional clauses, first person pronouns, second person pronouns, contractions, pronoun "it".

Written text, on the other hand, exhibits a high frequency of the following items:

nominalizations, prepositions, specific conjuncts, agentless passives, low type/ token ratio. (Biber 1988)

Flowerdew (1992c), in a comparison of two corpora, one made up of a biology lecture course to non-native speakers and the other consisting of the chapters from the textbook upon which the lecture course was based, broadly corroborated these distinctions as they relate specifically to academic lectures and textbooks.

It is clear from the above discussion of lexico-grammatical features of lectures that there is a need for the use of authentic lectures in academic listening teaching materials; scripted texts are obviously likely to present to learners a type of language that is not authentic.

Lecture input variables

There are two possible ways to help non-native speakers understand lectures in a second language. One is to improve their knowledge and skills in the target language until the comprehension process is no longer a problem. The other is somehow to modify the form of the lectures, to vary the input, so as to make them easier to comprehend. Research into the effect of input variables, as well as being of interest to teachers and course designers, who can make use of such modified input in developing teaching materials, can also be of value to content lecturers, who can incorporate these modifications into their own lectures to second language students, with a view to making them more comprehensible (see Lynch [this volume] for a discussion of these issues).

Input studies

Most of the early "input" studies were limited to creating taxonomies and quantifying modifications made by speakers to non-natives (see Chaudron 1988 for review). They did not attempt to measure any effects these modifications might have on comprehension. In addition, most of the input studies were based on informal interaction, not lectures. One tendency noted within this research, however, is that interactive aspects of modification (repair, negotiation of meaning, confirmation checks, back-channel cues, etc.) tend to be effective in increasing communication. It is thus possible that lectures of a more interactive nature, encouraging more audience participation, will be more easily comprehended by non-native speakers (although see Lynch [this volume] and earlier comments in this chapter, regarding potential drawbacks of interactive lecturing). In an unpublished study, Griffiths (personal communication) lent support to the hypothesis that more interactive lecturing might be beneficial. Using groups of Omani students as subjects, Griffiths presented a lecture in an interactive conversational style and in a non-interactive reading style. Subjects scored higher on both objective comprehension tests and a subjective self-rating instrument for the interactive style.

Another lecture-oriented input study, and one often quoted, investigated the effect on comprehension of pragmatic signalling devices, or discourse markers (Chaudron and Richards 1986). Chaudron and Richards (1986) presented subjects with the same lecture with and without discourse markers. On testing subjects after listening, they found that "macro-markers" (higher-order markers marking major transitions) had a greater effect on recall than did "micro-markers" (lower-order markers linking clauses and sentences). See also Dunkel and Davis (this volume), for contrasting findings on a similar experiment.

There are very few experimental studies such as those of Griffiths (personal communication) or Chaudron and Richards (1986), however. Much more empirical work of this type is needed on the effect of modifications to lecture input before meaningful recommendations can be made to ESL course designers and content lecturers.

Speech rate

One exception to the above statement concerning the paucity of experimental studies in lecture comprehension research is in the area of speech rate. Speech rate is an important area for lecture comprehension research. In the research already referred to into the lecture comprehension problems and strategies of mother-tongue Cantonese speakers listening to lectures in English by Flowerdew and Miller (1992), subjects were unanimous in rating speed of delivery as the greatest obstacle to understanding. When questioned why this should be so, subjects referred to the great amount of processing required of the incoming data in a very short space of time. Such evaluations are consistent with Griffiths's (1990: 56) comment that "[a] normal speed of delivery requires a great deal of work in a very restricted time".[1]

Important questions for speech rate studies are as follows:

1. What are the reasons for non-native speakers' difficulty with speed of delivery?
2. Can comprehension be improved by controlling speed of delivery?
3. If so, what are the optimum rates for different levels of learners?
4. Is it possible for lecturers consciously to control their rate of delivery?

1. What are the reasons for non-native speakers' difficulty with speed of delivery?

Based on experiments with time-compressed speech, Conrad (1989) found that native speakers, unable to comprehend fully a set of accelerated sentences, are more able than non-native speakers to get a maximum amount of information from the message by using their knowledge of the language to assign syntax and to predict which words would be content words. Non-native speaker comprehension is more hindered, therefore, than that of natives by a faster speech signal. In an earlier study, Henrichson (1984) showed that contraction and reduction had a much greater effect on the comprehension of non-native speakers, even at advanced levels, than it did on the comprehension of native speakers. This result was attributed to the much greater dependency of non-native speakers on a strategy in which they attempted perfect decoding. The studies by Conrad and Henrichson both show, therefore, that the reliance on decoding is a hindrance to non-native speakers' ability to cope with the incoming speech message, in contrast to the

---

[1] As two anonymous reviewers of this book pointed out, it is possible that speed of delivery is an *effect* of difficulty in comprehension, not a cause, i.e., non-native speakers have problems understanding and, therefore, perceive speech as fast, even though objectively it is not.

native speakers, who are able to apply inferential processing to make up for gaps in decoding. This is a reason also cited more anecdotally by Heaton (1977) and Jordan (1977).

2. Can comprehension be improved by controlling speed of delivery?

Grosjean (1972, reported in Griffiths 1990) found that non-native listeners scored markedly higher on comprehension tests based on texts modified in terms of articulation rate and pause frequency and duration. Likewise Conrad (1989), in her compressed speech experiments, found that non-native speakers scored better on comprehension tests as rates were decreased. Anderson-Hsieh and Koehler (1988) discovered that on passages read by both natives and non-natives, comprehension scores were significantly higher when the passages were read at slower rates. Overall, based on these findings, it would appear that slower rates enhance comprehension.

Griffiths (1990) showed that for lower intermediate listeners, although moderately fast speech rates (220 wpm) resulted in a significant reduction in comprehension, comprehension of slow rates (100 wpm) was not significantly greater than that of average rates (150 wpm). Similar lower comprehension levels for artificially slowed speech were found by Derwing (1990, reported in Brumfit and Mitchell 1991). Thus while comprehension can be enhanced by avoiding faster speech rates, it appears from these findings that there is no benefit to be derived from exaggeratedly slow delivery.

3. What are the optimum rates for different levels of learners?

The Griffiths (1990) study, cited above, suggested an optimum rate of delivery for his lower intermediate learners. As he pointed out, however, more studies are needed to establish optimum rates for different proficiency levels. Upper intermediate or advanced listeners presumably might have coped better with the faster rates in Griffiths's study. On the other hand, given the finding that artificially slow rates are a hindrance rather than a help (Griffiths 1990; Derwing 1990, reported in Brumfit and Mitchell 1991), beginners would have been unlikely to benefit from slower rates. In addition, the effect of text difficulty as a variable on comprehension at various speech rates needs to be investigated (Griffiths's research, for example, was based on simplified texts), as does the effect of different ways of slowing: by means of a machine, by slower articulation on the part of the speaker, by lengthening of pauses, or by insertion of extra pauses. Another factor that needs to be borne in mind in evaluating the research on speech rate is that much of this research is based on read text. For speech rate data to be of real value for research into academic listening, it would obviously be preferable to have data on conversational style lecturing. More research is needed in this area of speech rate studies before recommendations can be made to lecturers or materials developers regarding optimum rates of delivery.

4. Is it possible for lecturers consciously to control their rate of delivery?

Based on a sample of 22 lecturers using a conversational style of lecturing to non-native speakers, Tauroza and Allison (1990) showed a wide range of rates of delivery. In a controlled experiment, Griffiths and Beretta (1991) had six university lecturers give the same lecture to groups of native speakers, low-proficiency non-native speakers and high-proficiency non-native speakers. They found that lecturers made no significant adjustment to their speech rate when lecturing to the different groups. This finding, based, admittedly, on a small number of subjects, suggests that lecturers cannot necessarily be expected to modify their speech rate when lecturing to non-native speakers.[2] The question remains as to whether lecturers *are able to* moderate their speech rate, given training.

Accent

Accent is often singled out as a factor contributing to difficulties for non-native lecture comprehension (Kennedy 1978; Richards 1983; Bilbow 1989). It is true that non-native speakers studying through the medium of English are likely to encounter a range of accents, both native and non-native.

The research into the effect of accent on comprehension is quite clear-cut in supporting the commonsense view that unfamiliar accents cause difficulty in comprehension (Eisenstein and Berkowitz 1981; Smith and Bisazza 1982; Anderson-Hsieh and Koehler 1988). The concept of familiarity extends to the question of the comprehensibility of local vs. standard accents of English, local accents proving to be more comprehensible (Brown 1968; Ekong 1982; Smith and Bisazza 1982).

These findings on accent have clear implications for pedagogy. If non-native speakers have least difficulty with familiar accents, then, other things being equal, those lecturers who are likely to be most easily comprehended will be from the students' own language background. Next most comprehensible are likely to be those lecturers with the accent

---

[2] See Lynch (this volume) for further discussion of the study by Griffiths and Beretta and on the issue of lecturer training.

closest to the model learners have been exposed to in their studies and in society at large (e.g., American English in the United States, Taiwan, the Philippines; British English in the U.K., Hong Kong, Singapore). Where it is not possible to control the background of lecturers lecturing in English, then, where possible, students should be exposed to few lecturers over a longer period rather than many lecturers over a shorter period, so as to allow students to develop familiarity with their accents.

Conclusion

This paper has reviewed a large body of research of relevance to second language lecture studies. Some of the findings of this research are clear-cut, e.g., the research on accent. However, the majority of the work raises more questions than it answers. One thing that is clear from this review is that a lot more research is needed before we have a clear idea of what constitutes a successful second language lecture. A lot more information is needed – in terms of how a lecture is comprehended, in terms of what a lecture is made up of, and in terms of how the variable features of a lecture may be manipulated to ensure optimum comprehension – before meaningful statements can be made about many aspects of lectures which will have concrete effects on pedagogy.

One of the problems with the research base in second language lectures is that many of the studies which have been cited here as forming part of this base are not focussed on lectures *per se* (e.g., they have looked at comprehension in general or spoken discourse in general). Faster progress will, perhaps, be made if a research agenda is created which is specifically targeted at second language lectures. Such is the aim of the present collection, and it is hoped that the rest of the chapters in this book will be found to make at least a start in developing this agenda.

Acknowledgment

I am grateful to Steve Tauroza for his comments on an earlier version of this chapter.

References

Anderson, A., and T. Lynch. 1988. *Listening.* Oxford: Oxford University Press.
Anderson, J. R. 1983. *The Architecture of Cognition.* Cambridge, Mass.: Harvard University Press.
   1985. *Cognitive Psychology and its Implications* (2nd ed.). New York: Freeman.
Anderson-Hsieh, J., and K. Koehler. 1988. The effect of foreign accent and

speaking rate on native speaker comprehension. *Language Learning* 38: 561–613.

Benson, M. J. 1989. The academic listening task: a case study. *TESOL Quarterly* 23 (3): 421–445.

Biber, D. 1988. *Variation across Speech and Writing*. Cambridge: Cambridge University Press.

Bilbow, G. T. 1989. Towards an understanding of overseas students' difficulties in lectures: a phenomenographic approach. *Journal of Further and Higher Education* 13 (2): 85–99.

Brown, G. 1990. *Listening to Spoken English* (2nd ed.). London and New York: Longman.

Brown, G., and G. Yule. 1983. *Discourse Analysis*. New York: Cambridge University Press.

Brown, K. 1968. Intelligibility. In *Language Testing Symposium*, A. Davies (Ed.), 180–191. Oxford: Oxford University Press.

Brumfit, C. J., and R. Mitchell. 1991. Research in applied linguistics of relevance to language teaching. *Language Teaching* 24 (3): 137–142.

Buck, G. 1991. The testing of listening comprehension: an introspective study. *Language Testing* 8 (1): 67–91.

    1992. Listening comprehension: construct validity and trait characteristics. *Language Learning* 42 (3): 313–357.

Carrell, P., J. Devine, and D. Eskey. 1988. (Eds.). *Interactive Approaches to Reading*. Cambridge: Cambridge University Press.

Chaudron, C. 1988. *Second Language Classrooms*. Cambridge: Cambridge University Press.

Chaudron, C., and J. C. Richards. 1986. The effect of discourse markers on the comprehension of lectures. *Applied Linguistics* 7 (2): 113–127.

Clark, H., and E. Clark. 1977. *Psychology and Language*. New York: Harcourt, Brace, Jovanovich.

Conrad, L. 1989. The effects of time-compressed speech on native and EFL listening comprehension. *Studies in Second Language Acquisition* 11: 1–16.

Cook, J. R. S. 1975. A communicative approach to the analysis of extended monologue discourse and its relevance to the development of teaching materials for ESP. Unpublished M.Litt. thesis, University of Edinburgh.

Coulthard, M. 1975. Discourse analysis in English: a short review of the literature. *Language Teaching and Linguistics: Abstracts* 8 (2).

Coulthard, M., and M. Montgomery. 1981. The structure of monologue. In *Studies in Discourse Analysis*, M. Coulthard and M. Montgomery (Eds.), 31–39. London: Routledge and Kegan Paul.

DeCarrico, J., and J. R. Nattinger. 1988. Lexical phrases for the comprehension of academic lectures. *English for Specific Purposes* 7: 91–102.

Dudley-Evans, A., and T. Johns. 1981. A team teaching approach to lecture comprehension for overseas students. In *The Teaching of Listening Comprehension*. ELT Documents Special. London: The British Council.

Dunkel, P. 1988. The content of L1 and L2 students' lecture notes and their relation to test performance. *TESOL Quarterly* 22: 259–82.

Dunkel, P., and F. Pialorsi. 1982. *Advanced Listening Comprehension*. Rowley, Mass.: Newbury House.

Eisenstein, M., and D. Berkowitz. 1981. The effect of phonological variation on adult learner comprehension. *Studies in Second Language Acquisition* 4 (1): 75–80.

Ekong, P. 1982. On the use of an indigenous model for teaching English in Nigeria. *World Language English* 1 (2): 87–92.

Flowerdew, J. 1991. Pragmatic modifications on the "representative speech act" of defining. *Journal of Pragmatics* 15: 253–264.

— 1992a. The language of definitions in science lectures. *Applied Linguistics* 13 (2): 202–221.

— 1992b. Salience in the performance of one speech act: the case of definitions. *Discourse Processes* 15 (2): 165–181.

— 1992c. Contrasts across speech and writing in biology. Paper presented at international conference "Discourse and the Professions", Uppsala, Sweden, August.

— 1993. Concordancing as a tool in course design. *System* 21 (2): 231–244.

Flowerdew, J., and L. Miller. 1992. Student perceptions, problems and strategies in L2 lectures. *RELC Journal* 23 (2): 60–80.

Frederick, P. J. 1986. The lively lecture – 8 variations. *College Teaching* 34 (2): 43–50.

Goffman, E. 1981. The lecture. In *Forms of Talk*, E. Goffman, 162–195. Philadelphia, P.A.: University of Philadelphia Press.

Grice, H. P. 1975. The logic of conversation. In *Syntax and Semantics, Vol. 3: Speech Acts*, P. Cole and J. L. Morgan (eds.), 40–58.

Griffiths, R. 1990. Speech rate and NNS comprehension: a preliminary study in time-benefit analysis. *Language Learning* 40 (3): 311–336.

Griffiths, R., and A. Beretta. 1991. A controlled study of temporal variables in NS–NNS lectures. *RELC Journal* 22 (1): 1–19.

Grosjean, F. 1972. Le rôle joué par trois variables temporelles dans la compréhension orale de l'anglais étudié comme seconde langue et perception de la vitesse de lecteurs et d'auditeurs. Unpublished doctoral dissertation. Université de Paris VII, Paris, France.

Halliday, M. A. K. 1985/89. *Spoken and Written Language*. Oxford: Oxford University Press.

Heaton, J. B. 1977. Keep it short – note-taking for learners of English as a second language. In *English for Specific Purposes*, S. Holden (Ed.), 30–32. London: MEP.

Henrichson, L. 1984. Sandhi-variation: a filter of input for learners of ESL. *Language Learning* 34: 103–126.

Horowitz, R., and S. J. Samuels. 1987. *Comprehending Oral and Written Language*. London: Academic Press.

James, K. 1977. Note-taking in lectures: problems and strategies. In *English for Academic Purposes*, A. P. Cowie and J. B. Heaton (Eds.). Reading: BAAL/SELMOUS.

Johns, A. M. 1981. Necessary English: a faculty survey. *TESOL Quarterly* 15: 51–57.

Johns, T., and A. Dudley-Evans. 1980. An experiment in team-teaching of overseas postgraduate students of transportation and plant biology. *ELT Documents* No. 106: 6–23. London: British Council.

Jordan, R. R. 1977. Study skills and pre-sessional courses. In *English for Specific Purposes*, S. Holden (Ed.). London: Modern English Publications.

1989. English for academic purposes (EAP). *Language Teaching* 22 (3): 151–164.

Kelly, P. 1991. Lexical ignorance: the main obstacle to listening comprehension with advanced foreign language learners. *IRAL* XXIX (2): 135–149.

Kennedy, G. 1978. The testing of listening comprehension. RELC monograph series. Singapore: Singapore University Press.

Lebauer, R. S. 1984. Using lecture transcripts in EAP lecture comprehension courses. *TESOL Quarterly* 18 (1): 41–53.

Liberman, A. M., F. S. Cooper, D. P. Shankweiler, and M. Studdert-Kennedy. 1967. Perception of the speech code. *Psychological Review* 74: 431–461.

Long, D. 1989. Second language listening comprehension: a schema-theoretic perspective. *Modern Language Journal* 73 (1): 32–40.

Lund, R. J. 1991. A comparison of second language listening and reading comprehension. *Modern Language Journal* 75 (2): 196–204.

Mason, A. 1983. *Understanding Academic Lectures.* Englewood Cliffs, N.J.: Prentice Hall.

Montgomery, M. 1977. Some aspects of discourse structure and cohesion in selected science lectures. Unpublished M.A. thesis, University of Birmingham.

Morrison, J. W. 1974. An investigation of problems in listening comprehension encountered by overseas students in the first year of postgraduate studies in science at the University of Newcastle upon Tyne. Unpublished M.Ed. thesis, University of Newcastle upon Tyne.

Munby, J. 1978. *Communicative Syllabus Design.* Cambridge: Cambridge University Press.

Murphy, D. F., and C. N. Candlin. 1979. Engineering lecture discourse and listening comprehension. *Practical Papers in English Language Education* 2: 1–79. Lancaster: University of Lancaster.

McDonough, J. 1978. *Listening to Lectures.* Oxford: Oxford University Press.

Olsen, L. A., and T. N. Huckin. 1990. Point-driven understanding in engineering lecture comprehension. *English for Specific Purposes* 9: 33–47.

O'Malley, J. M., A. U. Chamot, and L. Kupper. 1989. Listening comprehension strategies in second language acquisition. *Applied Linguistics* 10 (4): 418–437.

Powers, D. E. 1986. Academic demands related to listening skills. *Language Testing* 3 (1): 1–38.

Richards, J. C. 1983. Listening comprehension: approach, design, procedure. *TESOL Quarterly* 17 (2): 219–39.

Rost, M. 1990. *Listening in language learning.* London: Longman.

Rounds, P. 1987. Characterizing successful classroom discourse for NNS teaching assistant training. *TESOL Quarterly* 21 (4): 643–671.

Ruetten, M. K. 1986. *Comprehending Academic Lectures.* New York: Macmillan.

Sinclair, J. McH., and M. Coulthard. 1975. *Towards an Analysis of Discourse: the English used by Teachers and Pupils.* Oxford: Oxford University Press.

Smith, L. E., and J. A. Bisazza. 1982. The comprehensibility of three varieties of English for college students in seven countries. *Language Learning* 32 (2): 129–269.

Sperber, D., and D. Wilson. 1986. *Relevance: Communication and Cognition.* Oxford: Blackwell.

Strodt-Lopez, B. 1987. Personal anecdotes in university classes. *Anthropological Linguistics* 29 (2): 194–258.

1991. Tying it all in: asides in university lectures. *Applied Linguistics* 12 (2): 117–140.

Swales, J. 1990. *Genre Analysis: English in Academic and Research Settings.* Cambridge: Cambridge University Press.

Tannen, D. (Ed.). 1982. *Spoken and Written Language: Exploring Orality and Literacy.* Norwood, N.J.: Ablex.

Tauroza, S., and D. Allison. 1990. Speech rates in British English. *Applied Linguistics* 11 (1): 90–105.

Tyler, A. E., A. A. Jefferies, and C. E. Davies. 1988. The effect of discourse structuring devices on listener perceptions of coherence in non-native university teachers' spoken discourse. *World Englishes* 7 (2): 101–110.

Ur, P. 1984. *Teaching Listening Comprehension.* Cambridge: Cambridge University Press.

Weir, C. 1990. *Communicative Language Testing.* London and New York: Prentice Hall.

Wijasuriya, B. S. 1971. The occurrence of discourse-markers and inter-sentence connectives in university lectures and their place in the testing and teaching of listening comprehension in English as a foreign language. M.Ed. thesis, University of Manchester.

PART II:
THE SECOND LANGUAGE ACADEMIC
LISTENING PROCESS

Editor's introduction to Part II

This section of the collection contains four chapters all concerned with different cognitive aspects of academic listening. In the first chapter, Tauroza and Allison report on a study in which subjects had difficulty understanding a lecture when its discourse structure varied from the type of structure with which they were most familiar. The most common discourse pattern in the subjects' field (informatics) is analyzed by the authors as a SITUATION–WHAT TO DO pattern (a variation on the Hoey (1983) PROBLEM–SOLUTION pattern), whereas the lecture the subjects listened to had a more complex PROBLEM–SOLUTION–EVALUATION pattern. It was the EVALUATION section which proved problematic. Although the authors are careful about reading too much into the relation between schemata (a psychological concept) and text structure, their findings nevertheless add support to the idea that schema theory applies as much to lecture comprehension as to other discourse genres, an idea which surprisingly has not been previously investigated empirically. Another feature of the Tauroza and Allison research worthy of mention is the large corpus of informatics lectures which the authors were able to draw on to establish what is a typical and what is a less typical discourse pattern of the lectures their subjects (informatics students) are normally exposed to. Such large corpora allow more generalizable statements to be made about the discourse of lectures than do some of the very small corpora on which previous research has been based.

The second chapter in this section, by Dunkel and Davis, is a report on an experiment which follows up on well-known previously conducted research by Chaudron and Richards (1986) in an L2 context and by Kintsch and Yarbrough (1982) and Hron et al. (1985) for L1. This previous research had shown a positive effect on comprehension of the presence of rhetorical signalling cues (i.e., micro-markers such as "well", "so", "now let's", and macro-markers such as, "Today I am going to be talking about . . . "). However, tests conducted by Dunkel and Davis on L1 and L2 subjects demonstrated no significant difference

31

in comprehension of a lecture when it was presented with and without rhetorical cues.

The reason for the discrepancy between the Dunkel and Davis research and the earlier studies, Dunkel and Davis suggest, might have been due to one of three differences: text type (the rhetorical pattern of their lecture might have been clearer and so signalling clues were less important), a different comprehension measure (Dunkel and Davis used written recall protocols, whereas Chaudron and Richards, for example, used comprehension questions and cloze test) and the fact that students were allowed to refer to notes when writing their protocols (previous studies had not allowed for note-taking). As well as providing a warning for ESL pedagogy not to place too much emphasis on the role of rhetorical signalling cues, at least until further studies are done which demonstrate more conclusively that rhetorical signalling clues do have an effect on comprehension, the wider value of this chapter is in showing how the results of empirical studies can vary significantly when the variables are changed. This points to a general need in the field of applied linguistics for more focussed research and numerous studies on particular issues before results are taken up in pedagogical application.

The third contribution to this section on the lecture comprehension process, by Chaudron, Loschky, and Cook, examines the interesting question of whether notes have a positive effect on lecture comprehension and recall. Although not statistically significant in terms of an overall positive effect, the results of Chaudron, Loschky, and Cook's experiment do suggest that over time notes do have a positive value (the time between listening to the lecture and performing the comprehension and recall test in the study was relatively short), and that *certain information* is retrieved better with the aid of notes (information which is required for answering specific questions, for example). Two important features of notes, if they are to be of value, are that they must be accurate and unambiguous.

The fourth and final chapter of this section, by Rost, describes a means of gaining access to L2 subjects' cognitive processes during academic listening. Summaries produced by L2 subjects on-line (i.e., when a video recording of a lecture is paused as they listen to it) are compared with summaries produced by native speakers. Discrepancies between the summaries of the two groups allow for the identification of L2 comprehension difficulties and of cognitive strategies employed. As well as providing a means of gaining insights into L2 subjects' cognitive processing, Rost suggests that the procedure he outlines can be applied in pedagogical contexts. On the one hand, insights gained from an analysis of student summaries suggest ways in which teachers can equip learners with strategies to overcome some of their processing problems. On the other hand, summaries can be used as a teaching tool, with learners analyzing their own summaries and evaluating them in the light of expert-produced summaries.

One interesting question raised by the four chapters in this section concerns the research methodology adopted. In each study, data on comprehension and recall is elicited by means of psychometric tests, a traditional tool of psychological and educational research. However, while Chaudron, Loschky, and Cook use the well-tried measures of multiple-choice comprehension questions and cloze test, the three other papers all use a more innovative and increasingly popular research tool, the summary protocol (Ericsson and Simon 1984). Worthy of attention are the different ways these protocols are elicited. In the case of Rost, subjects are required to write in English (their L2); in the case of Dunkel and Davis, they write in their L1; Tauroza and Allison elicit spoken, as opposed to written, summaries and allow subjects the choice of using either their L1 or their L2. Future researchers will be interested to consider which of these methods is most appropriate.

References

Chaudron, C., and J. C. Richards. 1986. The effect of discourse markers on the comprehension of lectures. *Applied Linguistics* 7 (2): 113–127.

Ericsson, K. A., and H. A. Simon. 1984. *Protocol Analysis: Verbal Reports as Data.* Cambridge, Mass.: MIT Press.

Hoey, M. 1983. *On the Surface of Discourse.* London: Allen and Unwin.

Hron, A., I. Kurbjuhn, H. Mandl, and W. Schnotz. 1985. Structural inferences in reading and listening. In *Inferences in Text Processing*, G. Rickheit, and H. Strohner (Eds.), 221–245. Amsterdam: North-Holland.

Kintsch, W., and J. C. Yarbrough. 1982. Role of rhetorical structure in text comprehension. *Journal of Educational Psychology* 74 (6): 828–834.

2 Expectation-driven understanding in information systems lecture comprehension[1]

Steve Tauroza and Desmond Allison

Abstract

This study explores the lecture comprehension of a group of first-year electronic engineering undergraduates taking a course on "The Human–Computer Interface" in Hong Kong. Following Olsen and Huckin (1990), we focus on the way that discourse structure relates to the comprehension of a lecturer's main points. Our subjects had relatively few difficulties in identifying most of the main points of a chosen lecture extract, which described how filtering can be used to offset information overload in human information processing. There were, however, frequent misrepresentations and omissions in subjects' summaries of one of the main points concerning a warning that errors might result from overuse or misuse of filtering. These misrepresentations appear to have been prompted by differences between the type of lecture format that the students expected and the actual format of the lecture. We describe the implications of our findings for lecture comprehension and EAP teaching.

Introduction

Olsen and Huckin (1990) conducted an exploratory research study into ESL students' comprehension of engineering lectures. They concluded that some of these students "may understand all the words of a lecture (including lexical connectives and other discourse markers) and yet fail to understand the lecturer's main points or logical argument" (p. 33). As an explanation of such outcomes, they argued that many students only expect to gain *information* from lectures, and thus fail to recognise and appreciate evidence of more complex speaker intentions. Olsen and Huckin (citing reading researchers) went on to posit the existence of contrasting "information-driven" and "point-driven" strategies in

[1] This research was funded by the University and Polytechnic Grants Committee of Hong Kong. We are particularly grateful to Ms. Anna Lee Sui Wan for the diligence she showed in all the translation work involved in this project.

35

lecture comprehension. They characterise students using an information-driven strategy as "simply trying to absorb facts" whereas students using a point-driven strategy are characterised as trying "to see the discourse as having a single overriding main point and a number of subordinate points supporting it" (1990: 41).

Olsen and Huckin noted that the students' behaviour is probably related to "a kind of disciplinary 'cultural' conditioning tied to methods of engineering instruction" (1990: 44). They assumed that science and engineering students were habituated to hearing lectures where a series of situations and facts were described. Furthermore, they suggested that in many lectures "problems" were isolated and presented as well-defined occasions for practice in selecting and applying formulae. Olsen and Huckin argued that this caused the students to have difficulties understanding lectures in which the speaker builds up an argument that reflects the workings of the scientific method; that is, lectures that focus on the resolution of a series of interlinked problems.

Olsen and Huckin's study is particularly interesting for two reasons. Firstly, it qualifies recent claims that lexical ignorance is the main obstacle to listening comprehension with advanced foreign language learners (see Kelly 1991). Secondly, it implies the existence of a problem that is educational as much as linguistic, and that may affect both first and second language users. If such a superordinate problem exists as regards the comprehension of lectures on the part of undergraduates, then it should be a key item on any EAP courses aimed at lecture comprehension. Hence, our decision to conduct a broader follow-up investigation of the area that Olsen and Huckin's study brought into focus.

Weaknesses in Olsen and Huckin's study

Olsen and Huckin's findings have already been cited as evidence of English L2 students' "inability to detect the main points [in a] lecture" (Chiang and Dunkel 1992). However, as Olsen and Huckin acknowledge, theirs was only an exploratory study. As such, while it serves to highlight an area that deserves consideration, it contains a number of weaknesses. For instance, only 14 subjects took part in the study.

Another weakness is that Olsen and Huckin use the term "main point" ambiguously. Initially, they talk of there being three main points in the lecture their subjects listened to (1990: 36). These main points matched the major discourse units within the structure of the lecture as described by Olsen and Huckin. The points and the sections of the discourse structure they relate to are as follows:

1. composite materials were prone to severe cracking (*the problem*);
2. it is necessary to increase the fracture toughness (*the solution*);
3. greater toughness can be achieved by weakening the bond between materials within a composite, leading to a trade off between adhesive and tensile strength (*an elaboration of how the solution operates with particular reference to an apparently paradoxical element*).

However, when discussing their results, Olsen and Huckin (1990: 41) refer to point (3) as the main point to which the other points are subordinate. Thus it is unclear when Olsen and Huckin write of students' failure to grasp the speaker's main points whether they mean all of the main points that they initially described or just point (3). This lack of clarity makes it difficult to interpret the degree to which Olsen and Huckin's results support their claim that the students were using an "information-driven" as opposed to a "point-driven" strategy.[2]

A further weakness concerns the methodology. Olsen and Huckin's subjects were asked to deliver oral summaries of the lecture in English. As the ability to speak in English is to some degree independent from the ability to listen and comprehend English, much of Olsen and Huckin's data is difficult to interpret because it is unclear to what degree the deficiencies in the subjects' summaries may relate to encoding as opposed to decoding abilities (see Rost 1990: 123–124 for a fuller description of this issue). This problem, admittedly, is not wholly eliminated by having subjects report in their L1 as this raises concerns regarding the process of translation. Nevertheless, allowing subjects the option to choose either L1 or L2 allows them access to a greater range of expression than confining them to either their L1 or L2.

The present study was designed to extend and improve on Olsen and Huckin's investigation by:

1. using a larger sample;
2. being consistent in our use of the term "main point" (that is, by using it in a manner analogous to Olsen and Huckin's initial usage);
3. allowing the subjects to report back either in English or in their L1.

In addition, we sampled a more homogenous population of learners than Olsen and Huckin's (our subjects were all first-year undergraduate students following the same course in a tertiary institution in Hong Kong).

---

[2] In addition, we are unconvinced as to the explanatory power of the notions of "information-driven" as opposed to "point-driven" strategies in accounting for students' observed difficulties. We return to this issue in our discussion.

Focus of investigation

We infer from Olsen and Huckin's arguments, and would ourselves anticipate, that ESL students, at least those on engineering courses, are likely to experience problems in dealing with any lecture which develops using the following structure, a fairly elaborate form of PROBLEM–SOLUTION discourse (for which see Hoey 1983: 31ff.):

SITUATION–PROBLEM–SOLUTION–EVALUATION (highlighting the need for another solution to deal with problems linked to the prior solution).

Here, the SITUATION is the context in which a complex PROBLEM or series of problems arises and is discussed. If students are more used to hearing lectures where a series of situations and facts is described, as Olsen and Huckin suggest, they might expect a less elaborate form of discourse structure, still within a general PROBLEM–SOLUTION mode, but more akin to the following:

SITUATION–WHAT TO DO–A DIFFERENT SITUATION–WHAT TO DO – (and so on).

Here, each SITUATION already implies or constitutes its own PROBLEM, but bears no particular relation to the next situation/problem in the series. Each description of (in our terms) WHAT TO DO offers a practical SOLUTION that receives no further EVALUATION.[3]

If students are indeed accustomed to hearing a series of facts and situations in their lectures, so that they expect a series of simple SITUATION–WHAT TO DO structures to predominate, we can certainly expect them to have greater difficulties with an EVALUATION section than with other sections of a more elaborate form of PROBLEM–SOLUTION discourse structure. Spoken summary protocols, used by Olsen and Huckin and in our own study, might then give evidence of such difficulties, either indirectly through the subjects' omission of the EVALUATION section, or more directly by the misrepresentation of information in the EVALUATION section (perhaps by treating it as just a further aspect of a recommended SOLUTION).

---

[3] We found that the terms "Situation" and "What to do" described the discourse structures we regularly encountered in our lecture corpus more aptly than "Problem/Solution". Frequently, the terms "Situation" and "What to do" fitted the data in our corpus of lectures without requiring any recourse to definitions beyond those associated with everyday usage. In contrast, the terms "Problem" and "Solution" could be applied to the structures in our corpus of lectures only by referring to the more extended definitions given to the terms in discourse analysis.

Methodology

An extract from a video-recorded lecture was selected for use in the experiment. The search for this extract was made within a corpus of videotaped lectures on computer science and information systems. Our sample consisted of nine lectures delivered by seven different speakers. Seven of these lectures lasted for two hours and two for one hour, giving a total of 16 lecture hours.[4] The lectures were delivered to first-year undergraduate students as a part of their normal courses at either the University of Hong Kong (HKU) or the City University of Hong Kong (CityU).

Of the 16 lecture hours analysed, we found only one clear instance of a speaker building up an argument. Most of the time was spent by the lecturers describing a situation or problem and then indicating a solution or trying to get the students to suggest a solution. This finding was in line with Olsen and Huckin's assumption that science students will be used to hearing a series of facts and situations described in their lectures. Our research thus suggests that developed argumentation may be relatively unusual in lectures to first-year undergraduates in informatics-related fields. Although the source of the difficulties may not be a common feature in lectures to first-year undergraduates, it could well create serious problems when it does occur if it affects the comprehension of large chunks of discourse. We expand on this issue in the concluding section of this paper.

The example of an argument-style discourse structure was found in a lecture on a course entitled "Fundamentals of Information Systems" for students majoring in Information Systems. The lecturer was a fluent non-native English speaker (L1 Cantonese) who had worked for 15 years in the United Kingdom before returning to Hong Kong.

Discourse structure of the lecture segment

The extract consisted of the first 16 minutes of the lecture. In the first 7 minutes of the extract, the lecturer reviews the topics covered in previous lectures and outlines the area that she will talk about in the current lecture on "Humans as Information Processors" (a topic that, ironically, proves of special interest, given the purposes of this research study). In the remaining 9 minutes of the extract, the lecturer states that humans have a limited capacity to process information, and that this leads to problems with information overload. The lecturer goes on to describe a solution to the problem, how the solution operates and then

---

[4] The sample was drawn from the Hong Kong Corpus of Computer Science and Information Systems Lectures (Tauroza, 1994).

TOPIC: Humans as Information Processors (c. 16 mins.)
INTRODUCTION (7 mins. 30 secs.): Reference to previous lectures; justification of today's topic; models of human information processing; description of the general model.
PROBLEM (1 min. 45 secs.): Limited capacity to process information leads to information overload.
SOLUTION (6 mins.): Filtering of information by way of 1. Frame of reference; 2. Normal decision making; 3. Decision making under stress.
EVALUATION (1 min.): Problem with the solution: Inconsistent but relevant data can be filtered out.

Figure 1   Structure of the first 16 minutes of the lecture

mentions a drawback to the solution. In this section, the lecture provides an exemplar of the Hoey (1983) problem–solution pattern of academic discourse, in that the speaker, having established a situation, highlights a problem, describes a solution and then, in an evaluation section, mentions a problem with the solution. The transcript of this 9-minute section appears in Appendix A; a diagram of the discourse structure is given in Figure 1.

The model in Figure 1 represents a consensus between the authors, following independent summarising and categorising of the lecture, and has also been endorsed by the lecturer herself. While this triple control guards against idiosyncrasy, we should recognise that it cannot preclude other modelling possibilities (possibly on the part of people less influenced than ourselves by the "Birmingham school" of discourse analysis).[5] The discourse structure of a lecture remains a construct, and is not a directly observed fact. This caution offers a reminder that all of us, not only students, are likely to relate textual material to our own expectations.

Subjects

The subjects were 50 first-year undergraduate students of electronic engineering at the CityU. Their level of proficiency was estimated to be in the 500–600 range on TOEFL.[6] They were taking a course on "The

---

[5] We are referring here to the body of literature in discourse analysis produced by academics influenced by the English Language Research Unit of the University of Birmingham, for example, Sinclair and Coulthard 1975; Coulthard 1977; Coulthard and Montgomery 1981; Stubbs 1983.
[6] This estimate is based on correlations between the TOEFL test and the grades awarded in the Hong Kong Certificate Examination in English (Syllabus B) and the Hong Kong Use of English examinations. The correlations are derived from comparability studies conducted by the Hong Kong Examination Authority.

Human–Computer Interface". The subjects were almost at the end of their first year of study when they viewed the lecture.

Procedure

The Principal Lecturer responsible for a course on the Human–Computer Interface (part of the Information Systems course) had previewed the 16-minute section of the tape and had timetabled it as input for his course; the extract offered relevant content as well as a change in mode of presentation (being a recorded lecture by another speaker). The students were taken to a Sony LLC–5510 MkII language laboratory. The lecturer explained that they were holding a lesson in the laboratory in order for them to watch a videotaped lecture on humans as information processors.

The subjects were given a handout. The handout stated that they were going to see a lecture entitled "Humans as Information Processors" and that they should listen and take notes in the same way as they would in a normal lecture. The subjects watched the video in individual booths, each with an individual monitor and Sony HS–95 headphones. The tape was relayed to the booths from an Akai VS–P9EV videocassette recorder. After the relevant section of the video was played (c. 16 minutes), the video was stopped and the subjects were given another handout containing the following instructions:

Imagine that you have met a very good friend who could not attend the lecture you have just seen. Your friend wants to know what was said in the lecture so that he or she can prepare fully for an examination. Imagine the situation and use the language that you would normally use when talking to a friend in this situation. You can give the explanation in Cantonese, English or a mixture of the two languages. Use your notes in the same way as you would in real life.

YOU CAN TAKE AS LONG AS YOU WANT OVER THIS BUT TRY TO BE REALISTIC, THAT IS, DO NOT SAY THINGS THAT YOU WOULD NOT SAY TO YOUR FRIEND IN THIS SITUATION IN REAL LIFE.

The handout also explained how to operate the audiocassette recorder which each booth contained. Both handouts given to the students were in English and Chinese. The immediate-recall summaries were recorded. The summaries were then translated, where necessary, and transcribed. The tapes and transcriptions were reviewed to check whether subjects reported ideas that reflected comprehension of the points shown in Figure 2.

While the development of ideas in the extract broadly follows the sequence shown in Figure 2, a study of the transcript in Appendix A will reveal some degree of backtracking and restatement. Certain idea units, including the "EVALUATION", nonetheless correspond clearly to recognisable sections of the lecture; the term "sections" will continue to be used at times when referring to such instances.

A. SITUATION: Humans have a limited capacity to process information.
B. PROBLEM: Information overload is a problem (performance decreases).
C. SOLUTION: We solve this problem by filtering.
D. HOW SOLUTION OPERATES INTRODUCED: Filtering operates in 3 ways:
   DETAILS OF SOLUTION:
   D1. Frame of reference
   D2. Normal decision-making
   D3. Decision-making under stress
E. EVALUATION (OF SOLUTION): However, there are problems/drawbacks connected to filtering (such as omission, distortion, inferences).

Figure 2   *Main ideas in the "PROBLEM", "SOLUTION" and*
"EVALUATION" sections of the lecture extract

Categorising the responses

Any doubtful responses were reviewed by both authors for a final decision on how they should be classified. Where a subject's response could not easily be classified, it was marked as an unclear response. The following are examples of such responses:

Regarding the SITUATION section:
– *However, humans' memory has limitation, when there is great limitation, the performance will decrease.*
Regarding the EVALUATION section:
– *The last point is talking about the filtering may use to block inconsistent datas leading to omit error.*

In the first example, it is unclear if the subject has erroneously confounded "memory" for "processing capacity" or has intentionally cited "memory" as the most probable place in human information processing where overload occurs. In the second example, it is unclear whether the subject means that filtering is a bad thing because it leads to errors of omission or whether she or he means that filtering is a good thing because it blocks inconsistent data that would lead to errors of omission. This type of ambiguity marked all six of the unclear responses to the EVALUATION section.[7]

---

[7] This problem was less evident among the subjects who elected to respond in Cantonese as the expressions they used for the concepts "is used" or "functions" clearly carried positive connotations. Hence there was no ambiguity when the subjects speaking Cantonese reported "*Filtering is used to block/functions by blocking inconsistent data leading to errors of omission or distortion*".

TABLE I. NUMBER OF SUBJECTS (50) X RESPONSES REGARDING IDEA UNITS

	Reported correctly	Not reported	Contradictory report	Not classifiable
Situation	35	13	0	2
Problem	13	33	0	4
Solution	9	41	0	0
Operation of solution introduced	12	37	0	1
Details of solution				
D1	30	15	0	5
D2	38	11	0	1
D3	37	12	0	1
Evaluation	3	29	12	6

Results

Eighteen of the subjects chose to give their summaries in English whereas 32 spoke in Cantonese. The results are shown in Table 1 above.

From Table 1, it can be seen that:

– 60% or more of the subjects correctly mentioned the SITUATION (70%) and each of the DETAILS OF SOLUTION: D1 (60%), D2 (76%) and D3 (74%);
– considerably fewer subjects correctly mentioned the PROBLEM (26%), the SOLUTION (18%) and the OPERATION OF SOLUTION INTRODUCED (24%);
– only 6% of the respondents correctly mentioned the EVALUATION section.

A complete breakdown of the results for each individual subject is given in Appendix B.

The EVALUATION section of the lecture thus clearly produced the lowest number of correct responses. This was one-third the number of correct responses given to the next lowest section (PROBLEM, with nine correct responses). In addition, EVALUATION was the only section where subjects reported the opposite of what the lecturer said (12 subjects). The following quotations show how the lecturer's warning about problems arising from the inappropriate use of filtering was, in fact, taken to be an additional comment regarding the benefits of the process:

1. *Another advantage of filter is used to block inconsistent data which will lead to error such as omission, distortion and interference.*
2. *The main function of filtering is to block inconsistent datas and also used to prevent of leading to error such as omission, distortion and some inference.*

In order to check if the students who mistook the import of the

TABLE 2. SUCCESS WITH OTHER IDEA UNITS COMPARED WITH RESPONSES
TO THE EVALUATION SECTION

No. of idea units	No. of students correctly responding	Evaluation section			
		correct	contra	unclass	not mentioned
8	0	0	0	0	0
7	2	1	0	0	1
6	4	1	0	0	3
5	9	0	2	2	5
4	15	1	6	4	4
3	8	0	4	0	4
2	2	0	0	0	2
1	4	0	0	0	4
0	6	0	0	0	6[8]
Sum	50	3	12	6	29

Note:
correct = correctly reflects what the speaker said;
contra = contradicting what the speaker said;
unclass = a response that could not be classified;
not mentioned = saying nothing relating to the section;
Sum = number of responses per column.

EVALUATION section also had excessive problems with the other ideas in the lecture, the subjects' success in responding to the other idea units was compared with their responses to the EVALUATION section. Table 2 presents these results and shows that none of the students who misunderstood the speaker's meaning in the EVALUATION section was among the worst performing 24% of the sample; that is, those subjects reporting fewer than three of the idea units correctly. In fact, all of the subjects who mistook the meaning of the EVALUATION section were among the 32 subjects who correctly reported between three to five of the other idea units. Therefore, there is no evidence of a link between the incorrect reports of the EVALUATION section and a general lack of success in reporting the ideas of the lecture. However, there is some evidence, albeit slender owing to the small number of subjects involved, that the more proficient subjects were more likely to correctly report

---

[8] One of the six subjects made remarks which partly reflected the ideas in the EVALUATION section but could not be counted as encompassing the overall idea unit. He mentioned filtering as a general function of the brain that allows humans to block out boring, irrelevant or erroneous things. He did not specify the details of filtering but did mention that it sometimes stops humans from getting the correct information.

what the speaker said in the EVALUATION section. This evidence stems from the fact that two of the three subjects who correctly reflected the speaker's point were among the six most "successful" subjects; that is, they correctly mentioned six or more of the eight idea units in the lecture extract.

Discussion

Our belief was that students would expect a recurring SITUATION–WHAT TO DO discourse structure and that this would render the recognition of information within a more complex SITUATION cum PROBLEM–SOLUTION–EVALUATION structure problematic. We were, therefore, looking for evidence of whether subjects had more difficulty with the EVALUATION section of the lecture than with other sections.

The results confirmed that this was the case. The EVALUATION section, where the lecturer sought to draw attention to the problems/drawbacks connected to filtering proved the most problematic among the main points. Only 3 out of 21 respondents referring to this aspect of the lecture mentioned it correctly; 12 responses made evident misrepresentations of the point being made, and 6 were unclear. The erroneous responses by 24% of all subjects (57% of those mentioning the section) showed that they were not comprehending the evaluative comment as a problem with the solution, but rather that they took the point as another positive feature of the filtering process. This is a serious error in that it involves not only the misunderstanding of the EVALUATION section but it also distorts the message the lecturer sought to convey about the SOLUTION. Instead of comprehending that filtering (the SOLUTION) has flaws and limitations, those students regarded it as being wholly beneficial.

Brown and Yule (1983: 58ff.) suggest that hearers follow a "principle of local interpretation", whereby they seek to understand what they hear by reference to its immediate context and co-text. Good hearers, though, recognise where such a principle fails to yield an interpretation that is consistent with textual evidence and wider context, and go on to refer to the more global context in order to reach a coherent interpretation consistent with textual evidence. It would appear that the 12 subjects who misinterpreted the EVALUATION section followed the principle of local interpretation. However, with this section of the lecture it proved to be inadequate. In order to be successful, listeners had to "go back" and recompute the initially wholly positive value assigned to "filtering" as the solution to a problem. The evidence of difficulty is important, as the evaluative comment carried implications for the future development of ideas on the topic in the lecture course. In fact, the phenomenon of omitting or distorting inconsistent data mentioned in the lecture is ironically attested in most student summaries as they relate to this very point.

The 28 instances in which the EVALUATION section was not mentioned at all in students' summaries cannot, in the absence of post-summary interviews, be unambiguously accounted for. We cannot be sure if an omission results from a failure to comprehend or from a decision that the information comprehended is irrelevant (perhaps because of signals that it would in any case be taken up in a later lecture). It appears noteworthy that the item was omitted by all subjects who only mentioned one or two of the main points in their summaries, but it was also absent from some otherwise quite comprehensive accounts.

A comparison of the sections from which the students reported more correct information with those from which the majority of students neglected to report information provides other support for our claim that our subjects expect relevant information in a lecture to be presented in a SITUATION–WHAT TO DO format. The claim is given credence by the high number of subjects, 60% or more, who correctly mentioned the SITUATION ("A" in Figure 2) as well as the details regarding how the solution operates (D1–3), in contrast with the low number of subjects (26% or less) mentioning the information relevant to the PROBLEM, SOLUTION, and INTRODUCTION TO DETAILS OF OPERATION sections of the lecture as well as the EVALUATION. From a subjective analysis of the language and concepts in these latter sections, there seems little reason to anticipate special comprehension difficulties for these parts of the lecture.

The notion that subjects expect relevant information in a lecture to be presented in a SITUATION–WHAT TO DO format explains why many of them might consider other information less important. For instance, if the subjects considered that the problem was inherent in the situation, they would regard mention of the problem as redundant following mention of the situation. Similarly, general statements about what-to-do (in the SOLUTION and INTRODUCTION TO THE WAY THE SOLUTION OPERATES sections) would be regarded as preparatory noises introducing the more substantial specifics about what is actually done (as described in sections D1–3).

Our findings regarding the miscomprehension of information in the EVALUATION section could be explained in terms of many students' activating inappropriate schemata as regards the discourse structure of the lecture. However the psychological status of "schemata" – or indeed of "strategies" – cannot be directly demonstrated by pointing to characteristics of textual products, be they written or oral summaries. We can, nevertheless, claim that the data are consistent with our belief that students tend to expect local discussion and resolution of "situations" in lectures, rather than seeking a more complex argumentative structure.[9]

Our findings coincide to a degree with those of Olsen and Huckin (1990) in affording further evidence that students often experience difficulty with stages in an argument that involve critical appraisal rather than simple solutions. In contrast with Olsen and Huckin, however, it is worth emphasising that our subjects had relatively few major problems in grasping the essential nature and operation of the solution that the lecturer was proposing to a problematic situation. Our results indicate that the role of "filtering" was fairly widely recognised as a response to difficulties related to humans' limited capacity to process information. Whereas the "unexpected" element in our lecture was a mention of possible drawbacks to the solution, the potentially surprising feature in the lecture used by Olsen and Huckin lay in the nature of the solution itself, and was thus more central to their lecturer's argument.

Our own findings are consistent with a belief that many students operate with a SITUATION–WHAT TO DO expectation when following their lectures. Such an expectation already goes well beyond the mere fact-grabbing that Olsen and Huckin imply by using the term "information-driven". The fact that students fail to recognise more complex forms of argumentation does not necessarily mean that students do not listen for a main point or line of argument. Our findings suggest that the failure can be explained by the difficulties students encounter when they try to fit information conveyed in an unfamiliar discourse structure into the pattern of a more familiar and less complex discourse structure. Indeed, one could adapt Olsen and Huckin's chosen terminology to argue that many learners in our own study had pursued a successful "point-driven strategy", since they had grasped the problem–solution (or situation–what to do) relation that was the main point of this lecture extract. Their problem, however, was prompted by the lecturer's presumably unexpected caveat concerning the solution she had described.

Implications for pedagogy

Problems that learners encounter in recognising information or ideas that are unexpected, and in reinterpreting other parts of a discourse in order to take the unexpected into account, will be matters of concern for those preparing learners for uses of language and for intellectual enquiry in academic contexts. Following Olsen and Huckin, we would imagine that most departments in polytechnics and universities will want their

---

[9] Considerations regarding how these expectations are structured, stored and retrieved, that is, schema theory, fall outside the scope of this paper.

students to develop cognitive abilities related to problem solving, including an appreciation of the imperfection of many "best" solutions to problems. Whether or not it is within the remit of an ESP course to facilitate this kind of cognitive development can still prove a controversial issue. Yet there seems to us to be every reason for ESP courses to address, with others, the kind of problem we are reporting. The case for incorporating such work in an English programme – in collaboration with, or at least alongside, initiatives taken in subject departments – is close to a tautology: an induction to language use in academic discourse communities ought to prepare students for aspects of language use that are characteristic in the intellectual practice of such communities.

If ESP teachers, among other educators, are to help learners adjust more effectively to unexpected moves in discourse, how might they go about this? Most suggestions seem to focus on changing learners' expectations at a general level. For example, Olsen and Huckin (1990: 42–44) suggest we need to prepare learners to focus on lecturers' intentions, and to take more account of the wider contexts of communication in their fields of study. Admirable as these goals are, it is not immediately clear how best to pursue them. Generalised exhortations will clearly not suffice, particularly when students are already attempting to follow a lecturer's main points (as was the case with many of our subjects). A serious pursuit of such broad goals will require sustained work at high levels of intellectual challenge, preferably in close collaboration with subject departments.

Are there more immediate steps for ESP teachers to take? One possibility is to raise students' awareness of formal schemata, such as Hoey's (1979 and 1983) Problem–Solution schema. However, explicit attempts to encourage learners to apply such a schema to samples of discourse, as proposed for written texts by Edge (1985), may prove frustrating for some learners. Edge's own work was with applied linguistics students, who were asked to apply a five-part model to TEFL articles. Allison (1989) reported less favourable responses to comparable work on the part of non-graduate teachers of English; a common problem was that cases of "lack of fit" between the model and actual discourse development caused dissatisfaction with the model or the task, rather than giving insight into the particular discourse. We would recommend, therefore, that work in applying idealised models to instances of discourse be conducted as a class activity with teacher guidance.

Recently, Tudor and Tuffs (1991) showed that actual practice in activating text-relevant formal schemata through an appropriate pre-listening task could enhance the comprehension and retention of the message content of a video recording. Such exercises might be useful in ESP courses if they allow students to become familiar with unfamiliar types of discourse structure that occur in academic lectures. The exercises might thereby ensure that students had fewer encounters with "unexpected" forms of argumentation.

A further possibility, when pursued sensitively and with respect for the learners' contributions, involves post-listening work in which students are led to discuss mismatches between their written summaries and parts of the lecture transcript. Such work can address particular problems that have arisen and will also serve other purposes, such as encouraging students to explain reasons for viewpoints. It seems to us that such specific text-focussed activities have their place, but we recognise that their "transfer" value for other occasions and tasks is difficult to demonstrate.

English teachers tend to equate communication problems with learner problems, yet learners are not the sole participants in the relevant activities. A final recommendation, therefore, is to make use of research findings and teacher experience in an effort to convince tertiary level lecturers of the need to signal clearly any deviations from a mode of lecture delivery – positive, factual, and without complex problems – that students in some educational contexts appear to expect. The main benefit of such a proposal will probably be indirect, in that it could lead lecturers to focus more on attested discourse problems during their own discussions with students.[10] Greater explicitness in the "tale" itself may reduce, though it will surely not eliminate, learners' difficulties with the unexpected.

Conclusion

Our results complement those of Olsen and Huckin (1990) in showing that L2 listeners have difficulties following argumentation that is developed in more complex discourse structures than they are used to. However, the results do not support Olsen and Huckin's claims concerning such students operating "information-driven" as opposed to "point-driven" strategies. Our subjects had few difficulties with the lecturer's main points except when one such point was introduced in a manner which they did not expect.

Although the source of the difficulties may not be a common feature in lectures to first-year undergraduates, it creates serious problems when it does occur as it affects the comprehension of large chunks of discourse. In addition, it may be a more frequent feature in lectures occurring later in courses. Furthermore, as Olsen and Huckin (1990: 43–44) point out, it is a feature of the type of lecture that university authorities believe

---

[10] Working with the lecturers rather than the students would be far more economical in terms of teaching resources.

lecturers should be delivering; that is, lectures that reflect the process of intellectual problem-solving. Therefore, one would expect it to occur more frequently earlier in courses if lecturers begin to pay lip service of a more audible variety to the notion that the overriding aim of university courses is to induce students to perfect intellectual problem-solving skills.

Appendix A
Transcript of the lecture excerpt:

Note: A slash, "/", = a pause

/ / / what is the implication of this model / the first implication is that / the capacity of humans to accept / inputs and produce outputs is limited / we all know that / er last week I think I told you / about the examp one of the examples I gave you is / er your concentration in a lecture / so I can talk to you for 2 hours nonstop / er probably I can / talk to you for 2 hours nonstop / but as human information processor / there is a certain limit you can actually take in / the information / and after you reach saturation / information is just not going into your heads / at all / I I remember I used a very good trick when I was in / well when I was working in the UK / er pe I think you probably / when you actually get your um language to a certain level / you can do the same too / because I was speaking English most of the time / during my working relationship with my friends and colleagues / and my native tongue is Chinese / so I have this ca cap capacity that I can switch off the English component if I want to / so if I don't want to listen to a conversation I actually switch it off / and then I can't hear what they are saying at all / so if I have one or two peop people behind me talking about things and I can still switch off / and can work on the computer and they thought it was great / it is great too but you actually have to reach a certain level / you actually reach a processing to a certain level / that you can actually switch off the component in your brain / this is actually quite fun / so we know that our capacity to process information is limited / and secondly / what we do is to prevent information overload / human filters the input into a manageable quantity / so / as the diagram shows us / what we have got here / is / some kind of filtering channel / when we know that we are actually getting too much information / something that we cannot deal with / what we do is / we actually tend to filter out the things that we think is irrelevant / or we think that we don't like so / / / er with one of the major um / degradation / of information overload is that your performance / actually decreases / er to go back to the example of your of your attention / when you actually start reaching information overload / and I don't give you a break / at the end of one hour / and I don't give you a break / I can actually tell that / whatever I said / is just not going in at all / I mean you have the eyes to look at me / you have the smile on your face / but I know the information is just can't / just is not getting through / so when information is reach is reaching overload point / I know that / your actually / your performance actually goes down / / so what do we d do to to actually re reduce information overload is / we actually um use filtering / with filtering / we use filtering techniques to actually / filter out the things we think is not relevant / and / / in order to / limit the quantity of information coming into our brains / and the filter may result from / we actually / how we actually do the filter / may result from / / frame of reference / of the individual / based on prior knowledge and experienced / and / normal decision making procedure / and / decision making under the stress / what is this saying is that / uh in order to filter the information and we uses three major methods to do it / we actually choose a frame of reference / we all work within some kind of frame of reference / according to our individual knowledge / and individual experience / and we also use some kind of pattern / we associate patterns / with things that are happening um / around us / one of the very good examples / which I actually noticed one morning / while I was getting dressed / I was I'm used to switching on the television as soon as I get up / so that I can listen to the news / and the weather report and everything / and this presenter / he was actually giving the weather report / on various cities in the world / you know they do it every morning / I don't know whether you do the same / if you switch on the television every morning they have news / and then they give weather report in Hong Kong / and then they give you the weather report all around the world / and then they repeat the same cycle about every 15 minutes or so / they repeat the same thing / so this guy was giving / um / er / the weather report / of of around the world / so he was saying Sydney fine day / er 5 degrees to 10 degrees / um / I don't know / er Peking / rainy day / zero degrees to um / to what / 2 degrees / he was actually giving this kind of pattern / so his brain is already / um trained into that pattern / that he will read the city first / then he will read the the condition / and then he will read the degrees / and then this morning / he was doing the same thing / and then he was saying London fine day 5 degrees to 5 degrees / and as soon as he said 5 degrees to 5 degrees / he im immediately said / oh means that it is actually going to stay at 5 degrees / but his brain is already working the condition / his frame of reference / is based on the fact that / you read the city / then you read the weather condition / and then you read the degrees / so even though it is written down 5 degrees / he still says / London er fine day today / 5 degrees to 5 degrees / but as soon as he read it out / he knew the mistake / so he actually shows you the kind of frame of reference that we are working on / the pattern / we also filter out the information because he was actually using some kind of filter / he really doesn't want to really read out the inform / to look at the information / to read it out / he's just actually using some kind of pattern / to know that he's actually doing the city / the weather condition / and the degrees / um we / filter the information also using normal decision procedures / so / decision making / under / er normal procedures tell us there is some kind of information that we don't need to read / other information are relevant to the process / and finally we have decision making under stress / now when we are / when we are pushed for a decision / what we tend to do is / to we do more and more filtering we tend to throw out more and more information / we we think are not relevant at the time / just to push pu / um just to push out a / a decision as the shortest possible time / / / and the stress of making decisions under time pressure will cause filtering to increase / so you actually tend to / um let less less data / and information come in / so that you can process the information at hand quicker / in order to turn out a decision quickly / / / / / frame of reference applies to both input and processing / over time the brain establishes / pattern or categories of data / which define the human understanding / of the nature of the environment / so again / when I referred you to the example which I told you that the presenter / is actually trained / to the um the reference or categories of data / that he will actually give the city / and he will give the weather condition / then he will give the degrees / from from one degree to another degree / he actually read it re / regardless of what is actually presented to him because his frame of reference is already trained on that thought / I think very often you might come across that / when you actually when your train of thought is on something / you're trained on something / it is difficult to actually to get you / to bombard you with other kind of information / because you tend to filter them out / your train of thought on one direction / and you're just going that way OK / / / filtering may also be used to block inconsistent data / leading to errors such as omission / distortion / and inferences / what this is saying is / um in terms of avoiding information overload / we use filtering / to actually make the amount of information presented to us / manageable / but / we might be using it to an extent that / we're actually blocking out information / wh or data / or information / which are inconsistent with the current situation / which w or which we / think / is inconsistent with the current situation / and in that case / then we tend to have errors or omission or distortion / because we think that is not important / or we think / we feel that is not relevant / but in a sense / it might still be relevant / OK / well we could actually come back to this about omission and distortion later on / when we talk about cognitives and style and things / / so this is the general model / and the next thing we want to look at / . . .

Appendix B: How individual subjects responded

S	SIT	PROB	SOL	OP:	D1	D2	D3	EVAL
E1	1	0	0	0	1	1	1	X
E2	1	1	0	0	1	1	1	1
E3	1	0	0	0	1	1	1	?
E4	1	1	1	0	1	1	1	0
E5	1	?	0	1	1	1	1	0
E6	1	0	0	0	?	1	1	1
E7	0	0	0	0	1	1	1	0
E8	1	0	0	0	1	1	1	?
E9	0	0	0	0	1	1	0	0
E10	0	0	0	0	0	0	0	0
E11	1	1	0	0	0	0	1	X
E12	0	0	0	0	0	1	1	0
E13	1	1	1	0	1	1	1	?
E14	1	1	1	1	1	1	1	1
E15	1	0	0	0	1	1	1	X
E16	1	?	0	0	1	1	1	?
E17	0	0	0	0	0	0	0	P
E18	?	0	0	0	0	0	0	0
C19	1	1	0	0	1	1	1	X
C20	1	0	0	0	0	0	0	0
C21	1	1	1	1	1	1	1	0
C22	0	0	1	1	1	1	1	X
V23	1	0	0	0	0	1	1	0
C24	1	0	0	1	0	1	1	0
C25	1	0	0	1	0	1	1	X
C26	?	0	0	0	0	0	0	0
C27	1	0	0	1	1	1	1	0
C28	1	?	0	0	1	1	1	?
C29	0	0	0	0	0	0	0	0
C30	0	0	0	1	?	1	1	0
C31	0	0	0	0	0	0	0	0
C32	1	?	0	0	0	0	0	0
C33	1	1	0	?	?	1	1	X
C34	0	0	0	0	1	1	1	X
C35	1	1	1	0	1	1	1	0
C36	1	0	0	1	1	1	1	0
C37	1	1	1	0	1	1	1	0
C38	1	1	0	0	1	1	1	0
C39	1	0	0	1	1	1	1	?
C40	0	0	0	1	1	1	1	0
C41	1	0	0	0	1	1	0	X
C42	1	0	0	0	1	1	1	X
C43	1	1	1	0	?	?	?	0
C44	0	0	0	1	1	1	1	X
C45	0	0	1	0	1	1	1	0
C46	1	0	0	0	0	0	0	0
C47	1	1	0	0	1	1	1	0
C48	1	0	0	0	0	0	0	0
C49	1	0	0	0	1	1	1	0
C50	1	0	0	0	?	1	1	X

Note:
Apart from the "S" (= subjects) above the first column, the other column headings relate to the row headings used in Table 1, that is, "Sit" = "Situation", and so on.

In the first column, the letters "E" and "C" next to the subject's number indicate whether the subject responded in English (E) or Cantonese (C).

1 = The subject correctly reported what the lecture said.
0 = The subject did not mention the point.
X = The subject contradicted what the lecturer said.
? = The subject's response could not be classified.

References

Allison, D. 1989. Helping teachers on INSET courses to read professional articles: when does intervention become interference? in *Language Teaching and Learning Styles Within and Across Cultures*, Bickley, V. (Ed.), 491–530. Hong Kong: Institute of Language in Education.

Brown, G., and G. Yule. 1983. *Discourse Analysis*. Cambridge: Cambridge University Press.

Chiang, C. S., and P. Dunkel. 1992. The effect of speech modification, prior knowledge, and listening proficiency on EFL lecture learning. *TESOL Quarterly* 26 (2): 345–374.

Coulthard, M. 1977. *An Introduction to Discourse Analysis*. Harlow: Longman.

Coulthard, M., and M. Montgomery. (Eds.). 1981. *Studies in Discourse Analysis*. London: Routledge and Kegan Paul.

Edge, J. 1985. Do TEFL articles solve problems? *ELT Journal* 39 (3): 153–157.

Hoey, M. P. 1979. *Signalling in Discourse*. (Discourse Analysis Monographs No. 6). Birmingham: English Language Research, University of Birmingham.

1983. *On the Surface of Discourse*. London: Allen and Unwin.

Kelly, P. 1991. Lexical ignorance: the main obstacle to listening comprehension with advanced foreign language learners. *IRAL XXIX* (2): 135–149.

Olsen, L. A., and T. N. Huckin. 1990. Point-driven understanding in engineering lecture comprehension. *English for Specific Purposes* 9: 33–47.

Rost, M. 1990. *Listening in Language Learning*. London: Longman.

Sinclair, J. McH., and M. Coulthard. 1975. *Towards an Analysis of Discourse*. Oxford: Oxford University Press.

Stubbs, M. 1983. *Discourse Analysis*. Oxford: Blackwell.

Tauroza, S. 1994. The Hong Kong Corpus of Computer Science and Information Systems Lectures. In Khoo, R. (Ed.). *The Practice of ESP*. Singapore: RELC.

Tudor, I., and R. Tuffs. 1991. Formal and content schemata in L2 viewing comprehension. *RELC Journal* 22 (2): 79–97.

3 The effects of rhetorical signaling cues on the recall of English lecture information by speakers of English as a native or second language

Patricia A. Dunkel and James N. Davis

Abstract

The study examined the differences between the lecture information recall of first-language listeners (native speakers of English studying Speech Communication) and second-language listeners (non-native speakers of English) relative to the presence or absence of rhetorical signaling cues in the discourse. Several studies (Chaudron and Richards 1986; Kintsch and Yarbrough 1982) have suggested that devices explicitly signaling text structure are important in both first- and second-language listening comprehension. In the present research, American students (native speakers of English) and international students (students of English as a second language) listened to a lecture on the sinking of the Titanic *and the* Andrea Doria. *The structure of the lecture was organized according to two major rhetorical patterns: narration and comparison-and-contrast. One form of the lecture (the evident form) contained explicit cues as to the rhetorical organizations used to convey the lecture information. In the nonevident form, these cues were omitted. The content remained the same for both forms of the lecture. During the lecture, subjects were encouraged to take notes in their native language. After the presentation, subjects were asked to write down all the information that they could recall in their native language. Both the English as a Second Language (ESL) and English as a Native Language (ENL) subjects were permitted to use their notes when they wrote their protocols. For purposes of analysis, the ESL protocols and notes were translated into English by native speakers of the foreign languages.*

Analysis of variance was conducted on the data in the protocols and notes. The main-effect results indicated the following: 1. ENL listeners took more lecture notes than did ESL listeners; 2. the quantity of notes taken was greater for subjects who had listened to the lecture containing rhetorical cues (i.e., the evident form); and 3. ENL listeners' recall protocols contained almost twice as much information as did ESL listeners' protocols in terms of: a. the number of information units in the recall protocols and b. the total number of words written in the protocols. The presence of the rhetorical signaling cues did not have a significant influence on the number of information units or the total number of words noted in the protocols.

Introduction

Research on the comprehension of spoken connected discourse has burgeoned in recent years, according to Carroll (1986), who suggests that the study of discourse comprehension provides researchers with a more natural unit of language to examine than does the study of isolated-sentence comprehension, since we rarely speak in isolated sentences. "The study of prose comprehension, conversation and related processes may thus provide a glimpse of language processing under more naturalistic circumstances," according to Carroll (1986: 212).

Research on the comprehension of spoken connected discourse by first-language (L1) listeners indicates that listening comprehension depends less on the meanings of the individual sentences contained in the discourse than on their apparent interrelatedness and their arrangement (or structure). As Carroll (1986) notes, it is quite possible for a group of meaningful sentences to be thrown together in a way that makes no sense whatsoever to even the L1 listener (or reader) if the sentences lack coherence, or an evident micro- and macrostructure.[1] Devices that explicitly signal micro- and macrostructures are thought to aid listeners with bottom-up and top-down processing of aurally received information. Referencing the considerable body of research on the cognitive processes underlying comprehension of L1 discourse (e.g., Clark and Clark 1977), Chaudron and Richards (1986) note that these two basic processes have been identified as catalyzing the comprehension of spoken and written text. Bottom-up processes help the listener/reader assign grammatical status to words on the basis of syntax and word order and the meanings of lexical items used in the message. Top-down processing allows the comprehender to use prior knowledge as part of the process of comprehension. The prior knowledge "may take many forms, including expectations about the topic and structure of a piece of discourse based on real-world knowledge and reference to various types of frames, schemas, and macrostructures . . . ," according to Chaudron

---

[1] According to Carroll (1986), discourse is coherent if "its sentences are easily related to one another. At the microstructural level, coherence is achieved primarily through the appropriate use of overlap between sentences" (p. 220). For example, a speaker provides discourse with coherent microstructure by ensuring that the utterances are interrelated in conventionally acceptable ways (e.g., with the use of pronouns, given a preceding context, etc.). Texts also have macrostructures, overall structures and meanings that are linked to a listener's (reader's) background knowledge; our knowledge of the macrostructure corresponding to birthdays would, for instance, enable us to comprehend discourse that describes a birthday celebration.

and Richards (1986: 113), who stress that the two levels of processing work in interactive fashion to enhance the comprehension of connected discourse by both L1 and L2 listeners.

With respect to the comprehension of connected discourse by L2 listeners, Chaudron and Richards (1986) stress that effective speakers make use of structuring and organizing cues while speaking so that the listener can apprehend the interrelated threads of meaning in the lecture information. Noting that the function of lectures is to instruct, by presenting information in such a way that a coherent body of information is presented, readily understood, and remembered,[2] they describe some of the ways in which the thread of information is continued and made coherent, and in which the rhetorical organization of the discourse is signaled with the use of connectives and discourse markers (i.e., signaling phrases and cues). According to Cook (cited in Chaudron and Richards 1986: 115), connectives and discourse markers serve as indicators of lecture topic continuation. They also signal the information structure of discourse by emphasizing directions and relations within discourse; phrases such as, "Now, getting back to our main point . . . " highlight such relations and directions. Murphy and Candlin (cited in Chaudron and Richards) identify a number of markers of the rhetorical organization of lecture discourse, "including what they refer to as markers (e.g., 'Well, right, now'), starters (e.g., 'Well, now, let's get on with . . . '), and metastatements (e.g., 'I want to mention two types of generator')" (Chaudron and Richards 1986: 115). Such cues signal the rhetorical organization of the lecture and help the listener understand and remember the threads of information contained in the discourse.

A number of experimental investigations have provided some rather convincing evidence that first-language (L1) listeners benefit from the presence of rhetorical signaling cues placed in discourse messages (see, for example, Kintsch and Yarbrough 1982), and that second language (L2) listeners, as well, benefit from the presence of certain types of text accentuation cues (macromarkers) incorporated into spoken text (see, for example, Chaudron and Richards 1986). However, it is not clear whether the inclusion or exclusion of English lecture discourse markers (rhetorical signaling cues) affect the comprehension of English lecture information by L1 listeners and L2 listeners in comparatively different ways. As a result, an investigation was undertaken to probe the comparative effect of providing or not providing ENL and ESL listeners

---

[2] Lecturing is a widely-accepted practice in American institutions of higher learning, as well as throughout the world (see Dunkel and Davis 1989). Although lecture learning is the predominant form of information transfer in American higher education, relatively few studies have addressed the empirical relationship between lecturers' English discourse and English as a Second Language learners' comprehension and recall of lecture material (see, for example, Dunkel 1988).

with discourse markers. The effect was examined in terms of the ENL and ESL listeners' recall of information contained in the English lecture, and in terms of the amount of notes each group took while listening to the lecture given in English.

Background

In their study of the comprehension and recall of written material, Kintsch and Yarbrough (1982) determined that the comprehension of text is influenced by the discourse and information processing strategies the reader/listener brings to the comprehension task. These strategies comprise pre-programmed plans that help "text processors" to perceive the organization of the text, to comprehend the inter-relationship between ideas, and to derive meaning from the text (Bever 1970; Clark and Clark 1977). According to van Dijk and Kintsch (1978), there are a number of rhetorical structures, such as cause-and-effect, comparison-and-contrast, classification and procedural description, which experienced Western readers and writers consciously and unconsciously employ to organize information and derive meaning during reading or writing.

In attempting to comprehend incoming information, the reader (or listener) calls into working memory the appropriate rhetorical structure that corresponds to the discourse type being used by the author or the speaker (Meyer and Freedle 1984). The rhetorical cues in the passage, which code coherence and provide a well-articulated organizational structure, allow the reader or listener to perceive the overall microstructure/macrostructure of the information, and its gist and main points. According to the Kintsch and van Dijk (1978) model of comprehension and recall, micro-processes of comprehension are concerned with the global comprehension and recall of text. A second level of verbal information processing, microprocessing, involves the local processing of incoming information and focuses on the under-standing and recall of information details.

The work of Kintsch and Yarbrough (1982) suggests that subjects are better able to answer gist and main-idea (macroprocessing) questions for texts that contain manifest rhetorical cues than for texts with identical content that do not contain evident rhetorical cues. Their findings imply that transparent rhetorical organization of information combined with the presence of evident rhetorical cues facilitates the global compre-hension and recall of information. The cues seem to activate appropriate rhetorical schemas and provide comprehenders with a familiar way of structuring the content of incoming information.

Additional support for various signaling cues emerged in the investi-gations of Hron, Kurbjuhn, Mandl and Schnotz (1985) and Chaudron and Richards (1985). Hron, Kurbjuhn, Mandl, and Schnotz (1985) presented science texts to native speakers of German in "accentuated" (i.e., evident) and "non-accentuated" (non-evident) versions. The accentuated variant of the text contained "content independent accentuation devices" (p. 227), which emphasized main points with techniques such as pointer words and summarizing statements. Half the subjects listened to the text, while the other half read it. Subjects receiving the accentuated version reproduced significantly more central information immediately after exposure than those receiving the non-accentuated lecture. On a retention test one week later, the text accentuation devices increased only the performance of readers. For listeners tested at a later time, the effect disappeared. Measures used included recall protocols written without reference to the stimulus text and nine open-ended factual questions. In a study of the effect of discourse markers on the comprehension of lecture text, Chaudron and Richards (1986) measured the listening comprehension of ESL learners at two instructional levels on four versions of the same text: 1. a baseline, which did not contain any markers of organization or sentence linking; 2. a "micro" version, which contained lower-level markers of such textual aspects as intersentential relations;[3] 3. a "macro" version, which signaled the relationship between the major propositions in the lecture;[4] and 4. a "micro-macro" version, which was a combination of the micro and macro versions described above. Comprehension was measured using cloze, true–false and multiple-choice tests. Across the groups, it was found that the macro-version led to better scores on the comprehension measures than either the micro or micro-macro versions.

In an attempt to explore further the relationship between modifications in oral discourse and their effects on listeners' comprehension of the information conveyed, the authors conducted the presented study. Specifically, they sought to add to the growing body of research on the effect of discourse markers, or signaling cues, on the comprehension, note-taking, and recall of native and non-native speakers of English during English lecture learning.

---

[3] Chaudron and Richards's list of micro-markers included markers signaling: 1. segmentation (e.g., "Well", "OK", "All right"); 2. time (e.g., "At that time", "After this"); 3. cause (e.g., "So", "Then")' 4. contrast (e.g. "But", "On the other hand"); and 5. emphasis (e.g., "You can see", "Unbelievably", "Obviously") (p. 127).

[4] The sample of the macro-markers used in the study included the following: "What I'm going to talk about today is something you probably know something about already"; "The problem here was that . . . "; "Another interesting development was . . . "; "And that's all we'll talk about today" (p. 127).

Method

Subjects

To test the effect of the presence or absence of English rhetorical cues in lecture discourse on the note-taking practices and information recall of non-native speakers of English, 26 university-level students studying ESL and 29 Speech Communication majors (native speakers of English) were asked to take part in the study. The subjects were tested in intact classes at The Pennsylvania State University; within the intact classes, subjects were randomly assigned to one of the experimental conditions of the study. In all, 14 ESL students (who were speakers of Arabic, Chinese, Japanese, Urdu and one additional language not named) and 14 ENL students were assigned to listen to the non-evident form of the lecture (the form containing no rhetorical signaling cues). Twelve ESL students (who were speakers of Spanish, Korean, Japanese, Greek and Urdu) and 15 ENL students were assigned to listen to the evident form of the lecture. A total of 55 subjects took part in the investigation.

Materials and procedures

Each group of students listened to an audiotaped lecture on the wreck and sinking of the transatlantic liners the *Titanic* and the *Andrea Doria*. The lectures followed two commonly-used rhetorical structures: narration and comparison-and-contrast. The first half of each lecture was framed in narrative rhetorical structure, and the second half was framed in comparison-and-contrast structure. The lecture in the evident form contained explicit cues indicating the two rhetorical structures, as well as denoting relations between sentences. These cues included brief pointer words (e.g., "first", "in contrast", and "similarly") as well as sentences highlighting textual relationships (e.g., "Let me note a few of the similarities between the sinking of the *Titanic* and the *Andrea Doria*"). In the non-evident form, these cues were deleted. The content remained basically the same for both forms.[5]

The lectures were recorded at the radio station at Penn State and were played back during subjects' regularly-scheduled classes. The length of the lecture in evident rhetorical form was approximately 10 minutes. It contained 1,263 words. The length of the lecture in non-evident rhetorical form was approximately 7 minutes and it contained 878 words. (See Appendix A for the scripts of the two lectures.)

---

[5] The evident form of the lecture contained one piece of information omitted from the non-evident form of the lecture – that a "court of inquiry into the accident blamed the shipping company for its negligence".

During the lecture, two groups of native speakers of English and two groups of non-native speakers of English listened to either the evident or the non-evident form of the lecture. Students were asked to listen to the lecture and concurrently to take notes on the information heard. Students were informed that they would take a quiz after the lecture ended, and that they would be asked to write down everything they could remember from the lecture. The non-native speakers of English were informed that they could take notes in their native language if they wished. Because empirical evidence (e.g., Lee 1986; Wolff 1987) suggests that writing recalls in the non-native language represents a possible confounding variable, non-native speakers were instructed to write their recalls in their native language. After the lecture, subjects were first asked to write down everything they recalled from the lecture. When they wrote the recall protocols, subjects had access to the notes they had taken during the lecture.

In order to quantify subject recall, the lecture scripts were divided into information units. An information unit equals the smallest unit of knowledge that can stand as a separate assertion and that can be judged true or false (Anderson 1980). The information unit in the protocol was matched to the corresponding unit in the lecture template. To measure the amount noted, the researchers counted the number of notations, including words, abbreviations, numbers, arrows, lines, dashes and colons (i.e., any mark which provided information). The non-native-speaker notes were translated into English by native speakers of these languages. The protocols of the ESL listeners were translated into English for tabulation of quantity of information recalled.

Statistical analysis

The data were analyzed by means of three 2 × 2 (language proficiency × lecture cuing form) analyses of variance (ANOVAs). Language proficiency (English as a native language *vs.* English as a second language) was combined with lecture form (evident rhetorical form *vs.* non-evident rhetorical form). Three separate ANOVAs were conducted. The dependent measures for each analysis were the following: 1. the total number of notations made, including symbols, abbreviations, and words; 2. the number of information units contained in the recall protocols; 3. the total number of words contained in the recall protocols. In order to take into account the difference in passage length (the evident script was longer than the non-evident), the raw scores were converted into proportions. The data were analyzed with the main-frame SPSSx Batch system.

TABLE I. ANOVA TABLE: 2 X 2 ANALYSES OF VARIANCE

Source	Notes: Proportional Quantity of Notations			Recall protocols: Proportional Number of Information Units			Recall protocols: Proportional Number of Words		
	df	MS	F	df	MS	F	df	MS	F
Main Effects	2	.062	21.59*	2	.227	30.47*	2	.085	26.34*
Language	1	.120	41.82*	1	.451	60.63*	1	.110	34.01*
Form	1	.007	2.31	1	.007	.98	1	.070	21.51*
2-Way Interactions (Language × Form)	1	.001	0.47	1	.009	1.17	1	.005	1.69
Residual	51	.003		51	.007		51	.003	
Total	54	.005		54	.016		54	.006	

$^*p < .01$

Results

Main effects were found for the language proficiency (language) variable with respect to the proportional quantity of notes taken during the lecture (i.e., the quantity of notes) $F (2, 54) = 21.59$, $p < .01$, and the number of information units contained in the recall protocols, $F (2, 54) = 30.47$, $p < .01$. Main effects were found for the language proficiency (language) variable as well as the form variable (evident *vs.* non-evident rhetorical cuing) with respect to the proportional number of words written down in the recall protocols $F (2, 54) = 26.34$, $p < .01$. However, no statistically significant F ratios were obtained for the interactions between the language proficiency and rhetorical cuing variables in the three analyses (see Table 1 for the F statistics for the main effects of the three analyses). Discussion of each of the three analyses is presented below.

The notes: proportional quantity of notations

Results of the analyses indicated the following: 1. English as a Native Language (ENL) listeners took a greater quantity of lecture notes than did the English as a Second Language (ESL) listeners $F (1, 54) = 41.82$, $p < .01$; and 2. those who listened to the lecture containing cues disclosing the rhetorical structure of the lecture did not take down a significantly greater quantity of information in their notes than did those who listened to the lecture without the cues $F (1, 54) = 2.31$ (n.s.d) (see Table 1 and Figures 1 and 2). Table 2 presents the means and standard deviations of the groups.

TABLE 2. MEANS AND STANDARD DEVIATIONS

	In Notes Quantity of Notations			*In Recall* *Protocols* Information Units			*In Recall* *Protocols* Number of Words		
	Mean	SD	N	Mean	SD		Mean	SD	N
Language									
ESL Listeners	.123	.049	26	.169	.060		.216	.065	26
ENL Listeners	.216	.058	29	.349	.104		.302	.069	29
Lecture Form									
Non-evident	.180	.079	26	.270	.136		.294	.081	28
Evident	.164	.062	29	.257	.116		.228	.063	27

The recall protocols: proportional number of information units

Analysis of the students' recall protocols in terms of the proportion of information units contained in the protocols revealed the important role language proficiency played in listeners' recall of the lecture information. ENL listeners' protocols contained twice as much information as did the ESL listeners' protocols $F (1, 54) = 60.63, p < .01$. The presence of evident rhetorical cues did not result in significant differences in the proportion of information units written down in the protocols by either group $F (1, 54) = .98$ (n.s.d) (see Table 1 and Figures 3 and 4). The means and standard deviations for the subjects are presented in Table 2.

The recall protocols: proportional number of words

Analysis of the students' recall protocols in terms of proportional number of words written in the protocols highlighted the critical role language proficiency plays in lecture information recall. Native speakers of English recalled almost twice as much as did the non-native speakers $F (1, 54) = 34.01, p < .01$. Unlike the other measures, however, rhetorical cues did make a significant difference in the quantity of information recalled $F (1, 54) = 21.51, p < .01$, if that quantity is indicative of the amount of information transcribed in writing. Rather surprisingly, both native and non-native recall was higher for the non-evident form of the lecture than for the evident form (see Table 1). The means and standard deviations are presented in Table 2.

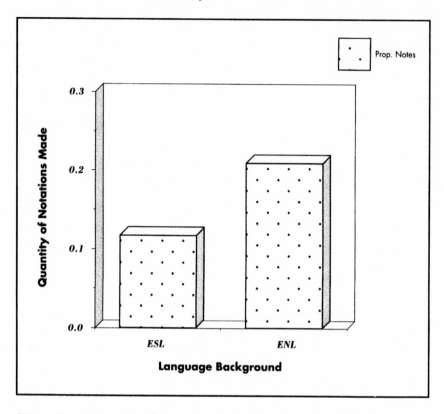

Figure 1   Proportional quantity of notations in notes: ESL vs. ENL

Discussion

The results indicated the following: 1. English as a Native Language (ENL) listeners took proportionally more lecture notes than did English as a Second Language (ESL) listeners during the lecture; 2. ENL listeners' recall protocols contained almost twice as much information as did ESL listeners' protocols in terms of the proportion of information units in the recall protocols; the total proportion of words written into the protocols was also greater from the ENL listeners. The presence of the rhetorical signaling cues had a significant, albeit slight, impact on the proportional number of words written in the protocols. Subjects receiving the non-evident form, lacking the rhetorical signals and cues, actually recorded more words in their protocols than did those hearing the evident form containing the cues.

On all three measures, a strong and consistent language effect emerged from the data. Although both groups of subjects, the ENL and ESL

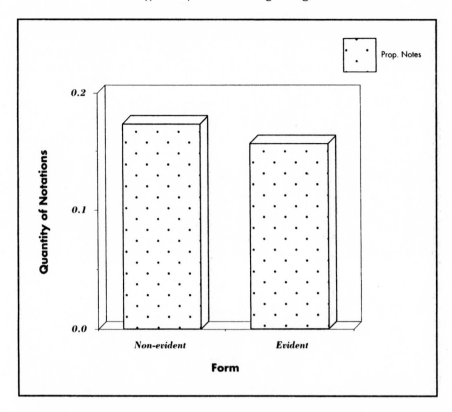

Figure 2   Proportional quantity of notations in notes: non-evident vs. evident forms

listeners, were matriculated students in a major research university where English is the language of instruction, it appears that the two groups do not have equivalent listening comprehension ability, possibly due to unequal language proficiency (i.e., native speakers were more proficient than non-native speakers). It is interesting to note that non-native English-speaking students whose TOEFL scores are sufficiently high for them to gain admission to study in a major research institution in the United States (TOEFL > 550) still seem to be at a distinct information-processing disadvantage vis-à-vis native speakers in such a setting. Furthermore, the ESL listeners' comprehension was not improved by the addition of rhetorical signals and cues. Thus, it is important that universities recognize the need to support non-native speakers' development of their listening proficiency, possibly by providing additional coursework in developing advanced listening skills (see Dunkel 1988).

An unexpected finding involved the greater quantity of words written

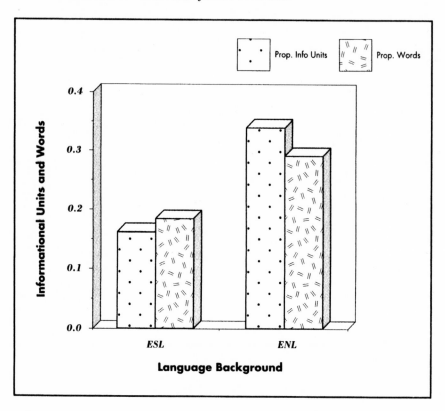

Figure 3   Informational units and words in protocols: ESL vs. ENL

by both ENL and ESL students hearing the non-evident form of the lecture, although no significant differences in the proportional number of information units were detected. An examination of the protocols revealed that many subjects in the non-evident-lecture condition added connectives to "fill in" missing markers, and they provided circumlocutions of the information. For instance, in the non-evident-form condition, subjects heard the sentences:

The *Andrea Doria* had radar to warn of the approach of another ship; the *Titanic* was not equipped with radar. Radar had, of course, not been invented at that time. The *Titanic* had only a lookout to warn of approaching ships and other potential hazards.

The sentences were reconstructed in several of the native-speaker protocols in the following fashions:

Unlike the *Titanic*, this ship [the *Andrea Doria*] had radar. The *Titanic* only had a lookout. No radar **because** radar wasn't invented yet.

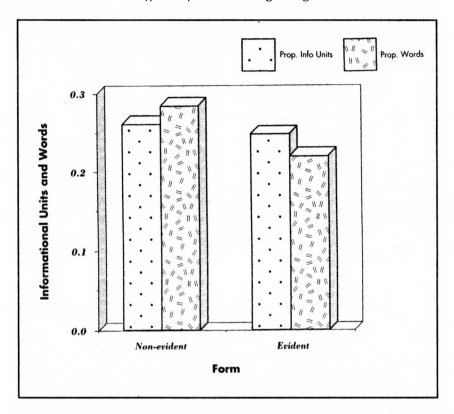

Figure 4   Informational units and words in protocols: non-evident vs. evident forms

Since there was no radar the only way to warn the *Titanic* of icebergs was for headquarters to radio to the captain that the *Titanic* was approaching icebergs.[6]

Another sentence in the non-evident form of the lecture, "When the *Titanic* sank, more than 1,500 people died" was written in a protocol of one subject as: "1500 plus people drowned or froze **as a result of** the *Titanic* disaster"; and in the protocol of another listener as, "Many people died, 1500, **because of** the cold and drowning." Such rewritings did not contain extra content information, and were not counted as additional information units. Thus, while a number of subjects in the

---

[6] The evident form lecture presented the same information with the following discourse: "Another contrast was that the *Andrea Doria* had radar to warn of the approach of another ship, but the *Titanic* was not equipped with radar. Radar had, of course, not been invented at the time, and so the *Titanic* had only a lookout to warn of approaching ships and other potential hazards."

non-evident condition appeared to be sensitive to the absence of macro-markers (as indicated by their addition of "because", "unlike", and "as a result of"), the number of information units (counting actual content) in these protocols was still unaffected by the provision or omission of accentuation cues (or form markers).

As cited above, Hron et al. as well as Chaudron and Richards found that the presence of macromarkers/text accentuation cues enhanced the listening comprehension of the ESL learners. Three differences between our study and the other two may explain these divergent findings. First, the narrative and comparison-and-contrast structures of our text, as well as intersentential relations, may have been sufficiently salient to listeners, so that signaling devices were not necessary for their recognition. Second, unlike Chaudron and Richards who used cloze, true–false, and multiple-choice tests, we used a different measure, written recall protocols (Bernhardt 1983). It is possible that this difference in method caused our results to diverge from those of Chaudron and Richards. Third, in contrast, with the Hron et al. experiment, which also used recall protocols, we allowed subjects to refer to their notes during the recall period. This difference in results suggests the need for continued research using a variety of texts, learners, methods and metrics to measure comprehension and retention of spoken academic discourse.

Another methodological issue concerns the writing of protocols and the taking of notes in the subjects' native language. To the best of our knowledge, no other researchers studying the comprehension and note-taking of ESL or EFL (English as a Foreign Language) subjects have examined the protocol recalls written in a number of different native languages. While we agree with Lee (1986) and Wolff (1987) that writing protocols in the second or foreign language may well confound L2 writing ability with L2 comprehension, many practical issues related to the quantifying of recall protocols and notes written in EFL listeners' native language merit further examination. For example, one of the questions that proved to be perplexing in the present study was the following: What exactly counts as a word (or notation) in languages such as Chinese, Urdu, and Arabic? For those ESL subjects who took notes in English (and several did), the translating of information heard into their native language in the protocols may have presented them with additional information-processing difficulties.

A limitation of this study is the lack of a verification of subjects' prior background knowledge of the content of the lecture. It is possible that the topic of the lectures was already familiar to many in both groups of subjects. If this was the case, then perhaps text structure was not an important factor influencing understanding. As Roller (1990), reviewing studies of text structure and L1 reading comprehension, has asserted,

"Text structure variables operate differently depending on the extent of the reader's knowledge of the topic of the text. Because structure variables highlight or make explicit ideas in the text, they exert their influence only in moderately unfamiliar text" (p. 86).

In conclusion, while it is thought that the listener benefits from the presence of signaling cues in discourse messages (Kintsch and Yarbrough 1982), the findings of the present study do not lend support to this contention if amount of notes made and quantity of information recalled in protocols are used as metrics of comprehension and retention of lecture information. The present study compared the comprehensibility of an elaborated spoken text (the evident form of the lecture) with a non-elaborated version (the non-evident form of the lecture) and found that the elaborated text did not augment comprehension and recall as measured by the amount of information units and words in the protocols of subjects. Further investigation of the interaction of text type (content and structure) with signaling devices is strongly advocated.

Appendix A
Scripts of the lectures

The *Titanic* and the *Andrea Doria*
(Non-evident form lacking rhetorical signaling cues)
Directions: You are going to listen to a mini-lecture on two famous disasters at sea. Please listen carefully to the information presented in the lecture. Take notes on the information as you listen to the lecture. After the lecture ends, you will be asked to look at your notes and to write down everything you can recall about the information contained in the lecture. But for now, just listen and take notes as you normally would during a lecture in class.

On the morning of April 10, 1912, the luxury liner the *Titanic* left England on a voyage to New York. Just four days later, the *Titanic* lay at the bottom of the Atlantic Ocean. On Wednesday July 18, 1956, the ocean liner the *Andrea Doria* left Italy. The *Andrea Doria* was also travelling to New York. Eight days later, this great ship also lay at the bottom of the Atlantic. The sinking of these two huge ships shocked the world.

The *Titanic* and the *Andrea Doria* were transatlantic ocean liners. They were also luxury liners. They carried many of the world's rich and famous people. As each ship was sinking, there were acts of heroism and villainy from the people on the ship. One man on the *Titanic* dressed up as a woman so that he could get into a lifeboat to save his life. The *Titanic* and the *Andrea Doria* were considered "unsinkable". It was inconceivable that they would ever sink even if they did have a collision at sea.

The *Titanic* was on her maiden voyage, that is, her first voyage across the Atlantic. The *Andrea Doria* was on her 101st transatlantic crossing. The *Titanic* struck an iceberg; the *Andrea Doria* collided with another ship. The *Andrea Doria* had radar to warn of the approach of another ship; the *Titanic* was not equipped with radar. Radar had, of course, not been invented at that time. The *Titanic* had only a lookout to warn of approaching ships and other potential hazards. When the *Titanic* sank, more than 1,500 people died. They drowned or froze to death in the icy North Atlantic water. More than 700 people survived the sinking. In the *Andrea Doria* accident, 60 people lost their lives, and about 1,650 lives were saved.

The *Titanic* sailed from England. The first five days of the journey were warm and clear. On Sunday, April 14th, the weather changed. It became much colder. The *Titanic* received several warnings that icebergs were seen in the shipping lanes. There were three messages about icebergs sent to the ship on the 14th. At 9:40 in the evening of the 14th, a message was received that there were a large number of icebergs in the area near the *Titanic*. The message was never delivered to the captain of the ship. At 11:40 p.m. on April 14th, a seaman, the lookout, spotted an iceberg. The ship swiped the iceberg, and a 300-foot hole was ripped in the side of the ship below the waterline. By 12:20 a.m. (about a half hour after it struck the iceberg), the ship began to sink. At 12:30 the women and children were ordered to leave the ship in the lifeboats. At 12:45 in the morning, the ship was listing so badly that many of the lifeboats could not be lowered. Passengers began to panic. At 2:20, the *Titanic* rose almost perpendicular to the ocean and began to slide beneath the ocean. A ship named the *Carpathia* arrived at the site of the sinking at 4:10 a.m. The captain expected to find the *Titanic* afloat. He saw no ship. The *Titanic* lay at the bottom of the ocean. In New York City, officials of the White Star shipping line refused to believe the ship had sunk. They steadfastly denied reports of the sinking until 8:30 on the night of April 15th. There was massive loss of life when the *Titanic* sank. There were only lifeboats for 1,178 people (in other words about ⅓ of the ship's passengers). Remember, the *Titanic* was thought to be "unsinkable". The available lifeboats were not used wisely during the sinking. There had been no lifeboat drills. The passengers did not know how to lower some of the lifeboats. The passengers had not been assigned to specific lifeboats in advance of the sailing. The *Titanic*'s speed was excessive in light of the fact that the captain had received warnings that icebergs were in the shipping lanes. A ship named the *Californian* was in the vicinity of the *Titanic* when it sank. The *Californian*'s radio operator had turned off the radio for the night when he went to bed. He did not hear the *Titanic*'s distress calls that it was sinking.

The sinking of the *Titanic* was a major blow to Britain's ship building, which, at the time, was considered the best in the world. It was thought that it was possible to build unsinkable ships. An ice patrol of the North Atlantic shipping lanes was begun. The United States Coast Guard began conducting an ice patrol. There are now requirements that the number of lifeboats on a ship has to be sufficient to hold the maximum possible number of people on board. Ship radio must now remain on 24 hours a day and cannot be turned off for the night.

In recent times, we have seen plane disasters occur in which hundreds of people are killed in one instant. We never stop hoping that someday, somehow, we will find better ways to transport people across distances in safety, if not always comfort. Whenever there are large numbers of people traveling together on a ship, the possibility of disaster is always present. The *Titanic* and the *Andrea Doria* sank. Today, people travel in greater safety across the ocean.

The *Titanic* and the *Andrea Doria* script
(Evident form containing rhetorical signaling cues)
Directions: You are going to listen to a mini-lecture on two famous disasters at sea. Please listen carefully to the information presented in the lecture. Take notes on the information as you listen to the lecture. After the lecture ends, you will be asked to look at your notes and to write down everything you can recall about the information contained in the lecture. But for now, just listen and take notes as you normally would during a lecture in class.

Today, I'd like to spend some time talking about the sinking of one of the world's greatest ships, the *Titanic*. But before we get to some of the details about that sinking, I'd like to mention another great shipwreck, the wreck of the *Andrea Doria*, and I'm going to talk about the wreck of the *Titanic* and the wreck of the *Andrea Doria*. Let me briefly compare these two disasters at sea.

On the morning of April 10, 1912, the luxury liner the *Titanic* left England on a voyage to New York. Just four days later she lay at the bottom of the Atlantic Ocean. On Wednesday July 18, 1956, the ocean liner the *Andrea Doria* left Italy. The *Andrea Doria* was also traveling to New York. Eight days later, this great ship also lay at the bottom of the Atlantic.

The sinking of these two huge ships shocked the world. When the *Andrea Doria* went down, people compared her sinking with that of the *Titanic*. There were similarities between the two disasters; however, there were also some important differences. What were some of the similarities and differences? How did the two events unfold? What were some of the causes and effects of the disaster? I will attempt to answer these questions in this short lecture.

What were some of the similarities between the two sinkings? Let me note a few of the similarities between the sinking of the *Titanic* and the *Andrea Doria*. For one thing, both ships were transatlantic ocean liners. In addition, they were both luxury liners. They carried many of the world's rich and famous people. Another similarity was that as each ship was sinking, there were acts of heroism and villainy from the people on the ship. One man on the *Titanic* dressed up as a woman so that he could get into a lifeboat to save his life. One last similarity was that both of the ships were considered "unsinkable". It was inconceivable that they would ever sink even if they did have a collision at sea.

Let me shift my attention for a moment and talk about the differences between the two ship disasters. To begin with, the *Titanic* was on her maiden voyage, that is, her first voyage across the Atlantic. The *Andrea Doria*, on the other hand, was on her 101st transatlantic crossing. Another difference was that the ships sank for different reasons. The *Titanic* struck an iceberg, whereas the *Andrea Doria* collided with another ship. Another contrast was that the *Andrea Doria* had radar to warn of the approach of another ship, but the *Titanic* was not equipped with radar. Radar had, of course, not been invented at that time, and so the *Titanic* had only a lookout to warn of approaching ships and other potential hazards. When the *Titanic* sank, more than 1,500 people died. They drowned or froze to death in the icy North Atlantic water. More than 700 people survived the sinking. In the *Andrea Doria* accident, 60 people lost their lives, and about 1,650 lives were saved.

I'm going to talk for a while about the actual sinking of the *Titanic*. I'll briefly narrate for you some of the chronological events that occurred before the *Titanic* struck the iceberg, and during its sinking. I'll begin with the start of the voyage from England. The first five days of the journey were calm and clear. However, on Sunday, April 14th, the weather changed. It became much colder. At this time, the *Titanic* received several warnings that icebergs were seen in the shipping lines. There were three messages about icebergs sent to the ship on the 14th. At 9:40 in the evening of the 14th, a message was received that there were a large number of icebergs in the area near the *Titanic*, but the message was never delivered to the captain of the ship. Just two hours later on April 14th, a seaman, the lookout, spotted an iceberg minutes before the ship sideswiped the mountain of ice. In a mere ten seconds of contact with the iceberg, a 300-foot hole was ripped in the side of the ship below the waterline. By 12:20 a.m. (about a half hour after it struck the iceberg), the ship began to sink. At 12:30, the women and children were ordered to leave the ship in lifeboats. At 12:45 in the morning, the ship was listing so badly that many of the lifeboats could not be lowered. Passengers began to panic. At 2:20, the *Titanic* rose almost perpendicular to the ocean and began to slide beneath the ocean. A ship named the *Carpathia* arrived at the site of the sinking at 4:10 a.m. The captain expected to find the *Titanic* afloat, but it saw no ship because the *Titanic* lay at the bottom of the ocean. In New York City, officials of the White Star shipping line refused to believe the ship had sunk, and steadfastly denied reports of the sinking until 8:30 on the night of April 15th.

There were many causes and effects of the sinking of the *Titanic*. A court of inquiry into the accident blamed the shipping company for its negligence. One of the causes of the massive loss of life was that there were only enough lifeboats for 1,178 people (in other words, for about ⅓ of the ship's passengers). Remember, the *Titanic* was thought to be "unsinkable". Another cause of the tragedy was that the available lifeboats were not used wisely during the sinking. There had been no lifeboat drills and the passengers did not know how to lower some of the lifeboats. The *Titanic*'s speed was another cause of the accident. It had been excessive in light of the fact that the captain had received warning that icebergs were in the shipping lanes. One other cause of the loss of life, however, was not the fault of the shipping company or the captain of the *Titanic*. There had been another ship, named the *Californian* in the vicinity of the *Titanic* when it sank, but the ship's radio operator had turned off the radio for the night when he went to bed. As a result, he did not hear the *Titanic*'s distress calls that it was sinking.

The sinking of the *Titanic* had several damaging results, and also several very good consequences. One of the damaging consequences was that the sinking was a major blow to Britain's ship building industry, which at the time was considered the best in the world. It was thought that it was possible to build unsinkable ships. One of the good consequences of the disaster was that an iceberg patrol of the North Atlantic shipping lanes was begun. The United States Coast Guard began conducting the ice patrol. Another effect of the disaster was the requirement that the numbers of lifeboats on a ship had to be sufficient to hold the maximum possible number of people on board. For another thing, ship radios must now remain on 24 hours a day, and cannot be turned off for the night.

In recent times, we have seen plane disasters occur in which hundreds of people are killed in one instant. However, we never stop hoping that someday, somehow, we will find better ways to transport people across distances in safety, if not always comfort. Whenever there are large numbers of people traveling together on a ship or a plane, the possibility of disaster is always present, but because of the sinking of the *Titanic*, people today travel in greater safety across the ocean.

References

Anderson, J. R. 1980. *Cognitive Psychology and its Implications*. San Francisco: Freeman.

Bernhardt, E. B. 1983. Three approaches to reading comprehension in intermediate German. *Modern Language Journal* 67 (2): 111–115.

Bever, T. G. 1970. The cognitive basis for linguistic structures. In *Cognition and the Development of Language*, J. R. Hayes (Ed.). New York: Wiley.

Carroll, D. W. 1986. *Psychology of Language*. Monterey, CA: Brooks/Cole Publishing.

Chaudron, C., and J. C. Richards. 1986. The effect of discourse markers on the comprehension of lectures. *Applied Linguistics* 7 (2): 113–127.

Clark. H. H., and E. V. Clark. 1977. *Psychology and Language*. New York: Harcourt, Brave, Jovanovich.

Dijk, T. A. van, and W. Kintsch. 1978. Cognitive psychology and discourse. In *Current Trends in Text Linguistics*, W. U. Dressler (Ed.). Berlin/New York: Walter de Gruyter.

Dunkel, P. 1988. The content of L1 and L2 students' lecture notes and its relation to test performance. *TESOL Quarterly* 22: 259–281.

Dunkel, P., and S. Davy. 1989. The heuristic of lecture notetaking: perceptions of American and international students regarding the value and practice of notetaking. *English for Specific Purposes* 8: 33–50.

Hron, A., I. Kurbjuhn, H. Mandl, and W. L. Schnotz. 1985. Structural inferences in reading and listening In *Inferences in Text Processing*, G. Rickheit and H. Strohner (Eds.), 221–245. Amsterdam: North-Holland.

Kintsch, W., and J. C. Yarbrough. 1982. Role of rhetorical structure in text comprehension. *Journal of Educational Psychology* 74 (6): 828–834.

Kintsch, W., and T. A. van Dijk. 1978. Toward a model of text comprehension and production. *Psychological Review* 85 (5): 363–394.

Lee, J. F. 1986. On the use of the recall task to measure L2 reading comprehension. *Studies in Second Language Acquisition* 8 (2): 201–211.

Meyer, B. J., and R. O. Freedle. 1984. Effects of discourse type on recall. *American Educational Research Journal* 21 (1): 121–143.

Roller, C. M. 1990. The interaction of knowledge and structure variables in the processing of expository prose. *Reading Research Quarterly* 25 (2): 79–89.

Wolff, D. 1987. Some assumptions about second language text comprehension. *Studies in Second Language Acquisition* 9 (3): 307–326.

4 Second language listening comprehension and lecture note-taking

Craig Chaudron, Lester Loschky and Janice Cook

Abstract

This study looks at the relationship between second language learners' notes taken while listening to audiotaped lectures and the learners' success on two different types of comprehension measures. A review of L1 and L2 literature on the effects of taking notes and retaining notes on students' recall of lecture information reveals several factors as important contributors to successful recall, such as quality of notes, and training in note-taking. In this study, the effect on comprehension tests of the availability of notes taken, and the quality of L2 learners' notes, was studied. Both multiple-choice and cloze listening comprehension measures were employed. Results indicate no favorable role for retaining or not retaining notes on short-term recall success, but complex relationships appeared between measures of lecture note quality and successful recall.

Introduction

The study of L2 lecture comprehension involves a number of important research questions. A considerable number of recent L2 studies have dealt with the analysis of lecture structure and its effect on L2 learners' comprehension, analyzing native speaker lecture style as well as non-native speakers' oral skills and comprehensibility (e.g., Chaudron and Richards 1986; Chaudry and Astika 1991; DeCarrico and Nattinger 1988; Tyler, Jefferies, and Davies 1988; Williams 1989). A much larger area of methodological prescription involves the training of L2 learners, in which an emphasis is put on such strategies as listening for main ideas and supporting details, paying attention to key phrases and words that signal discourse relevance, and, in note-taking, the use of abbreviations, and outlining or highlighting techniques (e.g., Brown 1978; Dunkel and Pialorsi 1982; James 1975; James, Jordan, and Matthews 1979; Lebauer 1988; Mason 1983; Otto 1979; Plaister 1976; Ruetten 1986). With respect to note-taking, we find that despite the common practice of encouraging L2 learners in academic settings to take lecture notes, little

Tasks while listening	*Tasks following listening*
1. No notes	With or without notes
2. Brief notes	1. Free recall
a. Schematic or non-schematic	2. Short answer (probed recall)
b. Guided or unguided	3. Other operations (*see first*
3. Complete notes (verbatim)	*column*)
4. Other operations	
a. Following instructions	
b. Multiple-choice	
c. True–false	
d. Fill-in sentences	
e. Cloze	
(fixed ratio or rational)	

Figure 1   Methods for obtaining learners' responses to listening material

research has been conducted to date to evaluate the extent to which doing so aids L2 learners' comprehension, or to determine the characteristics of good notes; most instructional practice and prescription is thus based on individual experiences and intuitions.

There exists, however, a considerable accumulation of literature on note-taking in first language (L1) educational research (see especially the reviews by Hartley and Davies 1978; Rickards 1979; Carrier and Titus 1979; and Ladas 1980), and a handful of relevant studies to our knowledge in a second language context (Dunkel 1988; Dunkel, Mishra, and Berliner 1989; for an ethnographic approach, see also Benson 1989, and King, this volume). Most methodological prescriptions on lecture note-taking are premised on at least one of two key assumptions about its value, and these same assumptions are reflected in the major distinction in L1 educational research on this topic. The first assumption, that note-taking aids in organizing lecture content while listening, is viewed as an effect of note-taking on encoding processes; the second, that note-taking is a useful record for later recall and reconstruction of lecture content when studying, is viewed as an effect of notes as an external storage stimulus for recall. Di Vesta and Gray (1972), and later researchers (Carrier and Titus 1979; Rickards and Friedman 1978) have characterized this distinction with the following arguments. First, note-taking aids the *encoding* process by increasing:

1. meaningful *chunking* and thereby encoding of information,
2. general level of attention,
3. general *effort*, and
4. *assimilation* of new and old information.

Second, note-taking provides an *external storage* of information:

1. it helps *rehearsal*, and
2. it provides mnemonics and information for *reconstruction* of memory.

In this study we review the L1 and L2 research on this distinction, following which we examine research on the quality of lecture notes and the effect of note-quality on comprehension performance. Our aims are first, to isolate the function and effectiveness of note-taking and use, and second, to determine the extent to which measures of quality of notes taken by learners in lectures correlate with their comprehension. The latter aim is intended to contribute to the goal of developing a research methodology for assessing learner comprehension in natural lecture contexts (see Figure 1, and cf. discussion of measures of intake in Chaudron 1985).

Pre-training

Test expectancy

    Multiple-choice, recall, essay, etc.

Encoding

                                               Conditions:

Taking own notes   Parallel
Following other notes/outline   Distributed
Listening – no notes   Delayed

Review/Rehearsal

                                             Conditions:

Own notes   Review
External notes   Elaboration
Mental review

Retrieval

                                             Conditions:

Recognition (multiple-choice)   Pacing
Free recall (recall protocol, summary)   Immediate
Cued recall (cloze, completion)   Delayed
                                             With notes
                                           Without notes

Figure 2 Stages in taking and using notes

Stages in taking and using notes

In Figure 2, we display the key stages of note-taking, and the principal factors that have been considered in the study of note-taking; we will use these headings as a framework for the first part of our review of the effectiveness of note-taking from the encoding and external storage points of view.

Pre-training in taking notes is an important factor for research to consider, for study of students' note-taking in which quality of notes is not assured risks introducing too much error into the measurement of note-taking effectiveness. Amazingly, however, the L1 research to date has not fully investigated this aspect. Carrier and Titus's study (1981), which found no effect for pre-training, employed too brief a training session. Peck and Hannafin (1983) found an interaction between instruction in note-taking and taking notes: when students were trained, they only performed better than untrained learners when they were allowed to take notes. When prohibited from taking notes, an untrained group was better in recall measures than the trained group.

Test expectancy is likely to be a factor in determining the sort of notes that will be taken. Carrier and Titus (1981) demonstrated that the pre-training condition stimulated higher quality notes only when students were informed of a coming multiple-choice test; when informed of an essay test, the pre-training group did worse. Rickards and Friedman (1978) found that essay expectancies influenced learners to record a higher level of information than a multiple-choice expectation. Generally, however, one should question whether test expectancy should be investigated as a critical factor, in that the most natural use of notes should be as a general source of information for study, rather than for immediate testing on lecture content.

The *encoding* process has been evaluated with respect to three sorts of note-taking opportunities for students: taking their own notes, following other provided notes or a lecture outline, and listening with no note-taking. The first two of these conditions can also be combined with at least three different conditions *when* notes are taken or followed; that is, notes can be taken or read totally in *parallel* with listening, *distributed* at intervals throughout the listening period, or *delayed* until after the listening.

The L1 literature has produced mixed findings as to the general advantage of students taking notes or not. Hartley and Davies (1978) state that 19 out of 38, that is 50% of studies which made such a comparison found no effect of note-taking. Even if there is an advantage, as several major studies have found (Barnett, Di Vesta, and Rogozinski 1981; Dyer, Riley, and Yekovich 1979; Fisher and Harris 1973), whether this supports the usefulness of taking one's own notes can be questioned, for several studies (Klemm 1976; Thomas 1978) found that using other or guided notes had superior effects to taking one's own. (However, Fisher and Harris 1973, found superior effects for one's own notes, and Annis and Davis 1975 found equal effects.) As one might expect, results on the whole appear to favor taking notes in parallel, rather than distributed or delayed note-taking, as argued in Thomas's (1978) study re-evaluating the effects of Aiken, Thomas, and Shennum (1975).

The condition of being able to *review* notes can be added to the opportunity to take them or not, which would further test the superiority of the encoding over an external storage advantage. The review of notes, which constitutes essentially another encoding opportunity, has been shown to lead to superior performance on tests when compared with just a mental review of lecture content, but this is *regardless of whether other notes or the student's own notes* were reviewed (Annis and Davis 1975; Barnett et al. 1981; Fisher and Harris 1973; Howe 1970). This suggests that an encoding effect, if it exists, has less to do with the encoding of the lecture while listening.

Moreover, Fisher and Harris (1973) found that subjects who did not take notes, but reviewed external notes, were superior in test performance to subjects who took their own notes, but also reviewed external notes. Such a result supports either the possibility that listening without the cognitive load of note-taking is simply a superior learning condition, or that the *conflict* between having taken one's own notes but then reviewing other notes results in difficulty for the latter group. The authors favor this second interpretation. Rickards and Friedman (1978) found, finally, that subjects with external notes performed better in recalling higher level information than subjects who took their own notes; this could of course be a matter of poor quality note-taking, due to inadequate training of the note-taking group. The authors argue, however, that this supports a "reconstruction" view of the value of external storage, in that any set of prompts to the learner's memory aids in the reconstruction of the main points.

Findings for the effect of *elaboration* in review, that is, the subjects' rehearsal and additional encoding of information derived from the notes, are difficult to interpret, largely owing to the inability of experimenters to control precisely how and what subjects elaborate. Barnett et al. (1981) found, in fact, a superior effect for an unguided review condition over elaboration.

The final stage in the process of note-taking and use is that of *retrieval* of information from notes. The type of retrieval required, which is dependent on the type of test measure (recognition, free or cued recall), and the pacing and delay in demand on retrieval, can all influence effectiveness. The L1 literature has not fully controlled for all these factors. In immediate recall, access to some notes appears generally to favor performance, thus supporting the external storage hypothesis. Furthermore, Barnett et al. (1981) found that delaying the test equally favored subjects who had been given other notes or took their own, over those who had no notes.

On the whole, then, resolution of the encoding versus external storage value of note-taking must await more extensive studies which incorporate more of the above factors in their design. The results to date tend to favor the external storage position, but this situation may be biased by the reliance of researchers on sometimes gross measures of lecture content recall, and their failure to develop more refined measures of learners' internal encoding and representation of lecture content. For this reason, the issue of quality of notes may play a more important role in future research.

Quality of notes

L1 and L2 research on note quality has examined a number of features, displayed in Figure 3. These features consider either the *quantity* or the *quality* of notes taken. In the following discussion, we will primarily discuss the extent to which the L1 literature has demonstrated a relationship between these features and test performance.

Fisher and Harris (1974) and Norton (1981) both found that total number of words in notes was significantly positively correlated with long-term recall of information. Thus far, only Dunkel's (1988) L2 study has found a positive correlation between number of "information units" (identified on the basis of lecture content) in notes and successful recall of concepts and details on multiple-choice tests.

Other measures of note quality dealt with in the literature involve various calculations of efficiency, completeness, and test answerability. Regarding efficiency, Aiken et al. (1975) found that a high ratio of ideas to total words was positively correlated with better recall; several other researchers have found similar positive relationships between "terseness" of notes and test performance (Fisher and Harris 1973, 1974; Howe 1974). Regarding "completeness", however, Kiewra (1985) found no relationship with performance.

One would expect test answerability, or the extent to which test items are included in notes, to be highly correlated with recall, and in fact, several studies have found this relationship to be as great as $r = .50$ (Dunkel 1988; Fisher and Harris 1974; Locke 1977; and cf. Howe 1970). Such a finding is actually one of the early sources of positive expectations for the value of note-taking. Thus, assuming that the researcher knows ahead of time what will be assessed as appropriate comprehension of lecture content, this measure in student notes could be used as a strong predictor of recall.

A final feature that has been shown to have some relationship to recall performance is the relative amounts of higher and lower level information recorded from lectures into notes. Rickards and Friedman (1978) found that subjects used higher level information to reconstruct lower

Quantity
1. Total words
   Can include abbreviations, symbols, etc. or these may be counted separately.
2. Total information units

Quality
3. "Efficiency or Density"
   a. Ratio of information units or ideas to total words
   b. Verbatim versus telegraphic or abbreviated forms
4. "Completeness"
   Ratio of total information units or ideas in notes to main information units or ideas in text
5. "Test answerability"
   Number of information units or ideas pertinent to test items
6. "Level of information"
   Number and proportion of high order information relative to low order from text
7. Organizational features:
   a. outlining
   b. diagrams
   c. symbols
   d. numbering
   e. evidence of examples
   f. titles

Figure 3   Measures of quantity and quality of notes

level information much more efficiently than the reverse; that is, amount of higher level information in notes correlated much more positively with total information recalled than amount of lower level information.

Many other possibilities deserve to be explored as to their relationship to total note quality. In the present study, the researchers' interest was in deriving reasonably *low-inference* measures of note quality that could be used regardless of specific lecture content.

L2 learners' note-taking

With the foregoing brief review as perspective (see Carrier and Titus 1979; Dunkel 1988; Dunkel et al. 1989; Hartley and Davies 1978; and Rickards 1979 for more detail and discussion), the present study is intended to address the following two research questions:

1. What is the effect of retaining notes on L2 students' comprehension (as measured by performance on multiple choice and cloze tests)?
2. What is the relationship between learners' comprehension and their note quality (as measured by test scores and low-inference measures of quantity and quality of notes)?

The present study should be viewed in the context of the research by Dunkel (1988), and Dunkel et al. (1989), both of which studied L2 learners of English in contrast to L1 English speakers. In Dunkel (1988), subjects were assigned to note-taking and no note-taking conditions, shown a 23-minute videotaped lecture, and then given a 30-item multiple-choice test immediately afterwards (without review of notes). Various measures of note quantity and quality were taken. No effect for note-taking condition was found, nor any interaction of this factor with native language. That is to say, there was no *encoding* effect as a result of having taken lecture notes.

This finding, coupled with the previous review of L1 literature, led to the design in the current study of allowing all subjects to take notes, in order to evaluate the *external storage effects* of retaining notes on test performance. Half the subjects had their notes removed prior to taking tests of lecture recall. However, it was hypothesized that *there would be no difference in performance between those who did and those who did not keep their notes*, largely due to the immediacy of the test administration following the lecture (scheduling of the experimental classes regrettably precluded a delayed measure).

The second research question was in fact the more important one, since this study constitutes one of a series of investigations into appropriate assessment procedures for content-specific listening comprehension (cf. Chaudron 1985; Chaudron, Lubin, Sasaki, and Grigg 1986). In stepwise regression, Dunkel (1988) had found significant relationships between the quantitative measures of number of information units – positively correlated with L2 learners' recall of concepts and details from the lecture – and total number of words – negatively correlated with concepts.

Consequently, in this study, several measures of quantity and quality of notes were assessed relative to learners' performance on the multiple-choice and cloze tests following listening to three different lectures. Several lectures were used in order to determine the generalizability of the measures across different lecture content. This analysis was exploratory in nature, so no hypotheses were made prior to the study. All analyses were conducted using the SPSS–X statistical package on an IBM 3081 computer.

Method

Subjects

The subjects in this study were 98 adult students of English as a second language who were studying listening comprehension in six sections of a university program for foreign students. They were predominantly from

TABLE I. STUDENTS' PROFICIENCY TEST SCORES

	N	Mean	Standard Deviation
TOEFL Listening Subtest	59	52.2	4.2
Total TOEFL	59	528	29

Asian and Pacific backgrounds, with a median length of residence in the U.S. of 16 months. Table 1 displays the TOEFL Total and Listening Subtest means and standard deviations for a subset of these learners, for whom these scores were available. Unfortunately, in later analyses, due to absenteeism, the results for each listening task involved fewer subjects. The attempt to maintain students' anonymity precluded assessment of the nature of the eventual samples. By the time of this experiment, the subjects had all had some training in note-taking as a regular part of their course content. No other control or pre-training of their note-taking skill was attempted.

Materials

The materials used in the study were three lectures on academic topics, with corresponding multiple-choice and cloze comprehension tests, which had been prepared and pilot tested in previous research conducted at the Center for Second Language Classroom Research (Chaudron et al. 1986). Each lecture was pre-recorded, about six to seven minutes long, spoken by male and female native speakers of English. The twenty, four-option multiple-choice items for each lecture were scored as right or wrong, and the twenty-item cloze tests were scored by an exact word method (see Chaudron et al. 1986, for details). The following are excerpts from the multiple-choice and cloze test formats:

Lecture Passage Excerpt:
Archeologists are scientists who study man's past history and cultures. But how do archeologists reveal facts about the past? Like detectives, they make use of old practices and of modern technology.

Multiple-choice:
1. Archeologists are scientists who study:
    a. man's past history and culture
    b. modern technology
    c. the surface of the earth
    d. natural phenomena

Cloze passage:
. . . Like detectives, they make use of old practices and of modern technology to _____*(reveal)*_____ facts about the past . . .

Only two of the three lectures were tested with the cloze method. Test means and reliabilities are reported below in Table 2. Note that the cloze test for Lecture 2 was very low in reliability; this was the only test which had not been pilot tested or revised prior to the study.[1]

Design

The design of the study involved the presentation of the three lectures to the same class groups on different days, usually with several days intervening between the first lecture and the next two. Several classes also listened to Lectures 1 and 2 a second time, in order to complete the listening cloze tests on those lectures. The +/− note-retention condition was randomized within classes. The principal effect to be tested was whether the note-retention condition aided success on test scores; this was determined by one-way analysis of variance on test scores with note-retention the independent variable. Secondary analyses, including multiple regression and factor analysis, were conducted on the quality and quantity of the notes taken, to determine whether these values bore any relationship to outcomes on tests, or were influential in success in the note-retention condition.

Note quality scoring

A system for evaluating note quantity and quality, developed by Hull (1986), was employed to score the subjects' notes on nine different dimensions. Details of this system and its development are given in Chaudron et al. (1988) and summarized in Table 3. Two raters collaborated in coding trial sets of notes in six cycles, until they had attained 90–100% agreement on all dimensions. They then each rated about half of the 339 sets of notes.

Procedure

Each class was given two practice trials in listening to short passages and completing multiple-choice answers, then later, cloze blanks, based on the passages. Note paper was distributed to the class, but no training or specific instructions were given as to how to take notes or what to

---

[1] In their generalizability study of lectures and comprehension task measures, Chaudron et al. (1986) had found comparably high reliabilities (*range* = .56 to .72, *median* = .69) for 20-item multiple-choice and rational deletion cloze passages on three different lectures (*n* = 51). The generalizability analysis suggested that slightly higher levels of prediction of students' variance in lecture comprehension would be obtained by increasing the number of lectures instead of increasing different tasks for lectures (e.g., 85% of variance explained by two tasks for four lectures).

include in the notes. The lecture was then played on a SONY CFS–43 cassette player, following which, notes were randomly collected from about half of each class, and the tests were distributed. The note-retention and no-note-retention ("no notes") students might have the opportunity to retain their notes for some lectures and to have them removed for others.

TABLE 2. TEST SCORES FOR RELIABILITIES BY TEST, LECTURE AND TREATMENT

	Mean	Standard Deviation	*n*	*r*	ANOVA
Multiple choice					
Lecture 1					
Notes	12.13	2.68	47		
No Notes	12.39	2.74	44		
Total	12.22	2.69	91	.54	n.s.
Lecture 2					
Notes	11.64	2.39	39		
No Notes	12.22	2.66	41		
Total	11.86	2.53	80	.36	n.s.
Lecture 3					
Notes	11.73	3.41	44		
No Notes	12.13	3.09	39		
Total	11.95	3.21	83	.60	n.s.
Cloze					
Lecture 1					
Notes	8.59	2.86	22		
No Notes	8.95	3.97	20		
Total	8.76	3.35	42	.70	n.s.
Lecture 2					
Notes	7.60	2.10	25		
No Notes	5.89	2.17	18		
Total	6.88	2.24	32	.27	p < .06

Note:
r = Chronbach's alpha; p = .05

Results

Differences in note-retention condition

Table 2 shows the n's, means, and standard deviations for the multiple-choice tests (Lectures 1, 2, and 3), and cloze tests (Lectures 1 and 2), with both overall totals, and broken down by note-retention condition, as well as measures of the reliability of the tests (for all tests, $k = 20$). Because the note-retention condition was re-randomized within class groups for each lecture, comparisons between lectures were not independent, and analyses were calculated separately by lecture.

Results of analysis of variance showed no significant differences between the $+/-$ note-retention groups. While the Lecture 2 cloze test differences approached significance ($p < .06$), this test had very low reliability (Cronbach's alpha = .27), so little stock can be placed in this result. The low reliability of this test also led us to remove it from other primary analyses.

TABLE 3. NOTE-TAKING QUALITY MEASURES: DESCRIPTIONS, SCORING, RANGES, AND MEDIANS

Measure	Description	Scoring
Title	provision of lecture title	0–1
Range = .41–.71	Median = .61	
Numbering	numbers of letters indicating a list	0–3
Range = .52–.99	Median = .71	
Outline	use of hierarchical outlining	0–3
Range = 1.23–1.35	Median = 1.30	
Examples	provision of signalled examples	0–3
Range = .68–1.28	Median = .99	
Verbatim	evidence of transcription, completeness	0–3
Range = .12–.67	Median = .30	
Diagrams	provision of sketches, figures, maps	frequency
Range = .00–.39	Median = .04	
Symbols	provision of arrows, boxes, etc.	frequency
Range = 2.25–5.07	Median = 2.51	
Abbreviations	provision of abbreviated words	frequency
Range = 8.66–11.61	Median = 9.21	
Words	all units not numbers, symbols or diagrams	frequency
Range = 60.15–70.95	Median = 63.71	

Measures of quantity and quality of notes

Although retaining their notes did not seem to affect learners' performance on post-lecture comprehension tests, the exploratory questions regarding the relationship between various note quality measures and test performance, as well as the interrelationships among note quantity and quality measures, were of interest in this study. Table 3 shows the definitions, scoring scheme, and ranges and medians for the five lectures in this study.

Correlations between the note quantity and quality measures and test scores, forward stepwise regression analysis, and factor analysis were calculated for each lecture test. These results are detailed in Chaudron et al. (1988); we will provide only a summary of relevant findings here.

There were few significant ($p < .05$) correlations between note quantity and quality measures and comprehension (multiple choice or cloze) test scores, with magnitudes being quite low (range of $r = .26$ to .37 for total group performance). However, in analyses of differences between learner groups who kept their notes and those who did not, only the former group revealed any significant correlations with comprehension scores, with the magnitudes being consistently higher than those for the total group (range of $r = .42$ to .59). This finding would suggest that in some cases, learners were able to take advantage of their notes in answering the test items.

Stepwise regression analyses demonstrated that with the entry of the quantity/quality measure with the strongest correlation to comprehension outcomes, no other measures were significant; this results from the fact that the note quantity/quality measures were highly inter-correlated among themselves.

A factor analysis (principal components analysis with Varimax rotation) of the intercorrelations among the measures of note quantity and quality for the total group on each lecture revealed three main factors. There were slightly different loadings for each lecture, and the total explained variance attributable to the three factors ranged from 64% to 72%. In general, total words and outline loaded consistently on Factor 1. Quantity of abbreviations and symbols also both loaded on Factor 1 in all but Lecture 3. For this reason, we judge Factor 1 to be a *quantity and organizational* factor. Factor 2 consistently had a loading for frequency of use of diagrams, and several times for use of numbering in lists, which suggests that it is a factor of *representational simplicity*. Factor 3 generally only had a loading for verbatim notes, which would suggest the opposite of simplicity, namely *elaborateness*. Speculation about the nature of these factors is tentative, however, since predictions from the factor models for the intercorrelations among quality measures were not strong. This imprecision might be resolved by the addition of some other note quantity/quality measures, such as the idea unit/efficiency measure used in Dunkel's (1988) study. We were attempting, however, to employ quick, objective measures that were as independent as possible from an analysis of lecture content.

Discussion

As stated above, the lack of any overall effect for note retention on lecture scores should be neither surprising nor a source of consternation. The results of specific correlations and regression analysis show that certain note quality measures are more related to successful comprehension performance than others, on a lecture-specific basis. What we will argue is that, although retaining their notes did not give these learners any *overall* advantage over the condition of not retaining them (likely due in part to the capacity of short-term memory to retain much of the lecture content), *certain information* in the lectures was better retrieved with the aid of notes.

Notes content

In order for the note-retaining condition to be useful for the student, the written notes should contain the necessary information for answering a specific question. Dunkel (1988) and others refer to this as "test answerability". Because some of the quality measures correlated with test scores, and because some test items appeared to differentiate between the note-retention condition and the no-notes condition, we examined the notes in more detail for those items. For each test item which showed a statistically significant difference between conditions, notes were examined to determine which students had included the answer to that item, including abbreviations or symbols for the required word or phrase. Next, for each of these subjects with the item in their notes, it was determined whether or not the subject had kept the notes during the test and then whether or not the item had been answered correctly. It should be noted that all cases in which correctly taking and then retaining a note aided test answerability involved cloze test items.[2] Two points which this analysis uncovered are summarized below.

1. Accuracy in note-taking was critical to the effectiveness of notes as external storage. Accurately noted key words (e.g., "touch", and "satisfactory") if included in kept notes, were easier to answer on a cloze test. Conversely, if errors occurred in noting down information, e.g., inaccurately noting numbers such as "15" for "50", retaining one's notes proved to be a disadvantage.
2. Information had to be noted unambiguously to be useable as external storage. Appropriate use of abbreviations is likely to aid note efficiency, and it did correlate highly with comprehension scores (both multiple-choice and cloze) for two lectures for the note-retention group. On the other hand, we found that in some cases, over-abbreviation or overuse of symbolic representation may have caused difficulty in retrieving the encoded information. For example, several students abbreviated and symbolized the information "intelligence is *passed from parents to their children*" as something like:

p → c par → child int. par → child

---

[2] See Chaudron et al. (1988) for analysis of individual test items favoring the note-retention condition.

Here, we found that such highly schematized notes (within an equally schematized set of notes) did not contain enough information to serve as effective recall cues in reconstructing the lecture information once the students' short-term memory limitations had been surpassed. Thus, if information essential to test answerability is noted in such a fashion, it will only be useful as external storage to the extent that the student has firm control of the meanings of the abbreviations and their relations within the entire passage.

Conclusion

On the whole, our results suggest that the external storage explanation of the value of lecture notes has some justification, although no significant effects were found overall. Our failure to detect any stronger effect of a note-retention condition was likely to have been caused by the short-term delay between listening and testing, in which case the L2 learners' memory for information was sufficient to neutralize the value of retaining notes. Further research should introduce longer delays before testing to measure the effect of note-retention as external storage.

It was also evident in our results that note quality varied considerably among subjects, to the extent that errors in the notes could lead to incorrect responses. To the extent that these errors were not due to poor listening proficiency, this observation leads to the suggestion that further research should attempt to train or promote higher quality notes in the subjects prior to experimentation. Clearly, if a researcher wishes to assess the value of retaining notes, the quality of the notes should be carefully controlled.

Furthermore, it is evident that lecture note quality (in a strictly formal sense) should not be considered directly as a measure of comprehension, i.e., no strong or consistent relationship between our quantity and quality measures and comprehension was observed. However, we recognize the importance of including more content-based measures of note quality in an assessment of degree of comprehension (as in Dunkel 1988).

Finally, we recognize that, ultimately, learners' comprehension of lecture content, however well it is processed by the learner and encoded in notes, will be influenced by the clarity of structure and presentation of the lecture. For this reason, further research on lecture note-taking should devote more attention to the growing literature on lecture style and quality cited in the introduction. By considering lecture structure and the combination of factors reviewed in the present study, researchers will gain greater insight into the process of learning a second language through exposure to it.

Acknowledgements

This paper is a revised version of an earlier technical report (Chaudron, Cook and Loschky 1988) conducted in the Center for Second Language Classroom Research, of the Social Science Research Institute at the University of Hawaii at Manoa.

We would like to thank the following people for their cooperation and assistance in collecting the data for this project: Bill Murdoch, Marisa Brooks, Ray Devenney, Ken Jackson, Gail Kimzin, and Jason Alter. Bill Murdoch also contributed extensively to compiling the data and to the early stages of development of the note-taking coding system. Jonathan Hull's work on the project (see Hull 1986) was invaluable in starting this line of inquiry. Finally, we thank the Department of ESL, University of Hawaii at Manoa, for many forms of support, material and otherwise.

References

Aiken, E. G., G. Thomas, and W. A. Shennum. 1975. Memory for a lecture: effects of notes, lecture rate, and informational density. *Journal of Educational Psychology* 67 (3): 439–444.

Annis, L., and J. Davis. 1975. The effects of encoding and an external memory device on note taking. *Journal of Experimental Education* 44 (2): 44–46.

Barnett, J., F. Di Vesta, and J. Rogozinski. 1981. What is learned in note taking? *Journal of Educational Psychology* 73 (2): 181–192.

Benson, M. J. 1989. The academic listening task: a case study. *TESOL Quarterly* 23 (3): 421–446.

Brown, G. K. 1978. *Lecturing and Explaining*. London: Methuen.

Carrier, C., and A. Titus. 1979. The effects of notetaking: a review of studies. *Contemporary Educational Psychology* 4 (4): 299–314.

———. 1981. Effects of notetaking pretraining and test mode expectations on learning from lectures. *American Educational Research Journal* 18 (94): 385–397.

Chaudron, C. 1985. A method for examining the input/intake distinction. In *Input in Second Language Acquisition*, S. Gass and C. Madden (Eds.), 285–300. Rowley, Mass.: Newbury House.

Chaudron, C., J. Cook, and L. Loschky. 1988. Quality of lecture notes and second language listening comprehension. Technical Report No. 7, Center for Second Language Classroom Research, Social Science Research Institute, University of Hawaii, Manoa.

Chaudron, C., J. Lubin, Y. Sasaki, and T. Grigg. 1986. An investigation of procedures for evaluating lecture listening comprehension. Technical Report No. 5, Center for Second Language Classroom Research, Social Science Research Institute, University of Hawaii, Manoa.

Chaudron, C., and J. R. Richards. 1986. The effect of discourse markers on the comprehension of lectures. *Applied Linguistics* 7 (2): 113–127.

Chaudry, L., and T. Astika. 1991. Effect of lecture types on comprehension.

Manuscript research paper for ESL 672, Department of ESL, University of Hawaii.

DeCarrico, J., and J. W. Nattinger. 1988. Lexical phrases for the comprehension of academic lectures. *English for Specific Purposes* 7: 91–102.

Di Vesta, F., and S. Gray. 1972. Listening and note taking. *Journal of Educational Psychology* 63 (1): 8–14.

Dunkel, P. 1988. The content of L1 and L2 students' lecture notes and its relation to test performance. *TESOL Quarterly* 22 (2): 259–282.

Dunkel, P., S. Mishra, and D. Berliner. 1989. Effects of note-taking, memory, and language proficiency on lecture learning for native and non-native speakers of English. *TESOL Quarterly* 23 (3): 543–550.

Dunkel, P., and F. Pialorsi. 1982. *Advanced Listening Comprehension*. Rowley, Mass.: Newbury House.

Dyer, J., J. Riley, and F. Yekovich. 1979. An analysis of three study skills: notetaking, summarizing, and rereading. *Journal of Educational Research* 73 (1): 3–7.

Fisher, J., and M. Harris. 1973. Effect of note-taking and review on recall. *Journal of Educational Psychology* 65 (3): 321–325.

1974. Effect of note-taking preference and type of notes taken on memory. *Psychological Reports* 35 (3): 384–386.

Hartley, J., and I. K. Davies. 1978. Note-taking: a critical review. *Programmed Learning and Educational Technology* 15 (3): 207–224.

Howe, M. 1970. Note-taking strategy, review, and long-term retention of verbal information. *Journal of Educational Research* 63 (6): 285.

1974. The utility of taking notes as an aid to learning. *Educational Research* 16: 222–227.

Hull, J. 1986. Note-taking from lectures and the second language learner: a review of the literature. ESL 750 term paper, manuscript. Department of English as a Second Language, University of Hawaii, Honolulu.

James, K. 1975. Note-taking in lectures: problems and strategies. In *English for Academic Purposes*, A. Cowie and J. Heaton (Eds.), 89–98. Reading: BAAL/SELMOUS.

James, K., R. Jordan, and A. Matthews. 1979. *Listening Comprehension and Note-Taking Course*. Glasgow: Collins.

Kiewra, K. 1985. Investigating notetaking and review; a depth of processing alternative. *Educational Psychologist* 20 (1): 23–32.

Klemm, W. 1976. Efficiency of handout skeleton notes in student learning. *Improving College and University Teaching* 24 (1): 10–12.

Ladas, H. 1980. Note-taking on lectures: an information-processing approach. *Educational Psychology* 15 (1): 44–53.

Lebauer, R. S. 1988. *Learn to Listen; Listen to Learn*. Englewood Cliffs, N.J.: Prentice Hall.

Locke, E. 1977. An empirical study of lecture notetaking among college students. *Journal of Educational Research* 71: 93–99.

Mason, A. 1983. *Understanding Academic Lectures*. Englewood Cliffs, N.J.: Prentice Hall.

Norton, L. S. 1981. The effects of notetaking and subsequent use on long-term recall. *Programmed Learning and Educational Technology* 18 (1): 16–22.

Otto, S. 1979. Listening for note-taking in EST. *TESOL Quarterly* 13 (3): 319–328.

Peck, K., and M. Hannafin. 1983. The effects of notetaking pretraining and the recording of notes on the retention of aural instruction. *Journal of Educational Research* 75 (2): 100–107.

Plaister, T. 1976. *Developing Listening Comprehension for ESL Students.* Englewood Cliffs, N.J.: Prentice Hall.

Rickards, J. 1979. Notetaking: theory and research. *Improving Human Performance Quarterly* 8 (3): 152–161.

Rickards, J., and F. Friedman. 1978. The encoding versus the external storage hypothesis in note-taking. *Contemporary Educational Psychology* 3 (2): 136–143.

Ruetten, M. K. 1986. *Comprehending Academic Lectures.* New York: Macmillan.

Thomas, G. S. 1978. Use of student notes and lecture summaries as study guides for recall. *Journal of Educational Research* 71 (6): 316–319.

Tyler, A. K., A. A. Jefferies, and C. Davies. 1988. The effect of discourse structuring devices on listener perceptions of coherence in non-native university teachers' spoken discourse. *World Englishes* 7 (2): 101–110.

Williams, J. 1989. The elaboration of discourse marking and intelligibility. Paper presented at the American Association for Applied Linguistics, Washington, D.C.

5 On-line summaries as representations of lecture understanding

Michael Rost

Abstract

This chapter proposes a cognitive view of lecture comprehension instruction which includes use of "on-line" listener reports. The chapter first illustrates a method for accessing listener comprehension processes during lectures, and reports on a study in which a videotaped lecture was presented to 36 non-native speaker (NNS) subjects in a university preparation program. Summaries were elicited "on-line" – at pauses during the lecture. The summaries were analyzed by comparing them with ones written by expert native speaker (NS) listeners in order to assess comprehensibility of the lecture segments and to identify a range of strategies in lecture understanding. The chapter suggests pedagogic applications which incorporate the use of summaries.

Background issues

Investigating listening processes

This study starts with a simple question: How can we find out what listeners are understanding during a lecture? One of the challenges of investigating understanding processes in any discourse setting is trying to get inside the listener's mind, to understand the subjective nature of the listener's task. This challenge is quite pronounced in lecture settings, where the discourse is markedly asymmetrical – the listeners have few opportunities to demonstrate comprehension or confusion and little chance to interrupt or redirect the discourse.

Models of speaker encoding and production processes may serve as a rough mirror of understanding, but there are severe limitations to paralleling production and comprehension processes. Lecturers' behavior and the resultant input text to listeners can be analyzed in order to describe speaker production – the composing, simplifying, and encoding processes that the lecturer undertakes. However, it is misleading to assume that the lecturer "packs" the lecture with information and the listener "unpacks" it in a complementary fashion. The processes

93

by which the lecture input is converted to memorable intake are largely inferential, and cannot be modeled solely by reference to the speaker.

For example, text analyses of macrostructure – the hierarchical organization of information in the text (see text comprehension studies by Meyer 1985 and Kintsch and van Dijk 1978) – do not tell us how listeners might infer the hierarchy of information in a text since it is rarely signalled explicitly by the speaker. Similarly, organization and style analyses of lecturers (see the extensive categorizations done by George Brown [1978]) do not tell us how listeners construct an internal organization of the lecture content or an evaluation of the lecturer's style. In the same vein, studies of simplification of lecture content (see the study by Chaudron and Richards [1986] on use of discourse markers) do not tell us how the listeners come to simplify content when they form a mental representation of it. In sum, there is no valid way to assume that the composing or encoding processes of the lecturer reflect a parallel model of decoding or comprehension processes that the listener undertakes when attending to the lecture.

The fundamental question of how oral input is converted to meaningful intake is a vital one in psycholinguistics and applied linguistics. Two complementary models have been used to characterize this intake process and to explain how listeners come to understand and recall complex texts. These models serve as a starting point for addressing the question of how listeners make sense of lectures as they listen.

The first model is based on information-processing paradigms used in experimental psychology since the 1950s (see Shannon and Weaver 1949; Schramm 1954; Johnson and Klare 1961). The information processing paradigm is essentially "bottom-up": it posits that human comprehension is driven by the listener's need or desire to process "input data" accurately. Information processing models are used to explain how information, initially in the form of phonological signals, is transformed in the listener's memory as it undergoes storage and retrieval conversions. A central tenet of this model is that listening is a sequential process initiated by incoming data:

1. Listener takes in raw speech and retains a phonological representation of it in working memory.
2. Listener immediately tries to organize phonological representation, identifying its content and function.
3. As Listener identifies each constituent, Listener uses it to construct underlying propositions, building continually into a hierarchical representation of propositions.
4. Once Listener has identified the propositions for a constituent, Listener retains them in working memory and at some point purges memory of the phonological representation. (Based on Clark and Clark 1977: 49)

The second model is based on paradigms used in pragmatics to explain how communication occurs in actual social contexts. Pragmatic models tend to be "top-down" in that they posit that comprehension is goal-driven: participants in any interaction pay attention only to information which seems to them relevant to their purposes or needs. A pragmatic model can be used to explain how language users find relevance in situations and texts through activation of expectations and use of selective attention. "Relevance theory" and its applications to discourse comprehension have been best articulated by Sperber and Wilson (1986), with a model of transactional (lecture-type) listening based on it adapted in Rost (1990). A central tenet of this model is that the "stages" are overlapping and interdependent.

1. Listener activates probable knowledge base needed to interpret incoming utterances.
2. Listener attends to utterances selectively, interpreting the propositional meaning of utterances through phonological-syntactic-lexical analysis.
3. Listener interprets a possible pragmatic meaning for utterances, that is, a plausible intention for the speaker in making the utterances in the particular context.
4. Listener orders interpreted propositions into a hierarchical representation to be retained in long-term memory.

Both models are essential in addressing our initial question – How can we find out how a listener comes to understand a lecture? Both models intersect at the critical stage of "forming a hierarchical representation" – deciding what is most important or most relevant. (See also Flowerdew, this volume.) Forming a hierarchical representation is an inferential process of formulating an organization pattern for the input so that it will be maximally memorable and meaningful.

Forming mental representations of a lecture

To investigate this inferential process, it is important to recognize the time constraints in the use of memory. The time span over which actual inference processes take place is usually called the working memory, which is typically fifteen to sixty seconds in duration (Baddeley 1986). There appears to be an optimal amount of information in the working memory in order to affect integration of new text information into the text which has already been processed. If the working memory is confronted with too much new information, only little old information can be held in working memory.

Important old information, which may be necessary for integration of new information, must then be suppressed from working memory and only after a time-consuming search can it be recalled again. Further, there seems to be a fixed amount of new information that can remain in working memory: two to four propositions seem to be the optimal unit for establishing local coherence of the text and incorporating new information into working memory (Rickheit, Schnotz, and Strohner 1985: 16).

While the initial processing of new information takes place in short-term memory, the essential construct in assessment of language comprehension is long-term memory. Long-term memory consists of a network of images and propositional representations, initially formed through experience with external stimuli, but transformed into mnemonic representations which will permit us to reconstruct these representations when access to them is required (Schacter 1982). Long-term memory cannot be activated until at least 30–60 seconds after the presentation of a stimulus, since this is the time required by working memory to sort out the essential elements of incoming stimuli. Actual entry into long-term memory will be dependent on both rehearsal ("effort to remember") and learned organizational schemes (Bostrom and Waldhart 1988).

Access to internal representations

In order to access listener processes while these inference processes in memory are taking place – or as close as possible to the time when they are taking place – we need to design a reliable introspection or reflection task that will allow listeners to reveal the "content" of their internal representations. Introspection techniques have been used before, with some success, to tap the thoughts of L2 learners. Murphy (1987, 1989), for instance, has tried one-on-one interviewing as subjects listened to audio tapes, in order to identify areas of attention and interest. O'Malley, Chamot, and Kupper (1989), among other learning-style researchers in L2 education, have interviewed students (orally and via written questionnaires) in order to discover common techniques and comprehension strategies students use in listening classes.

Researchers using introspection methods invariably encounter challenges in interpreting protocols, as has been recognized by Ericsson and Simon (1984):

1. The subject's perception of the criteria for success in the reporting task influences the quality (and quantity) of the report. For example, knowing that they will be asked to write a summary of a lecture, the listeners may look for more macrostructure (global organization) than they ordinarily would when they listen without such task directions. Similarly, listeners may "stretch" to show more comprehension than they actually experience, and avoid revealing the areas of confusion that are actually part of their internal

representation, if they feel that their summaries are being evaluated by traditional academic criteria. On the other hand, some learners may perceive that the summarizing task will not be evaluated and will under-report what they do understand.

2. The subject's expression ability influences the quality (and quantity) of the report. Subjects who speak or write more coherently and with greater command of the language will appear to have superior comprehension and recall. These more proficient subjects will be able to talk around confusions or partial understandings and embellish their accounts with related information. More proficient subjects are able to produce what Dolitsky (1984) has called "self-enhancing texts". The problem of interpreting the subjects' ideas in self-reports is compounded in L2 studies since, as McLaughlin (1987) has noted, non-native speakers expend much of their cognitive resources on syntactic and lexical processing that non-native speakers can devote to processing the gist and creative construction. Flottum (1985), in a study dealing with evaluation of L2 summaries, has termed this the "language loading factor".

3. The subject's prior knowledge of a topic area influences the quality and quantity of the report – subjects will report what they *know* about a topic, rather than what they understood during a particular experience. As Findahl and Hoijer (1982), Eckhardt, Wood, and Jackobvitz (1991), and Rost (1987) have shown in their listening and memory studies, what subjects had previously known about a topic area enhanced their apparent recall of the discourse they had just heard. Experts in a topic area generally remember more of what they heard, not because of superior language or recall ability, but because of:
   a. previously established schemata for organizing information,
   b. familiarity with facts and ideas that non-experts may consider "new information", and
   c. prior practice with drawing inferences in a particular topic area.

Since all of these factors can play a role in our interpreting the content and style of self-reports, it is important to utilize concrete means of countering the possible distortions:

1. Recognize, in advance, that a self-report will provide clues to the subject's mental representations, and not a clear "reading" of them.
2. Provide structure to the self-reporting task in order to give it more face validity. That is, make the self-reporting task resemble another more commonly used task in the same situation.
3. Utilize the same texts for all subjects so that subjects' individual representations can be compared against a common text base.
4. Establish base-line data, using the self-reports of an expert group for comparison.

By implementing these techniques in the gathering of self-reports, we increase the reliability of the reports, and thereby their unique value in our coming to understand the internal representations of listeners during lectures.

Methodology

Reporting task to reveal mental representation of lecture

A task was devised to provide information about the following questions:

1. Which aspects of a lecture are most salient in the mind of the listener?
2. What type of ordering does the listener perceive?
3. How coherent is the lecture? Does the lecture make sense?

A reporting task was devised and pilot-tested which required the subjects to report "on-line", while they were listening to a lecture, what they currently understood.

Subjects

Thirty-six non-native speaker students at the intermediate level in a university preparation program in Japan were selected randomly to be part of an experimental content class on social psychology. The major component of this class was listening to a series of five pre-recorded videotapes on the topic of social psychology, taking notes, participating in discussions and passing tests on the content of the lectures. The students were aged 18–20 and had studied English in high school for three to six years, and in the preparation program for six to twelve months. Their average TOEFL score was 440 (range 420–470).

Materials (text)

Five videotapes were part of a social psychology lecture series (from Rost 1987). The tapes had an average length of 12 minutes. Each tape was accompanied by readings, discussion worksheets, and follow-up tests. The fourth tape of the series, "Attitudes and Behavior", was selected for this study (see Appendix A for a full transcript).

Elicitations of base-line data

In order to derive base-line data against which student summaries could be evaluated, an "expert group" of ten native speakers listened to the lecture and wrote summaries under the identical conditions that the students would face. They were instructed to listen to the lecture and when the tape was paused to, "write down what you think is important in the lecture". The tape was played and paused at logical breaks in the

TABLE 1. COMMON POINTS IN "MASTERY GROUP" SUMMARIES

These statements (or paraphrases) are found in all expert group summaries.

Part One

1. Norms are *accepted standards* of behavior or thinking.
2. All societies have norms for *basic survival elements*, such as food.
3. Some norms, such as "hierarchies of address" are *universal*.
4. Some norms, called "rituals", are *complex*; these are sequences of action in a fixed order.

Part Two

5. Roles provide *expectations* for appropriate attitudes and behaviors.
6. Role *reversals* lead to changes in attitudes and behavior.

Part Three

7. *Exposure* to attitudes and ideas *influences* us to accept those attitudes and ideas as normal.
8. *Pressure to conform* to group standards *influences* us to think and act in ways that may be contrary to our own judgement.
9. *In-group bias* is the tendency to *favor* members of our own group.

TABLE 2. TOKENS OF SUMMARIZING STRATEGIES IN EXPERT GROUP SUMMARIES

1. *Reporting* fact or idea (Some norms are universal . . . we change our way of behaving to fit the new role)
2. *Framing*: providing a framework for the summary to give it greater cohesion. (The lecturer talks about . . . He deals with . . . He continues by . . . Then he introduces . . .)
3. *Embedding* ideas: providing an order of importance for ideas (The main point is . . . Another point is . . . , which is a type of . . .)

---

text after approximately four minutes, six minutes, and ten minutes. (See transcript for pause points.) The statements included by each native speaker were listed, and from these ten lists, an intersecting set was made to represent the main ideas of the lecture (see Table 1). In addition, these ten native-speaker summaries were scanned for stylistic features that seemed to describe an "expert" summarizing style. The most commonly observed of these stylistic features served as strategy tokens for writing summaries under the experimental conditions (see Table 2). Taking the two aspects of the analysis into account, it was possible to define eight main ideas in the lecture and three main aspects of summarizing style.

Elicitation of student summaries

During a regularly scheduled class period, the non-native speaker subjects viewed the tape and during three pauses in the lecture were given two minutes to write a summary of the part of the lecture they had just seen. Specifically, the subjects were told to write down, in English, whatever they thought was important in the lecture. They were allowed to use notes that they had taken during the lecture. These "on-line" summaries were collected at the end of the lecture, photocopied, and returned to the students during the following class. The summaries were typed and two raters (the author and an ESL teacher colleague) independently read the summaries and evaluated them against specific criteria for content and style (see Table 3).

TABLE 3. PROCEDURES FOR RATING SUMMARIES

---

1. *Content*
   Which of the nine main ideas (see Table 1) were noted by the subjects?

   Each subject was given a content score. Two points were given if an idea was clear and complete (maximum 18 points overall); one point given if key words were included, but the idea was not clear or complete; no points given if no key words or paraphrase of idea were attempted.

2. *Summarizing style*
   Which of the three strategy tokens (see Table 2) were used by the subjects?

   Each subject was given a summarizing profile based on comments by the two raters. The profiles reflected the most apparent style in the summaries:

   Reporting-style – tending to provide lists of lexical items or strings of statements (but without rendering ideas or apparent attempt to provide cohesive summary)
   Framing style tending to write cohesive paragraphs, using time sequence markers
   Embedding style – tending to reorganize ideas in lecture hierarchically

---

Analysis procedures

Individual profiles

Each of the 36 summaries was analyzed individually for both content and style. Reading individual summaries produced unique pictures of how each student independently understood and summarized the lecture. In each summary, the raters were able to identify focuses on particular topics, as well as omissions of other topics. They were able to identify topics and ideas that were clearly understood and others that seemed to be only partially understood or completely misunderstood.

In addition, they encountered a wide range of writing abilities and strategies for writing summaries. Sample summaries by native speakers and the non-native speaker subjects are included in Appendix B.

Group profiles

For the purpose of this analysis of inferencing processes by listeners, however, the summaries were considered as a group. The 36 summaries were analyzed collectively for patterns of content and style. Discernible patterns of content that related most closely to the theme of inferencing were: 1. inclusions and omissions of main ideas and 2. misunderstandings and confusion of main ideas. Patterns of style identified were: 1. reporting, 2. framing, and 3. embedding.

Content analysis

Content analysis is based on interpreting several aspects of the listener's representation of a segment of the lecture in terms of: accuracy, completeness, familiarity with concepts, and confusion of concepts. The content analysis of the summaries consisted of noting 1. the relative inclusion and omission of main ideas, 2. apparent mishearings of key words, and 3. frequently misunderstood ideas. Results of the inclusion and omission of main ideas are given in some detail below to demonstrate the most general problem faced by the raters in interpreting the accuracy and completeness of summaries. The most commonly noted apparent mishearings are presented to demonstrate one of the specific interpretation problems in deciding upon the degree of the student's familiarity with a concept. Selected misunderstandings are presented to demonstrate the problem of interpreting a student's confusion with some concepts during the lecture.

1. Inclusion and omission of main ideas

In the time allotted for summarizing, most students were able to include two ideas in their summaries of each section. The average summary content score for the 36 subjects in the study was 11.3 (out of a maximum 18 points), with a range from 4 to 18 points. Some of the nine main ideas were more frequently reported, while others were less commonly reported on (see Table 4). Most summary writers received partial credit (one point) for the main ideas they included, as they were often judged to have provided a key word or phrase, but were not explicit. All summary writers had some idea omissions, with omissions ranging from one idea to six (of the total nine) ideas (see Appendix B for a sample of the student and native-speaker summaries).

TABLE 4. MOST FREQUENTLY REPORTED MAIN IDEAS IN STUDENT
SUMMARIES

---

1. (Idea number 1) Norms are *accepted standards* of behavior or thinking. – mentioned by 94% of subjects.
2. (Idea number 7) *Exposure* to attitudes and ideas *influences* us to accept those attitudes and ideas as normal. – mentioned by 89% of subjects.
3. (Idea number 5) Roles provide *expectations* for appropriate attitudes and behaviors. – mentioned by 78% of subjects.
4. (Idea number 6) Role *reversals* lead to changes in attitudes and behavior. – mentioned by 69% of subjects.
5. (Idea number 2) All societies have norms for *basic survival elements*, such as food. – mentioned by 62% of subjects.
6. (Idea number 8) *Pressure to conform* to group standards *influences* us to think and act in ways that may be contrary to our own judgement. – mentioned by 56% of subjects.
7. (Idea number 9) *In-group bias* is the tendency to *favor* members of our own group. – mentioned by 43% of subjects.
8. (Idea number 4) Some norms, called "rituals", are *complex*; these are sequences of action in a fixed order. – mentioned by 32% of subjects.
9. (Idea number 3) Some norms, such as "hierarchies of address" are *universal*. – mentioned by 18% of subjects.

The idea that was reported most clearly and completely concerned "norms", which was the first idea in the lecture, and which is a concept that students were apparently familiar with prior to the lecture. Example statements (*note:* S1 refers to Subject number 1, etc.):

(S15) Norm is for food, clothes, survival.
(S1) Norms are applied to food, clothes, ways of walking, way of behavior.

The idea that was second most clearly articulated concerned "exposure", which occurred at the beginning of the third section of the lecture. Again, interpreting summary statements related to this topic was typically non-problematic. For example:

(S16) Of course, group influences us in several ways. One is proximity – we choose idea of our near group.
(S11) "proximity effect" – adapt to norm principle of the family or certain group.

By contrast, the least commonly reported main idea concerned "universals", which was dealt with two minutes into the lecture, and which was apparently a new concept for most listeners. Interpreting problems for the raters increased dramatically in evaluating summary statements dealing with this topic (*note:* comments in brackets are made by raters).

(S35) There are several traditional behaves in the world, universal and districal. [recognizes distinction, unique use of "behaves" and "districal"]
(S36) The speaker gave us an idea of different addressing too. [recognizes topic, but unclear]

Many summary statements for these ideas included vague, incomplete, or overgeneralized ideas. For example:

(S17) Dr. Brown's universal norm hierarchies of address. [topic only, incomplete statement]
(S25) And he said about example of social norm, and other hierarchy. [mentions topic only]
(S23) He said conformity and bias tends to influence our behavior. [very general]

Sometimes, the "ideas" reported were little more than lists of the key words (or approximations of them) associated with the main ideas. This style of presentation posed problems for the raters, who often could not decide if the listener understood the concept or merely noted down the word from the board. For example:

(S24, part one)   social psychology norms culture and behavior [list only]
(S13, part two)   roles roles receival pygmalon effect [list only]

The second least commonly reported idea concerned "rituals", which appeared near the end of the first section of the lecture, and which was an elaboration on an earlier idea ("norms"). Again, many summaries which did attempt to report on rituals also included vague or incomplete statements:

(S33) Each society have ritual things about their behavior. [vague, no elaboration]
(S3)   About social skill there are some differences. {no elaboration]
(S18) Ritual is more than norm. [not clear, in what way more than?]

Some of the summaries included the example given to illustrate a "ritual", but gave no explicit statement of the main idea it supported. For example:

(S35) Especially, when new neighbors come, people behavior toward them is specified one. ["especially" may be used to show contrast between norm and ritual?]
(S29) A person's characteristics is shown in his behavior such as greeting. [unclear; may be a new construction: no discussion of person's characteristics in the lecture]

2. Mishearings of words

One type of misunderstanding is a lexical misunderstanding, cued by an inaccurate perception of the form and meaning of a particular word. The raters found that several of the key words in the lecture were identified as critical to the lecture, but were apparently unfamiliar to the subjects. Even though most key words were written on the board (within the video), many subjects provided alternative spellings. The following are examples of mishearings:

Pygmalion Effect	*Hierarchy*
pigmallion effect	herchy
pigmillion effect	hierchy
pygmarion effort	hierarcky

In-group bias	*Behavior*
in group vias	beheaves
group vice	heaves
group decides	behaves
group by decide	
in group best	
group base	
group boast	
non-group bias	

These misspellings in the summaries would seem to indicate lack of familiarity with the terms.

3. Misunderstanding and partial understanding of ideas

An additional interpretation problem for the raters concerned apparent misunderstandings. The raters concurred that within numerous summaries, even though partial credit was to be given for inclusion of key words, many misunderstandings were taking place. The two most commonly misunderstood points were:

– Some norms, such as "hierarchies of address" are universal. (Idea number 3)
– Some norms, called "rituals", are complex; these are sequences of action in a fixed order. (Idea number 4)

Although misunderstanding of these concepts may be most apparent in the form of omissions in the summaries (these ideas were attempted by only a third of the summary writers), those students who did attempt summaries of these ideas often misstated the point. For example:

(S31) He gave us an example about hierarchy of address which meant how to be neighbors in the location. [seems to mix examples of taxi driver and new neighbor ritual?]

This summary fuses two examples – the taxi driver asking for directions in a "neighborhood" (lines 59–83 in the lecture) and the "new neighbor ritual" (lines 101–156 in the lecture). Other summaries also fused key words from the lecture to provide summary statements. Another subject confused the more common use of "address" (i.e., street address) with the usage in the lecture (i.e., way of presenting self to another person):

(S10) He told example of hierachy of address. This is what taxi drivers ask to find the address in a new neighborhood.

Other subjects seemed to confuse the "learning the new neighbor ritual" with "being an acceptable member of society" by equating the example with the definition, rather than viewing the example as subordinate to the definition. For example:

(S9) Especially, when new neighbors come, people behavior toward them is specified one. [probably means that: specified one = determined by social rules?]

Most subjects received only partial credit for their main ideas reported. This "partial understanding" judgement was made when summary statements included vague words or when there was little or no elaboration following a general statement. For example:

(S5) Role reverse is relationship.
(S17) Proximity effect means same causes by some different attitude people.
(S2) Proximity effect is what style of thinking or acting of people.

In many of these summary statements, we see apparent expression difficulties the writers are having with syntax and lexis.

Style analysis

Style analysis is based on the impressions formed by the raters in reading individual summaries and comparing them to group norms in terms of readability. Style analysis consists of interpreting the patterns and strategies the subjects used to write the summaries. The subjects utilized all three tokens of summarizing style noted in the expert group summaries.

1. Reporting

Reporting moves, reiterating or rephrasing facts from the lecture, appear very often in the student summaries. Reporting moves are considered to be a sign of selective listening: the listener selects the most important propositions to report. Most student summaries utilized only reporting moves, with little, if any, framing or embedding. For example:

(S1) Norms are necessary in a group, for example greeting door, visitor admire house, farewell, and so on. Norms are distincted by age, sex, and occupation. [clear statement of main idea, but example from neighbor ritual seems misplaced here. Original use of word: distincted.]

(S9) Proximity effect is that people grow up and expect the style of act which is commonly good. [Idea "which is commonly good" is probably meant as "common acts" = "good acts"?]

The majority of summary writers utilized the words, propositions, and examples heard in the lecture. These summary writers tended not to introduce synonyms, paraphrases, and similar examples to clarify ideas in the lecture. This is viewed as a low-risk strategy, although the juxtaposition of (apparently difficult) terms often led to vague or anomalous usages. For example:

(S25) Role reversal depend on attitude and behavior. [vague]
(S28) Term is hierarchy of characteristics about people [unclear]

By contrast, the expert group tended to use more paraphrases. For example:

(NS1) An other example is given about teacher's bias toward their own students. Again, there seems to be a strong effect – or a strong desire – for people to conform to what their group thinks is normal or correct.

(NS2) For example, we may think that some foods are normal and others taboo, but this is arbitrary = other groups may have different norms.

In these summaries, the terms "strong desire", "taboo", and "arbitrary" are considered paraphrases as these words did not appear in the lecture text.

2. Framing

Framing is making explicit the organization or the overall structure and goals of the lecture. Framing is considered to be a clear sign of inferencing: the listener has provided a logical grouping for ideas. Framing moves appear in less than half of the student summaries. For example:

(S14) This lecture is about "influence on behavior". There are many classifications in it.

Framing is most easily recognized in the form of sequence markers. For example:

(S17) ... Next, the lecture is about role expectation, which is ...
(S22) At last the lecture talk about ...

Explicit framing was used more frequently in the expert group summaries:

(NS1) ... The lecturer continues with a discussion of ...
(NS2) ... This part of the lecture deals with ...

3. Embedding

Embedding is the presentation of facts or ideas in a hierarchical order. Embedding is considered to be a sign of inferencing: the listener has selected and then reorganized ideas in an order of importance. Clear embedding moves appear in less than a third of the summaries.

(S8)   At last the lecture talk about exposure and conformity. There are three case in them. One is exposure to family idea. If mother says dress this way, we wear those clothes. Another case is group says, "say this way", and we say that way. Another case is group is equal, but we say, "my group is best". These thing also influence attitudes and behavior [signals example]
(S31) He gave us three types of exposure and conformity: proximity effect, group pressure, and group bias. [provides grouping]

An ambiguous case of embedding is the use of chronological markers. It is difficult to know if the summarizer is viewing the statements as of equal value or is simply reporting in a paratactic fashion. The following excerpt, on the one hand, shows that the summary writer perceives the three cases (proximity effect, pressure of groups, and in-group bias) as subordinate to the main heading (exposure and conformity):

(S19) Exposure and conformity (These affects people's behaviors and attitudes).
       – proximity effect – go as group standard
       – pressure of groups; if all members except you agree with something, you tend to be agree with it.
       – in group bias you tend to make man who like, graduated. [embeds ideas under main heading]

On the other hand, the following excerpt clearly suggests some subordination of ideas, but does not show how the listener constructs the subordination:

(S25) Social psychology studys about influence, attitudes, and behavior of people. We must think about foods, clothes, something ways of talking, and ways of treating people – all is influence to us. And he said about example of social norms and other hierarchy. [seems to embed "social norms" and "other hierarchy" under influences . . .]

It is possible to detect an implicit embedding in the majority of summaries if we look into single statements to see how different lexical concepts are subordinated. For example, in the following summary statement, the summarizer apparently subordinates "social skills" and "ritual" to "norms":

(S11) A concept of "norms". All (society/culture) has now (elements standards) to survive. We see this as basic elements – norms of food, clothes, house. There are "social skills" – he call it "ritual" – not to survive, but to be comfortable for our society. [seems to order ideas well; own construction in use of "comfortable", which isn't in lecture, ties in earlier idea of "survival"]

This summary statement does seem to provide implicit ordering of ideas, partly through order of mention ("norm" first and "ritual" later) and partly through elaboration and contrast to earlier ideas ("ritual is not to survive"). The following summary is a similar case:

(S35) There are several traditional behaves in the world, universal and districal. They range from eating and working to acting to other people . . .

Here the examples of eating, working, and acting toward other people are embedded into the main idea: there are traditional (i.e., normal) ways of behaving. Other summary statements, through the apparent decision of the writer to collapse all of the lecture content into one or two brief statements, indicate a global sort of embedding. For example:

(S32) Group pressure influences us. We behave by group's impact and follow their idea. [original construction of "impact"]

In this summary, the writer has collapsed all of the ideas into one main idea statement and one elaboration statement.

The most difficult cases of interpreting possible embedding in the subjects' summaries occurred when the summary statements were brief and unelaborated:

(S9)   We behave to many people in several ways. [doesn't elaborate]
(S10) Exposure means particular type. [unclear; no elaboration – type of what?]
(S5)   Ritual is a complex situation. [no elaboration]

These create the impression of overgeneralizing, rather than embedding, since abstract words (such as "complex", "particular", "environment") are being used to define key terms, which the subject apparently does not understand clearly.

Non-embedding

Although many summary statements were ambiguous about how the listener was subordinating ideas, some summary writers appeared not to be attempting subordination at all. Some summaries allotted considerable space to listing details of examples, often in the absence of superordinate ideas. For example:

(S18) In rituals, we learn greeting at the door, how to admire house, how to serve tea and biscuits, how to give farewell. [uses whole sequence from example]
(S20) There are exposure and conformity. Same a social group – which is longer? A or B or C? Why? Because most of group say this. [uses actual example from lecture]
(S27) Group makes you say "A is longer than B" even this is not true. [uses actual example]
(S13) Influence of behaviors – visitor at door, ways of talking [unclear grouping]

Self-monitoring

Some of the statements made in the summaries by both the NNS students and the NS experts could not be classified by the three style tokens of reporting, framing, and embedding. At times, the writers gave self-monitoring comments – reports on what they were thinking of the lecture or their comprehension of the ideas in it. For example:

(S23) He said we have norms for everything. But what are norms? I didn't concentrate. [self-monitoring]
(S34) Role expectations – I couldn't understand what he explain. [self-monitoring]
(S14) He explained something, but I didn't get it. [self-monitoring]

This parallels the use of self-monitoring statements by the native speakers:

(NS1) One point seems to be that once we acquire a new role (like foreman) we begin to change our ways of behaving to fit the new role – we feel a very strong pressure to do this – perhaps something in our human make-up responds to social pressure?
(NS2) The example of *My Fair Lady* was brought up, since she went through a role reversal and began to be treated differently. (It's not clear how this relates to norms.)

Discussion

Comprehension of lecture content

The content aspect of the summaries may be discussed quantitatively, in terms of how much the subjects did or did not understand, or qualitatively, in terms of the strategies the listeners used in trying to understand and trying to summarize the main ideas. Looking at the summaries as a quantifiable product, we can evaluate the writers' performances as relatively "effective" or "ineffective". Since the average summary score, against a baseline of expert summaries, was little over 50%, we might simply conclude that most subjects' performances were ineffective – the lecture was too difficult or the students were ill-prepared for the lecture, or the summary task was too challenging. However, looking at the task results more qualitatively – in terms of strategies for understanding – it is apparent that nearly all students were engaged actively in trying to understand the lecture and to select and order the ideas in their summaries. The great majority of students (over 78%) successfully reported at least three key ideas from the lecture:

1. (Idea number 1) Norms are accepted standards of behavior or thinking – mentioned by 94% of subjects.
2. (Idea number 7) Exposure to attitudes and ideas influences us to accept those attitudes and ideas as normal – mentioned by 89% of subjects.
3. (Idea number 5) Roles provide expectations for appropriate attitudes and behaviors – mentioned by 78% of subjects.

This consistency of reporting suggests that the lecture was comprehensible in some degree – the lecture succeeded in conveying three important ideas against the backdrop of numerous expansions, examples, and tangents.

Ideas that were misunderstood or omitted from the summaries suggest that the students had either insufficient background knowledge or insufficient opportunities to seek clarification or, more simply, that there was an overload of new concepts to understand and report. This overloading could have led not only to the students' missing these extra points, but also to their confusing the points they did understand initially.

In many cases, it is difficult to judge a student's comprehension. One reason is the wide use of a "juxtaposition strategy" in the summaries. Students often posed two key words together with only a vague link between the words (for example, (S36) "behavior is a hierarchy"). This is an extreme form of what Brown and Day (1983) call a copy and delete strategy, what Flottum (1985) calls the "zero strategy", and what Kintsch and van Dijk (1978) call a verbatim strategy. In essence, the listener takes a low-risk strategy by assuming that two key words, closely juxtaposed in the lecture text, will effectively communicate the main idea. Often, of course, this strategy leads to creative anomalies, as seen in many of the summary samples.

Summarizing style

Summarizing style can be viewed from the perspective of task expectations and demands, or from the aspect of language development. In terms of task expectation, it is feasible that most students perceived that the task was asking them to report what they had understood – in terms of statements that they could recall. This would explain the relative paucity of framing moves and attempts to organize facts in a hierarchical order of importance. Therefore, even if many students were capable of expressing greater comprehension of the lecture through use of framing and embedding styles, they may have chosen the reporting style for the sake of simplicity.

In terms of task demands, the two minutes allotted to summary writing at each pause may have forced students to select the most economical strategy – emptying out the contents of working memory onto the summary page. Thinking through one's ideas and searching through notes may have been considered too time-consuming for the task. With additional practice, many students may have found that the summary writing time was indeed sufficient to recall, organize, and embed ideas more effectively.

Looking at summarizing style from the perspective of language development, we can readily see that many of the difficulties in interpreting the summaries are due in part to the writing abilities of the students. Many students are evidently attempting to write down ideas that are unfamiliar to them, using words they do not understand and grammatical structures that they have not yet mastered.

Conclusions

Effectiveness of on-line summaries as representations

The initial question of the study was: How can we find out what listeners are understanding during a lecture? A method employing on-line summaries was proposed to assist us in exploring this question. The study has shown both the problems and promises of employing this methodology in actual lectures or in experimental settings.

A number of problems arise in using this methodology. The first is the obvious issue of face validity: lecturers typically do not stop their lectures and ask for summaries or reflections, so the methodology introduces an element of surprise or strangeness into the discourse setting. The pausing itself introduced an opportunity for reflection that is not often found in actual lectures, and this opportunity may have enhanced comprehension for some subjects and interfered with comprehension for others. As such, it is not clear to what extent the summaries reflect "normal" comprehension processes.

The second problem is the issue of interpretability of the summaries. As readers of the summaries will note, it is not always apparent what the summary writers mean. Considering the subjects' difficulties with second language expression, in addition to their difficulties with organizing the lecture information and handling the time constraints of the task, the readers tended to be overly accepting of a summary ("Yes, this subject truly understands the lecture"). This attitude, natural as it may be, often interfered with the goals of the study – to find out what the listeners are understanding. Utilizing a more "objective" set of criteria – scoring main idea inclusions, noting misunderstandings, counting strategy tokens – helped in neutralizing this interference. However, it could never be eliminated entirely, since it became apparent to the readers that the criteria for "scoring" the summaries did not capture all of the dynamics of the listening–summarizing event.

In spite of these problems, the on-line summaries do provide promise for revealing listener representations of the lecture. The first advantage of the on-line summary is that it allows the student and teacher (or researcher) to get closer to the window of time during which long-term memory associations are formed. If critical memory associations are being formed *during* the lecture as new ideas are constructed by the listener, then it is important for us to note how these associations are being made. Waiting until after the lecture is simply too late for us to assess this process, and too late to intervene to remedy confusion or to repair partial understanding.

The second advantage of the on-line summary method is that it is effective in demonstrating (to the teacher or the researcher) an area of focus for the listener. Completeness or correctness of comprehension may *not* be the goal for listeners *while* they are listening to a lecture. A more common goal, and perhaps a more appropriate one, may be to find one area of salience within the lecture from which to construct new knowledge. On-line summaries seem to be effective at finding that area of salience, or focus, for the listener.

The third advantage of the method lies in its effectiveness in identifying confusion, misunderstandings, and partially understood ideas. Representations that listeners form from lectures typically contain confusions and misunderstandings, and not simply a sterile hierarchy of "new information". Thus, while on-line summaries may be "messy" to look at, they may reflect more closely the actual understanding processes that the listener is undertaking. To the extent that these unrehearsed summaries do reflect understanding processes, the summaries serve as a reference for interviewing individual listeners about causes of confusion and misunderstanding.

Implications for pedagogy

From the perspective of the learner, this study may seem to project a rather pessimistic picture of L2 learners groping in confusion as they listen to authentic lectures. However, from the perspective of the teacher, this study allows for lecturers to L2 learners to develop realistic strategies for instruction. Many learners, particularly in the lengthy years of the intermediate stages of language learning, regularly experience confusion in lectures. The task for pedagogy is to help learners stay the course – to find ways to deal with the partial understanding and misunderstanding they experience during lectures.

1. Promotion of a cognitive view of instruction

In order to prepare L2 students to deal with confusion during lectures, instructors can help equip their students with concrete strategies:

1. Self-monitoring: checking one's own comprehension and sense of satisfaction during the lecture (see Resnick 1984; Chan et al. 1987)
2. Questioning: formulating types of questions that will lead to clarification and greater comprehension (see Rost and Ross 1991; Jonz 1987)
3. Forming hierarchies: guided note-taking (see Robin et al. 1977; Carrier and Titus 1981) leading students to list ideas in lectures in order to search for subordination and hierarchical ordering, searching for logical connective relationships rather than amassing details
4. Building a lexical base for lecture instruction: generating lists of key terms for students to prepare prior to a lecture. Being familiar with the common meanings of these terms will allow the listeners to comprehend and make inferences during the lecture. (See Rost 1987)

2. Use of self-report protocols to teach listening strategies

In order to assist students in updating and revising their understanding of lecture content, instructors can instigate some type of self-report or summarizing protocol. The technique which was used with students who participated in this study was the comparison of student and expert summaries. In this application, students receive several different summaries and evaluate them by:

1. counting the number of ideas presented;
2. underlining the main points and circling supporting points;
3. comparing (rank ordering) the summaries in terms of effectiveness.

This use of summaries allows learners a chance to see how effective summary writers – and by analogy, effective listeners – identify a macrostructure in the lecture. (See Voss 1988 and Zabrucky 1986 for approaches to teaching macrostructure analysis to students.) Principles for writing effective summaries include:

1. Generalizing: synthesizing high level information from various parts of the text and "reducing" the text to a general principle, fact, or argument. In order to help students achieve this aim, the lecturer may need to pause at key points to indicate that synthesizing is appropriate, and to guide students in doing it effectively.
2. Clarifying arguments: subordinating information and introducing terms or concepts that effectively characterize the speaker's intended meaning. To develop this skill, the lecturer will need to encourage student paraphrasing of sections of the lecture.
3. Identifying the speaker's modality (or intention): supplying "meta-statements" about the speaker's reasoning and decisions for structuring the text in a particular way. To develop this skill, the lecturer may need to pose "meta-questions" (such as, "What do you think about this idea?" "What is your opinion about this?") to take the students "outside the text". These questions may help the students detect speaker attitudes such as hyperbole, sarcasm, and amusement that may assist them in understanding the lecture.
4. Evaluating the text (and speaker) in terms of effectiveness: supplying judgements of the clarity and effectiveness of the lecturer in getting points across to the audience. To develop this skill, the lecturer will need to become interactive, probing the students at certain points in the lecture about the effectiveness of examples and explanations in expressing new ideas.

Mindful consideration of these basic issues in L2 lecture pedagogy – promotion of a cognitive view of instruction and use of self-report protocols (such as summarizing) to promote macrostructural thinking – is likely to increase the quality of our instruction to L2 learners and lead them to adopt more active comprehension skills and strategies.

Appendix A

Lecture transcript
Note on conventions for this transcription: Line groupings indicate pause units, with underlined words and phrases showing phonological prominence of the speaker. Intonation, gaze, gestures and other cues, such as writing on the board, are not noted in this version of the transcript.

1.   hello <u>everybody</u>/
2.   today I would like to <u>continue</u>
     our discussions of social psychology/
3.   by talking about some of the <u>major influences</u> on our attitudes/

4. and on our <u>behaviors</u>/
5. I think the place to <u>start</u> is by introducing the idea or the <u>concept</u> of a <u>norm</u>/
6. <u>n o r m</u>/
7. and I'm sure you're all <u>familiar with this</u> concept/
8. a norm is an accepted or expected <u>standard</u> of behavior/
9. or standard of <u>thinking</u> in a given group of people/
10. and we find that <u>all groups</u> of people have norms/
11. for an <u>array of things</u>/
12. for basic things like the <u>food they eat</u>/
13. the <u>clothes they wear</u>/
14. to much more <u>complex types</u> of/
15. behavior and <u>decisions</u>// –
16. I would like to <u>give you an example</u> of a norm/
17. OK first I'm going to give you some <u>names</u> of some food items/
18. see if you've <u>heard</u> of these/
19. or have <u>eaten</u> these before/
20. here they are <u>oysters snails</u>   .
21. <u>locusts fish pork beef snakes</u>/
22. OK now all of these are <u>food items</u>/
23. that are <u>part of the norm</u> within given societies/
24. for example, <u>Americans eat oysters</u>/
25. but they <u>don't eat snails</u> OK/
26. the <u>French eat</u> snails/
27. but they <u>don't eat</u> locusts/
28. the Zulu in Africa <u>eat locusts</u>/
29. but they <u>don't eat</u> fish/
30. the <u>Egyptians eat fish</u>/
31. but they <u>don't eat</u> pork
32. <u>Indians will eat</u> pork/
33. but they <u>won't eat</u> beef/
34. <u>Russians</u> will eat beef/
35. but they <u>won't eat</u> snakes/
36. the <u>Chinese will</u> eat snakes/ –
37. and they <u>don't eat oysters</u> for example/
38. do you <u>see what</u> I mean/ –
39. that different types of food are <u>part</u> of one group's norm/
40. but <u>not another group's</u> norm/
41. so that each group has <u>different</u> norms/
42. for <u>things like food</u>/ –
43. OK now that it seems in <u>every culture</u>/
44. we do have <u>standards</u> for these kinds of things/
45. that relate to the very <u>basic elements</u> of survival/
46. such as <u>food</u>/

47. and our basic <u>habits</u> such as the way that we get dressed/
48. the <u>way that we talk</u> to people/
49. in <u>different situations</u>//
50. now some people claim that there are <u>universal norms</u>/
51. norms that <u>all societies</u> have/
52. one <u>example</u> of a universal norm/
53. is a norm for <u>hierarchies of address</u>/
54. an American psychologist named Roger <u>Brown</u> has talked about
55. the <u>hierarchies of address</u>/
56. the ways or <u>standards of addressing</u>/
57. the standards we use for addressing <u>different people</u> in our society/
58. as being a <u>universal</u>/
59. let me give you an <u>example of this</u>/
60. recently <u>I was in a taxi</u> in Tokyo/
61. or actually I believe it was <u>Nagoya</u>/
62. and I <u>hadn't been</u> to this place/
63. and <u>neither had</u> the taxi driver apparently/
64. so as we <u>got in the neighborhood</u>/
65. we had to <u>stop the car</u>/
66. and ask in turn <u>several different people</u>/
67. if they had ever <u>heard of this particular</u> building/
68. and the taxi driver stopped and <u>asked</u>
69. about four or <u>five different</u> people/
70. a <u>housewife</u> in maybe her early <u>thirties</u>/
71. an elderly woman maybe in her <u>seventies</u>/
72. a <u>businessman</u> maybe in his forties/
73. and a group of <u>schoolchildren</u>/
74. say around ten or <u>twelve years old</u>/
75. and the way that he addressed these people was really <u>quite different</u>/
76. the way that he <u>approached them</u>/
77. the way that he <u>opened the conversation</u>/
78. was very <u>different</u>/
79. because the people were of <u>different ages</u>/
80. different <u>sexes</u> different <u>social</u> positions/
81. so this is an example of a <u>hierarchy</u> of address/
82. which is a <u>type of norm</u>/
83. and it is <u>claimed to be</u> a universal norm//
84. OK now so far I have mentioned norms about about <u>very basic things</u>/
85. I've mentioned some norms for things like <u>talking</u>/
86. things like <u>eating</u>/
87. and these are rather <u>simple norms</u>/
88. there are of course more <u>complex ones</u>/

89. which involve a <u>series of actions</u>/
90. or a <u>series of</u> behaviors/
91. and these norms are called <u>rituals</u>//
92. all right rituals are a set or <u>series of actions</u> which/
93. take place in a <u>certain order</u>/
94. and they <u>together</u> form a certain kind of norm//
95. one example of this is quoted by <u>a British psychologist</u> named Michael <u>Argyle</u>/
96. Argyle had studied the rituals in <u>various societies</u>/
97. including <u>British</u> society/
98. and he has identified a <u>number of steps</u>/
99. that <u>take place</u> in different rituals/
100. one ritual that I'd like <u>to mention</u> is called/
101. is what he calls the <u>new neighbor ritual</u>/
102. all right in the <u>new neighbor ritual</u>/
103. as he <u>calls</u> it/
104. we have a <u>typical</u> set of/
105. <u>set of</u> behaviors//
106. when a new family <u>moves into</u> a neighborhood/
107. shortly <u>after</u> that/
108. the <u>housewives in the immediate area</u> will come over to the house/
109. and through a <u>series of actions</u>/
110. <u>introduce themselves</u> to the new housewife in the <u>neighborhood</u>/
111. and according to Argyle these are the <u>steps</u>/
112. OK these are the <u>steps</u> in this particular ritual/
113. first there is the <u>invitation</u>/
114. an old neighbor <u>invites</u> the new neighbor to come over/
115. OK that's the <u>first</u> step/
116. the second step is that there is the <u>greeting</u> at the door/
117. <u>hello</u> how <u>are you</u> please <u>come in</u>/
118. the visitor is <u>invited</u> into the house/
119. that's the <u>third</u> step
120. the fourth step the visitor has <u>to admire the</u> house/
121. gee that's a <u>lovely</u>/
122. lovely <u>furniture</u> you have here/
123. next the hostess will serve <u>tea and biscuits</u>/
124. then they will <u>sit down</u>/
125. and will <u>exchange information</u>/
126. <u>essential</u> in this exchange/
127. they must exchange information about their <u>husbands</u>/
128. what their husbands <u>do</u>/
129. where their husbands <u>work</u>/
130. what their husbands like to do in their <u>free time</u>/
131. and <u>finally</u>/

132. after a <u>fixed</u> period of time/
133. maybe fifteen minutes is <u>appropriate</u>/
134. the new neighbor <u>must take</u> the initiative/
135. and say it's <u>time to go</u>/
136. <u>gets up</u>/
137. says <u>farewell</u>/
138. we'll have to see each other <u>again</u>/
139. OK now these <u>steps together</u> form what we call/
140. a <u>ritual</u>/
141. or a ritualized <u>norm</u>/
142. OK <u>not only</u>/
143. in a ritual <u>not only</u> must all the steps <u>be there</u>/
144. but they must be there in a <u>certain order</u>/
145. for example in the <u>new neighbor ritual</u>/
146. the hostess won't <u>immediately</u> serve tea and biscuits/
147. without giving <u>a tour of the house</u>/
148. nor will the person who <u>comes to the house</u>/
149. immediately start talking about her <u>husband</u>/
150. OK the point here is that in <u>a ritual the</u> steps must be there/
151. and must be there in a <u>certain order</u>/
152. Argyle the British psychologist and <u>others</u>/
153. claim that it is <u>knowledge of rituals</u> that make/
154. us <u>skillful</u>/
155. that make us socially <u>skillful in a given society</u>/
156. so learning the rituals is part of learning to be an <u>acceptable member</u> of our society/

PAUSE ONE

157. OK now in the case of a <u>housewife</u>/
158. or in the case of a <u>student</u>/
159. or in the case of the <u>boss of a company</u>/
160. all of the <u>individuals</u> in a society/
161. have learned a <u>number</u> of norms and a <u>number</u> of rituals
162. and we may say that together all of this knowledge forms part of their <u>role</u>/
163. <u>r o l e</u>/
164. or their role <u>expectation</u>/
165. what they are expected to <u>do in</u> a given position in their group//
166. <u>all right</u>/
167. you will remember that <u>earlier</u>/
168. I talked about the roles of <u>a foreman</u> or a <u>union steward</u> inside a factory/
169. OK and we found that when people are <u>promoted</u> to
170. uh a certain <u>job</u>/

171. they begin to <u>change</u> their attitudes and behaviors/
172. they begin to <u>fit the expectations</u> of their new role/
173. OK so that the case in which someone <u>is promoted</u> into a new job/
174. is an example of a <u>role</u>/
175. how role expectations are an <u>influence</u> on our behavior//
176. Now an interesting <u>phenomenon</u> that we observe in social psychology/
177. is what is called a role <u>reversal</u>/
178. right when we suddenly <u>shift someone's role</u> from a student to a teacher/
179. or a <u>prisoner</u> to a prison <u>guard</u>/
180. all right or an <u>employee</u> to a <u>boss</u>/
181. we find that simply by <u>changing the roles</u>/
182. that is when the person's role has <u>changed</u>/
183. other people will begin to <u>treat you differently</u>/
184. as you assume the <u>aspects of the new role</u>/
185. this is what has been called the <u>Pygmalion effect</u>//
186. OK the Pygmalion effect is based on a literary <u>concept</u> by George Bernard <u>Shaw</u>/
187. and even <u>before</u>/
188. Shaw based his concept on an earlier <u>Greek</u> phenomenon/
189. <u>effect</u>/
190. this is called the <u>Pygmalion effect</u>/
191. in a play by Shaw called <u>Pygmalion</u>/
192. a young girl named <u>Eliza Doolittle</u>/
193. maybe you've <u>heard</u>/
194. or <u>read</u> this play/
195. is just a <u>poor little flower</u> vendor/
196. and through a <u>series of actions</u>/
197. she's taken into a <u>rich person's</u> society/
198. and she is taught the behaviors of a <u>rich proper woman</u> in British society/
199. and she finds much to her <u>surprise</u>/
200. that people begin to <u>treat her</u> very differently/
201. and this effect of role <u>reversal</u>/
202. and people starting to treat you <u>differently</u> is what is called/
203. the <u>Pygmalion effect</u>/
204. so when we talk about role <u>reversal</u>/
205. we often refer <u>to this</u>/
206. the <u>Pygmalion effect</u>/

PAUSE TWO

207. OK next let's turn to two more <u>effects</u>/
208. on our <u>attitudes</u> and behavior/

209. these <u>two</u> effects are/
210. what we'll call <u>exposure</u> and <u>conformity</u>/
211. both exposure and conformity have a <u>profound</u> effect/
212. on our attitudes and our <u>behavior</u>/
213. OK one of the exposure phenomena is called the <u>proximity</u> effect/
214. according to the <u>proximity effect</u>/
215. if we are <u>close to</u> something/
216. or in <u>contact</u> with something/
217. an attitude or system of <u>behavior</u>/
218. we will tend to <u>adopt that system</u> of behavior/
219. or that system of <u>thinking</u>//

220. one <u>example</u> of this is something like/
221. for instance if you were to grow up in a family in the southern <u>United States</u>/
222. and say your father is a <u>member</u> of a group called the <u>Ku Klux Klan</u>/
223. which believes that <u>white people</u>/
224. should be in <u>control</u> of the United States/
225. in <u>every aspect</u> of the culture and society/
226. probably if you <u>grow up</u> in a family
227. like that/ you will go to certain kinds of <u>meetings</u>/
228. certain kinds of even <u>church groups</u>/
229. in which these ideas are <u>presented and discussed</u>/
230. directly and <u>indirectly</u>/
231. and perhaps by the time you are an <u>adolescent</u>/
232. say thirteen or <u>fifteen years old</u>/
233. you yourself will have <u>internalized</u> these attitudes/
234. simply because you were in <u>contact with them</u>/
235. OK this is the principle of the <u>proximity effect</u>/
236. that the mere <u>exposure</u> and proximity to a phenomenon/
237. is in <u>some</u> cases/
238. a <u>cause</u> for a person to <u>internalize</u> these attitudes and behavior//
239. Another principle in social psychology is <u>group pressure</u>/
240. this is <u>related</u> to conformity/
241. the principle of group <u>pressure</u> or group/
242. conformity is <u>simply</u> that/

243. we tend to react to the pressure we <u>feel</u> in a group/
244. to think or to <u>act in a certain way</u>/
245. all right <u>even if</u>/
246. even if we believe that the standards of the group are <u>wrong</u> or <u>ineffective</u>/
247. OK there is a rather <u>well-known study</u>/
248. one of the <u>classic</u> studies/

249. by a psychologist named <u>Asch</u>/
250. <u>a s c h</u>/
251. he did his studies some <u>twenty</u> or twenty-five years ago/
252. and in his <u>experiments</u>/
253. he showed that people will indeed <u>change</u> their behavior/
254. if the group puts <u>pressure</u> on them/
255. very <u>indirect</u> pressure in fact/
256. to <u>do</u> so//
257. One classic experiment involved a <u>group of seven</u> people/
258. now in this group of <u>seven people</u>/
259. six of the subjects were <u>cooperating</u> with the experimenter/
260. this is what we <u>say</u>/
261. they're <u>stooges</u>/
262. they are <u>paid</u> by the experimenter to <u>act</u> in a certain way/
263. these people in a sense will <u>form the group</u>/
264. now the <u>seventh</u> subject comes in/
265. and <u>he does not know</u> that the other six subjects are <u>different</u> from him/
266. he thinks that all six people are <u>participating</u> in this experiment/
267. all <u>right</u>/
268. and in this <u>experiment</u>/
269. it's a very <u>simple</u> experiment/
270. the subjects are shown <u>three lines</u>/
271. <u>a b c</u>/
272. OK they're shown <u>these on a screen</u>/
273. for a <u>short</u> time/
274. maybe the a line is <u>one meter</u> long/
275. the b line is <u>70 centimeters</u> long/
276. the c line is <u>40 centimeters</u> long/
277. and they're shown the lines in different <u>sequences</u>/
278. and after each set of lines is <u>shown</u>/
279. the experimenter <u>says</u>/
280. OK please <u>tell me</u> which line was the <u>longest</u>/
281. and he goes <u>around</u> the table/
282. and the subjects <u>answer</u>/
283. now in <u>some</u> of these experiments/
284. the three lines would be <u>presented</u>/
285. and perhaps the <u>a line</u> would be much longer than b or c/
286. and he <u>would</u>/
287. the experimenter would <u>go around</u> the table/
288. and say which line was the <u>longest</u>/
289. and this person would say <u>c is</u> the longest/
290. <u>c is</u> the longest/
291. <u>c is</u> the longest/

292. and when they get to the <u>real</u> subject/
293. remember the <u>real</u> subject/
294. he shows some <u>real concern</u>/
295. because he <u>saw</u>/
296. and he's <u>certain</u> that <u>a</u> was the longest line/
297. but because the <u>other</u> people said that c was the longest/
298. in most cases the subject would <u>change</u> his opinion/
299. or change his judgement to <u>conform</u> to the group's judgement/
300. to the group's <u>decision</u>//
301. so in <u>experiments</u> and in <u>real life</u>/
302. we can often see that a person will <u>change</u> his or her opinion/
303. or his or her <u>judgement</u>/
304. to conform to what the people in the <u>group say</u> is the <u>norm</u>/
305. or is the <u>standard</u>/ for that type of <u>decision</u>/
306. OK the last principle that is <u>related</u> to this/
307. is called <u>in-group bias</u>/
308. in group bias is <u>related</u> to the idea of group pressure/
309. in in group bias the principle is that we tend to <u>judge</u> the people in our <u>own group</u>/
310. own <u>family</u> our own <u>society</u> our own <u>class</u> our own <u>social</u> group/
311. as <u>superior</u> to other people/
312. even if <u>even if we do not know</u> the people in the other group/
313. still there seems to be a tendency for people to <u>be biased</u>/
314. toward the <u>group they're in</u>//
315. one example of this is that we found in some <u>classroom</u> studies/
316. say at <u>this school</u>/
317. that when teachers correct the <u>papers</u>/
318. the compositions of <u>their own students</u>/
319. they tend to mark these <u>higher</u>/
320. they give them <u>higher marks</u>/
321. higher <u>scores</u>/
322. higher <u>grades</u>/
323. than if they're correcting papers by <u>someone</u>/
324. in <u>another</u> group/
325. OK if they're correcting <u>other students</u> compositions/
326. and if someone <u>corrects</u>/
327. who is <u>not associated</u> with either group corrects them/
328. that person might find them to be <u>exactly equal</u>/
329. but because the teacher says ah <u>this is my class</u>/
330. they're evaluated <u>more highly</u>/
331. OK so it seems that the principle here is we/
332. are <u>prejudiced</u> or <u>biased</u> toward the members of our own group//
333. OK I think we can <u>stop here</u> for the time being/
334. we've introduced here several <u>concepts</u>/

335. several <u>ideas</u>/
336. what types of things are <u>influential</u> on our attitudes and behavior/
337. OK so let's <u>stop</u> there/
338. and see if you have any <u>questions</u>//

Appendix B

Samples of non-native speaker and native speaker summaries

Sample of non-native speaker summaries

S1

Norms are applied to food, clothes, ways of talking, way of behavior. All groups have norms which govern both simple and complex behaviors. For example, clothes are different between men and women, and between culture 1 and culture 2. The difference between norm and ritual in the complex way is norm. Example is way to greet neighbor – it has special steps.

We must play a role in society. For example, student, housewomen, boss, assistant. Our role is main influence to our way of behavior. If our role suddenly change in the society – for example, we marry a rich man, suddenly we become different role. People behave to us by new role.

Proximity effect is that individual learns the way of behavior at young age from family or country, etc. Group conformity is that individuals will be changed by group influence even when group's idea is silly or wrong one. Group bias is that individuals will be changed by group influence too because they always think this group is best one.

S7

Norms are for all people in society. Japanese society have norms for food (example: fish, rice, pickles). All Japanese know norm and must follow it. Americans or British are different in norms.

Role expectation is what all people must do as part of job, family, career. We behave by our role. Role change suddenly, we bring pygamalion effect. Other people notice our changed role. They are surprised and treat differently.

We know what to believe is positive from childhood, by proximity effect. We see way of others and believe it is positive. Group pressure cause us sometimes to change idea or thought in group. Group pressure is strong for decision. Bias is teacher thinks his class is better because he likes them best. Generally, more exposure of groups results in a more positive attitude.

S11

A concept of "norms". All (society/culture) has now (elements standards) to survive. We see this as basic elements – norms of food, clothes, house. There are "social skills" – he call it "ritual" – not to survive, but to be comfortable for our society.

Role expectation. We are expected to act in a certain way. Example: student in student's way, etc. We don't even think about that. Role reversal "the pygmalion effect" – Shaw's play "pygmailion" is example – people are treated in a different ways when they show some sign of new role position.

Exposure and conformity. A "proximity effect" – adapt to norm principle of the family or certain group. A "group pressure" – ex. one is subject, others is not, effected by judgement of majority. A "in group bias" only by being in certain group, one gets a bias. All is automatical.

S19

Social environment affect people's behavior. About norm. Some part of world has a certain culture. And social system, like ritual, is various too.

Role expectation: role of people influences one's behavior and attitudes. Example of role is student, housewife, and so on. Role reversal: We change by pygmalion effect.

Exposure and conformity (These affects people's behaviors and attitudes).
– proximity effect – go as group standard
– pressure of groups; if all members except you agree with something, you tend to be agree with it.
– in group bias you tend to make man who like, graduated.

Sample of native speaker summaries

NS1

The lecturer talks about norms, providing a definition and some examples dealing with food, forms of address in Japanese, and social interaction (meeting a new neighbor). The main point seems to be that some norms are universal. Another point is that some norms are more complex than others – these are called rituals.

The lecturer continues with a discussion of rituals and shows how roles require learning of specific rituals. One point seems to be that once we acquire a new role (like foreman) we begin to change our ways of behaving to fit the new role – we feel a very strong pressure to do this – perhaps something in our human make-up responds to social pressure? He introduces the term Pygmalion effect to say that people treat you differently based on how you act.

The lecture continues with more about attitudes and behavior. Here he talks about different effects of exposure to attitudes and behavior and to being a member of a group. An example is given of a child brought up in a racist family coming to internalize these attitudes and to believe that they are "normal". Another example, of a psychology experiment, is given to show that people conform to group standards, even when they think the group may be wrong. Another example is given about teacher's bias toward their own students. Again, there seems to be a strong effect – or a strong desire – for people to conform to what their group thinks is normal or correct.

NS2

This part of the lecture deals with a definition of norms = accepted standard of thought or behavior. For example, we may think that some foods are normal and others taboo, but this is arbitrary = other groups may have different norms. Some norms, however, are universal = one example is "forms of address" – we tend to see people in a hierarchy and develop different ways of talking to them. Still other norms are complex = they require learning of intricate steps, etc. Nevertheless, we manage to learn these – such as the "good neighbor" routine.

This part of the lecture deals with roles = the expected behavior from someone who has a certain job or social position. Roles are powerful influences on how we think and feel and act = if we change roles (for example from worker to boss), we suddenly start to act differently. (This, too, though seems to be a learned behavior, since we probably act as we have seen others in that position act.) This is called role reversal. The example of My Fair Lady was brought up, since she went through a role reversal and began to be treated differently. (It's not clear how this relates to norms.)

This part of the lecture deals with effects of exposure and also conformity. Exposure has a strong effect on our attitudes, since we come to believe that the most common attitudes we see are normal = acceptable and right. Even if we later learn these are wrong, it may be hard to change them. Group conformity = the pressure to accept the group's ideas (even if we suspect they're wrong!). An interesting example – the experiment with forcing someone to change what he saw in order to conform to the group opinion.

References

Baddeley, A. D. 1986. *Working Memory*. New York: Oxford University Press.
Bostrom, R., and E. Waldhart. 1988. Memory models and the measurement of listening. *Communication Education* 37: 1–13.
Brown, G. K. 1978. *Lecturing and Explaining*. London: Methuen.
Brown, A., and J. Day. 1983. Macrorules in summarizing texts. *Journal of Memory and Language* 22: 1–14.
Carrier, C. A., and A. Titus. 1981. Effects of notetaking pretraining and test mode expectations on learning from lectures. *American Research Journal* 18 (4): 383–397.
Chan, L. K. S., P. G. Cole, and S. Barfett. 1987. Comprehension monitoring:

detection and identification of text inconsistencies. *Learning Disability Quarterly* 10 (2): 114–124.

Chaudron, C., and J. R. Richards. 1986. The effect of discourse markers on the comprehension of lectures. *Applied Linguistics* 7 (2): 113–27.

Clark, H., and E. Clark. 1977. *Psychology and Language.* New York: Harcourt, Brace, Jovanovich.

Dolitsky, M. 1984. *Under the Tumtum Tree: From Sense to Nonsense, a Study of Non-Automatic Comprehension.* Amsterdam: John Benjamins.

Eckhardt, B. B., M. R. Wood, and R. S. Jacobvitz. 1991. Verbal ability and prior knowledge. *Communications Research* 18 (5): 636–649.

Ericsson, K. A., and H. A. Simon. 1984. *Protocol Analysis.* Cambridge, Mass.: MIT Press.

Findahl, D., and B. Hoijer. 1982. The problem of comprehension and recall of broadcast news. In *Language and Comprehension*, J. LeNy, and W. Kintsch (Eds.). Amsterdam: North-Holland.

Flottum, K. 1985. Methodological problems in the analysis of student summaries. *Text* 5 (4): 291–308.

Johnson, F., and G. Klare. 1961. General models of communication research: a survey of a decade. *Journal of Communication* 11: 13–26.

Jonz, J. 1987. Textual cohesion and second-language comprehension. *Language Learning* 37 (3): 409–441.

Kintsch, W., and T. A. van Dijk. 1978. Toward a model of text comprehension and production. *Psychological Review* 85 (5): 363–394.

McLaughlin, B. 1987. *Theories of Second-Language Learning.* London: Arnold.

Meyer, B. J. F. 1985. Prose analysis: procedures, purposes, and problems. In *Analyzing and Understanding Expository Text*, B. Britton, and J. Black (Eds.), 11–64. Hillsdale, N.J.: Erlbaum.

Murphy, J. M. 1987. The listening strategies of ESL college students. *Research and Teaching in Developmental Education* 4 (1): 27–46.

1989. Listening in a second language: hermeneutics and inner speech. *TESL Canada Journal* 6: 39–40.

O'Malley, J. M., A. U. Chamot, and L. Kupper. 1989. Listening comprehension strategies in second language acquisition. *Applied Linguistics* 10 (4): 418–437.

Resnick, L. B. 1984. Comprehending and learning: implications for a cognitive theory of instruction. In *Learning and Comprehension of Text*, H. Mandl, N. Stein, and T. Trabasso (Eds.). Hillsdale, N.J.: Erlbaum.

Rickheit, G., W. L. Schnotz, and H. Strohner. 1985. The concept of inference in discourse comprehension. In *Inferences in Text Processing*, Rickheit and Strohner (Eds.). Amsterdam: North-Holland.

Robin, A., R. M. Fox, J. Martello, and C. Archable. 1977. Teaching note-taking skills to underachieving college students. *Journal of Educational Research* 71 (2): 81–85.

Rost, M. 1987. The interaction of listening, speaker, text, and task. Unpublished Ph.D. thesis, University of Lancaster.

1990. *Listening in Language Learning.* London: Longman.

Rost, M., and S. Ross. 1991. Learner strategies in interaction: typology and teachability. *Language Learning* 41 (2): 235–273.

Schacter, D. 1982. The psychology of memory. In *Mind and Brain: Dialogues in*

Cognitive Neuroscience, J. E. LeDoux and W. Hirst (Eds.). Cambridge: Cambridge University Press.

Schramm, W. 1954. How communication works. In *The Process and Effects of Mass Communication*, W. Schramm (Ed.). Urbana: University of Illinois Press.

Shannon, C., and C. Weaver. 1949. *The Mathematical Model of Communication*. Urbana: University of Illinois Press.

Sperber, D., and D. Wilson. 1986. *Relevance: Communication and Cognition*. Oxford: Blackwell.

Voss, J. 1988. On learning and learning from text. Manuscript. Learning Research and Development Center, University of Pittsburgh.

Zabrucky, K. 1986. The role of factual coherence in discourse comprehension. *Discourse Processes* 9: 197–220.

PART III:
DISCOURSE OF ACADEMIC LECTURES

Editor's introduction to Part III

Discourse analysis is the research methodology which has probably been most applied in relation to L2 lecture comprehension (see the background chapter by Flowerdew to this collection). Discourse analysis of lectures is important because knowledge concerning the macro- and micro-structuring of lectures will, on the one hand, allow content lecturers to structure their lectures in an optimal fashion (a number of contributors to this volume have noted how content lecturers have found analysis of their lectures useful (Tauroza and Allison, Dudley-Evans); on the other hand, it will aid ESL materials designers to produce instructional materials which familiarize learners with the form of authentic lectures.

This section of the book makes a further contribution in the area of discourse analysis of lectures, presenting three chapters which analyze lecture discourse from different perspectives, and which show how the tools of discourse analysis can provide insights for pedagogy.

Hansen, in her chapter, presents a model of lecture discourse based on the notion of discourse topic. Combining two approaches to the notion of topic, that of sentential topic and that of topic framework, Hansen shows how a lecture can be broken down into its constituent parts, according to a hierarchy of major topics, subtopics and minor points. Hansen shows how the analysis of a lecture according to this method can be used as a measure of completeness and correctness of student notes. This chapter can be usefully compared with those of Chaudron, Loschky, and Cook and of King (this volume), which also deal with note-taking, but in rather different ways.

Dudley-Evans's chapter makes the important point that lecture discourse structure may differ depending upon the discipline concerned. Such variation is illustrated with reference to lectures in plant biology and highway engineering, where the former typically follows an "information-driven", or listing, type of structure (Olsen and Huckin 1990) and the latter a "problem–solution", or argument building, type of structure (Hoey 1983). Based on the analysis of these lectures,

Dudley-Evans makes an important point for pedagogy. Rather than being initiated into a range of generalized listening strategies that apply to all lectures, as is the methodology applied in a number of current English for Academic Purposes (EAP) listening texts, learners should be made aware that lecture discourse varies according to the disciplinary procedures and agendas of the subject area concerned. The results of the chapter provide support for the subject-specific, team-teaching approach to EAP used by the author and his colleagues at the University of Birmingham. An example of the sort of material used, based on a lecture extract, is provided.

Young's chapter, "University lectures – macro-structure and micro-features" is particularly interesting for a number of reasons. First, it analyzes lectures using the methodology of systemic/functional linguistics – a powerful model, as Young points out, in relating situational/contextual features and language choices. Second, in relating the notion of macro-structure to schema theory, like Tauroza and Allison, Young suggests a relation between knowledge of macro-structure and discourse processing. Third, the system of analysis and the model of lecture macro-structure which is developed applies to different fields, both technical and non-technical. This point may seem contrary to the findings of Dudley-Evans, who, as mentioned above, emphasized the differences in lecture macro-structure across disciplines. However, the strength of Young's model is that while all lectures are made up of a number of what she calls "phases", it is the way the individual phases are realized which distinguishes the different disciplines.

References

Hoey, M. 1983. *On the Surface of Discourse*. London: Allen and Unwin.
Olsen, L. A., and T. N. Huckin. 1990. Point-driven understanding in engineering lecture comprehension. *English for Specific Purposes* 9: 33–47.

6 Topic identification in lecture discourse

Christa Hansen

Abstract

Neither the issue of the role of notetaking in the lecture learning process, nor the issue of what is effective notetaking has been fully determined in first or second language listening. This chapter describes an approach to discourse analysis which identifies the major topics, subtopics and minor points of a lecture. The results of the analysis, a topic hierarchy of the lecture, can be used to evaluate the qualitative completeness of students' notes, that is, whether students have noted the important points of the lecture. The approach is demonstrated in the analysis of a graduate-level lecture on language teaching. Two topic analysis methods are employed: a topic identification method that combines elements from T. Givon's (1979) sentential topic continuity measurements to identify the discourse markers that signal topic shift, and a topic framework method (Brown and Yule 1983) that incorporates the textual and contextual elements of the discourse situation that the speaker and students have access to. The topic hierarchy that results from the analysis is then compared against the notes of the students in the class, five L1 graduate students and two L2 graduate students, to evaluate their notes for completeness and correctness of information.

Introduction

One of the issues to be dealt with in understanding the lecture learning process is determining the function of notetaking for students, and more specifically what notetaking methods help students succeed academically. The correspondence between notetaking and lecture learning for first language (L1) learners has been a matter of exploration for educational psychologists for the past seventy years. Among the first questions that was explored was whether notetaking is more effective for mastering lecture information than just listening to the lecture. Crawford (1925) found not only that notetaking was indeed a more effective learning strategy for L1 students than just listening to a lecture,

131

but also that there is a positive correlation between the number of lecture points found in students' notes and the number of points recalled on quizzes. From evidence gathered in their experiments, Aiken, Thomas, and Shennum (1975) posited that notetaking facilitates learning by causing L1 listeners to process the lecture content; that is, listeners have to interpret the lecture, infer information from it, condense auditory input and paraphrase the lecture material in order to take notes. They found that an additional benefit of notetaking is that notes store the lecture information externally and can be used for reviewing lecture material, a feature that further improves students' recall of lecture material. Kiewra, DuBois, Christian, McShane, Meyerhoffer, and Roskelley (1991) found that notetaking is a complex integrative process that calls for the L1 listener to listen continuously and simultaneously to the lecture, select its important ideas, hold and manipulate lecture ideas, interpret information, decide what to transcribe, and then actually to record notes. As pointed out by Aiken, Thomas, and Shennum (1975), it is this process of holding ideas, interpreting information, and deciding what to transcribe that enhances the lecture learning process for L1 students. Almost 70 years later Kiewra, DuBois, Christian, McShane, Meyerhoffer, and Roskelley (1991) came to the same conclusion as Crawford (1925): completeness of notes is positively related to test performance.

The question we face in L2 lecture learning performance is: Do the findings on lecture learning and notetaking for L1 listeners have validity for L2 listeners? Dunkel and others (see especially Chaudron, Loschky, and Cook, this volume) have begun to explore this question. In contrast to the findings of Crawford and Kiewra at al. that completeness of notes is positively related to L1 test performance, Dunkel (1988) found that notes which contain answers to test questions are better predictors of L1 and L2 students' performance in recalling lecture details than other measurements that she used, including total number of words in the notes, information unit counts, and a completeness and efficiency ratio. The completeness ratio consisted of the total number of possible information units in a lecture, divided by the number of all the information units written in students' notes (1988: 265). This method does not take into consideration the quality of the information that is recorded in students' notes.

This chapter will build on previous work done by L1 and L2 researchers by describing a method to compare students' notes to the hierarchy of **major topics, subtopics** and **minor points**[1] in a lecture to determine the completeness of their notes, thus making it possible

---

[1] Appendix A is a glossary of technical terms used in this chapter and printed in bold face.

to ascertain whether key information is missing. In order to do this, first some of the considerations that make focusing on lecture topics so linguistically challenging will be pointed out. Next, the topic identification method developed to analyze lectures will be described. Following this, the analysis of a lecture will be presented and major topics, subtopics and minor points of the lecture will be compared to L1 and L2 students' notes. Finally, the findings and their implications will be discussed.

Topic identification in lectures

Linguists use the word "topic" in relation to a sentence, the **sentential topic**; a group of sentences, the **sequential topic**; and the theme of a piece of discourse, the **discourse topic** (Brown and Yule 1983; Givon 1979; Grimes 1975; Hockett 1958; Keenan and Schieffelin 1976; van Dijk and Kintsch 1983). The sentential topic is a "function assigned to a part of the semantic representation of the sentence, often marked in surface structure by initial position (in English)" (van Dijk and Kintsch 1983: 169). The sequential topic represents a participant over a series of sentences. The discourse topic consists of **macropropositions**, semantic representations of the global content of the discourse which is organized in a **macrostructure**, or an overall structure of the discourse. These macropropositions are derived from sentence level semantic propositions. As can be seen, discourse topic and sequential topic are loosely related to the sentential topics of the text, but this does not mean that topics at each level will be identical (van Dijk and Kintsch 1983). In addition, semantically, the topic may hold the position of agent or subject in the surface structure of a sentence. The term "topic" is also used to refer to new information which is highlighted in contrast to the given or old information, especially at sentence level. In cognitive processing, topic is the element identical to the element from previous sentences that is held in the short-term memory for linking one sentence to another to make a coherent text.

Because of the complexity of the relationships among different topic levels and the lack of visual signals like titles, headings, and subheadings that are used in written discourse to signal topic shift, a discourse analysis method whose purpose is to identify the major topics and subtopics in a lecture requires a combination of different treatments of the textual material. The focus adopted here is on identifying discourse markers that signal the point at which there is a change from one topic to another in two contiguous pieces of discourse. Identification of these discourse markers, referred to here as **topic-shift markers**, should provide a structural basis for dividing up the lecture into smaller units on separate topics. Brown and Yule (1983) have found that, in conversation, new discourse topics are often signaled by topic-shift markers which are used as closing brackets for the old topic and/or opening brackets for the new topic. Topic-shift markers are expected to be used in the same way in lectures.

A combination of Givon's sentential topic continuity measurements (1979), identification of topic-shift discourse markers, and the use of a **topic framework** as described by Brown and Yule (1983), will be used for the analysis. The sentential topic continuity measurements will be used to divide the lecture into smaller units on separate topics and to identify points of topic shift. The measurements will also identify noun phrases that might be candidates for topics. The topic framework will use the elements of the lecture text and the shared physical context of the lecture situation to limit the analysis to the elements that are shared by the speaker and listeners. By doing so, the framework will be able to shed light on the choice of language that is used and the speaker/listener expectations that are reflected in the language used. Identification of the topic-shift markers will be particularly useful for identifying the major topics of the lecture because major topics are often signaled by topic-shift markers that are actually topic titling devices.

This method of topic identification is a structural analysis of the lecture material. The topic hierarchy that will be identified and compared to students' notes consists of major topics, subtopics, and minor points in the lecture. Major topic refers to the theme of the lecture, the main ideas of the lecture, the major points of the lecture. Subtopics are the supporting information for the major topic; they delineate the different facets of the major topic. And finally, the minor points are the less important details of the lecture, the information that modifies the subtopic. A previous study (Hansen 1991) identified the topic hierarchy and the topic-shift markers that were used to signal topic shifts in an undergraduate lecture. The results of the analysis were compared to the speaker's notes to validate the lecture topic hierarchy which had been created. As a final step, the topic hierarchy was compared to the notes of six L1 students; it proved to be an effective method for evaluating the completeness of their notes. In that analysis, it was found that major topics in the lecture were headed by topic-shift markers that could be characterized as topic titling devices. Subtopics were marked overtly with topic-shift markers; the chunks that were identified as subtopics extended across more than two clauses with continued appearances of a topic noun phrase. It was found that minor points in the lecture referred to chunks that only extended across two noun phrases and were often not marked as strongly with topic-shift markers as major topics and subtopics.

Analysis method

The lecture transcript was divided into clauses and a modified version of Givon's (1979) sentential topic continuity measurements was applied; these are measurements which were originally used to study the continued appearance of sentential topics in a piece of discourse. The first modification made was to use only the **referential distance** measurement and the **topic persistence** measurement. Referential distance is the distance from the present mention of the topic noun phrase and the last clause to the left where the same referent was a semantic argument. Topic persistence is the number of clauses to the right from the locus under study in which the same topic/reference persists in discourse register as an argument of some clause (Givon 1979). In contrast to Givon, it was found that assuming the grammatical subject of a sentence would be the topic of the sentence was not reliable. In lectures speakers often create a shared discourse environment with their listeners by filling the subject position in sentences with noun phrases or pronouns that are inclusive of the speaker and the audience. These sentence subjects are usually not the topic of the sentence but are indicators of speakers' interactions with and awareness of their audience (Chafe 1982). The speakers use them to draw the audience's attention to the topic that they are introducing. To combat that problem, the referential distance and topic persistence measurements were applied to all the noun phrases in the lecture. Any noun phrase that persisted for at least two clauses had the potential to be the topic of a chunk of discourse that was set off by topic-shift discourse markers. Interestingly, van Dijk and Kintsch's work supports the decision to use noun phrase persistence to identify topics. They found that topic continuity rather than semantic agency or subject position is a more reliable identifier of sentential topics (1983). The referential distance measurement was useful for identifying the larger chunks of discourse like major topics and subtopics because it could be used to account for the reappearance of a noun phrase.

After dividing the lecture into chunks per Givon's topic continuity measurements, the chunks were examined to see if there were topic-shift markers that signaled the beginning or the end of a chunk. Topic-shift markers, discourse markers that signal a change or shift in topic, are one subset of discourse markers. Schiffrin has defined **discourse markers** as "sequentially dependent elements which bracket units of talk", and which "index an utterance to the local context in which the utterances are produced and in which they are to be interpreted" (1987: 31 and 326). She has developed a list of conditions that identify an expression as a discourse marker:

- It has to be syntactically detachable from a sentence.
- It has to be commonly used in the initial position of an utterance.
- It has to have a range of prosodic contours, e.g., tonic stress and [be] followed by a pause, phonological reduction.
- It has to be able to operate at both local and global levels of discourse, and on different planes of discourse; this means that it either has to have no meaning, a vague meaning, or to be reflexive (of the language, of the speaker). (1987: 328)

It was found that the opening bracket discourse markers *there, but, uh,* and *now* could be used alone to signal topic shift at minor points in a lecture. They can also be coupled with topic-shift markers that signal change in major topics (Hansen 1991).

One type of discourse marker that is often used to signal topic shift, particularly at the major junctures in the discourse is the **meta-talk marker**. These markers are used by speakers for identification and/or evaluation of chunks of propositional information in their discourse (Schiffrin 1980). There are three types of meta-talk markers: **meta-linguistic referents, meta-linguistic operators,** and **meta-linguistic verbs**. Meta-linguistic referents point to the language itself, entities in the text itself, or an item in the text. Terms of discourse deixis that relate utterances to the spatial and temporal coordinates of an utterance, and demonstrative pronouns pointing to items in the text itself rather than to items in the world outside the text are examples of meta-linguistic reference. Meta-linguistic operators such as *right, wrong, I mean, for example* and *like* perform an informative or evaluative function by indicating either the modification or the combination of propositions into more complex forms in ways that parallel logical operations. Meta-linguistic verbs are verbs that name acts of speech, indicate something that will be done to a piece of talk or name a speech event. *Say, ask, tell, assert, clarify, define, argue* and *joke* are examples of meta-linguistic verbs (Schiffrin 1980).

The third element of the analysis method that is utilized to identify the lecture topics, Brown and Yule's topic framework (1983), provides a viable way to incorporate the contextual and textual elements of the discourse situation into the analysis. "The topic framework consists of elements derivable from the physical context and from the discourse domain for any discourse fragment." (Brown and Yule 1983: 79) Only the elements that are relevant to the interpretation of what is being said, not everything the speaker and listener may have access to, are included in the topic framework. Elements of the physical context that influence what is being said are aspects of time and place of the discourse and facts about the speaker and hearer, including the speaker's assumptions about the hearer's knowledge. Elements from the discourse domain include previously mentioned information that is directly reflected in the text (Brown and Yule 1983).

Results of analysis of lecture

A graduate-level class on language teaching methodology was audio-taped and the notes of the seven graduate students who attended the lecture that day were collected. There were five L1 students and two L2 students, all of whom were training to be ESL teachers or teachers of other languages. The L2 students had attained at least a 590 on the TOEFL. After the audiotape was transcribed verbatim, the transcript was divided into clauses, and Givon's referential distance and topic persistence measurements were applied to all the noun phrases. The transcript was then divided into chunks based on the persistence of noun phrases across clauses.

At this point in the analysis, the topic framework proved to be very useful. The following elements of the physical context of the lecture are reflected in the language that the speaker uses. The lecture was given in a classroom with a blackboard at the front and permanently positioned seating for 35 with the seats arranged in a horseshoe shape on three levels. Students could seat themselves anywhere in the room. This class had a traditional lecture monologue format; speaker–listener interaction was minimal.

The topic framework also provides the following contextual information: Despite the lack of interaction the speaker signals involvement with his audience by using phrases such as "we teachers" and "our students". The use of the blackboard, references to reading material and specific classroom procedures are all contextual elements of the lecture that are directly reflected in the language the lecture is encoded in. The speaker's informational goals are also reflected in the language of the lecture. His main goal appears to be addressing what teachers have to control, what they should know about language learning, and what their students' needs and abilities are in the area of grammar instruction. He often shifts from presenting information from the perspective of what teachers have to do in a classroom to how students learn. The speaker even occasionally verbalizes students' thought processes to illustrate points he is trying to make about the students' perspective more fully. This changing perspective from teacher viewpoint to student viewpoint is often the only clue that minor topic change has happened.

Measuring the continuous appearance of topic noun phrases proved to be a nonproductive way to identify the major topics of the lecture because major topics in this lecture could actually be characterized as titles for sections of the lecture with the discourse following their introduction being a delineation of points to be made about the topic.

These topics are usually introduced by the speaker with meta-talk expressions like "the things I'm going to have to say . . . ", or with other topic titling expressions like "there are two main ways . . . ". In addition to introducing major topics by such topic titling expressions, the speaker writes key information on the blackboard and refers back to it at different points in the lecture. He then discusses supporting details or subtopics of the major topic rather than talking about the topic itself. The speaker also uses a lot of silence and extremely long pauses as closing brackets. He has a pattern of information presentation that consists of presenting a series of different facets or supporting ideas of a major topic. He then ends the presentation of that topic with a concluding sentence that begins with *this*. The *this* refers back to all of the previous sentences on the topic. The speaker changes topics after he has enumerated the points he has just made about a topic and summarized them in a concluding sentence.

Givon's measurement system was helpful in identifying the following devices that are used to signal topic shifts within major juncture boundaries: topic titles, summaries, use of the blackboard, change of viewpoint, syntactic contrast and pauses. Pauses, topic titling, blackboard references, syntactic contrast, change of perspective, summarizing and the use of *there* are all used to signal topic shift at the subtopic level. The most prevalent device is the topic titling device, followed by the summary, as might be expected by the speaker's presentation pattern. Noun phrase counts are helpful for identifying subtopics; that is, supporting information subsumed under a major topic title.

In addition to major topics and subtopics, minor points in the lecture were also identified. These points had at least two continuous noun phrases and could be identified as a point of topic shift under the domain of the subtopic. Minor topic changes are signaled by topic titles, change of viewpoint, summaries, and pauses.

Presented below in Figure 1 is a chart of the major topics, subtopics and minor points identified in the lecture. The actual topic-shift marker is given under the example column.

Analysis of students' notes

After the lecture was analyzed, and the major topics, subtopics and minor points of the lecture had been identified, the students' notes were studied to determine how many of the propositions subsumed under major topic, subtopic and minor points in the lecture analysis were represented in the students' notes (see Table 1). Table 1 shows that of the nine major topics identified by means of topic-shift markers, four of the five L1 students were found to have 5 of the major topics in their notes; the fifth student only had 3 major topics. One L2 student had 4 major

TABLE I. TOPICS FROM ANALYSIS REPRESENTED IN STUDENTS' NOTES

	Main topic	*Subtopic*	*Minor point*	*Other information*
L1S1	5	12	20	3
L1S2	5	14	23	3
L1S3	5	14	19	4
L1S4	5	14	19	6
L1S5	3	13	17	2
L2S1	4	12	17	6
L2S2	3	11	10	3

Note: L1 = native speaker of English; L2 = non-native speaker of English; other information = number of propositions in students' notes not analyzed as a topic.

topics, and the other had 3 major topics in the notes. Twenty-one subtopics were identified in the analysis. Three L1 students recorded 14 subtopics in their notes, one recorded 13 subtopics and the fifth L1 student recorded 12 subtopics. In contrast to the L1 students, one L2 student recorded 12 subtopics and the other recorded 11 subtopics. And finally, of the 26 minor points identified through the analysis, the L1 students noted from 23 to 17 points, and the L2 students noted 17 and 10 minor points.

The students' notes were also looked at to determine if they contained extraneous information, that is, information that was not a major topic, subtopic or minor point of the lecture topic itself. For most of the students, extraneous information was taken down at the beginning of the lecture. The extraneous information is interpreted as indicating that these students were unsure as to how the speaker would approach the topic of grammar instruction and what information was important.

The points in students' notes where the students misunderstood the speaker and wrote down wrong information were also noted. Only the L2 students recorded wrong- information. One misunderstood information in a subtopic and the other misunderstood minor points in the lecture. Below is the speaker's text and the student's notes showing the subtopic misinformation.

Speaker: We need something specifically for the form and this is where the "M" comes in. It could be another kind of model. I just use it nowadays as some use the word "memory". Something, uh, a sentence that will say . . . "I'm not going to forget any of the words, I'm going to get the order right, I'm going to get all the words right. And this is going to be something that will really stick in my mind." Our model we want to be fairly orthodox. We'd like it to be attractive to the students, if possible to be memorable, certainly to be clear . . . but our primary focus is not going to be on how the students

Topic-shift marker	Major topic	Subtopic	Minor point	Example
Meta-talk	X			I expect you handle it this way.
	X			I'll insert at this point.
	X			gotta couple of minutes. I'm always showing off cartoons.
	X			the things I'm going to have to say
Meta-talk + blackboard	X			so the first I write down
Topic title + blackboard	X			the other acronym [write on board]
		X		the other [point to board]
			X	meaningful practice [write on board]
			X	communicative practice [write on board]
Topic title	X			there are two main ways
	X			two kinds of review
			X	one of them
			X	and one of the
			X	one of the problems
			X	what they will need to work from
			X	this first one
			X	this is where
			X	the exceptional use of language
			X	the grammar reference
Topic title			X	two ways you can go
			X	one of them
			X	the other
			X	the other side is
			X	this is where
			X	what can you attach this new grammar point to
Topic title + summary		X		one of them [+ summary statement]
			X	this is what
Topic title + pause		X		. . . this difference
		X		. . . sometimes they're reminders
Topic title + summary + blackboard	X			how do we go about presenting the lesson? [write on board + final summary statement]

Topic-shift marker	Major topic	Subtopic	Minor point	Example
Topic title + blackboard + pause			X	. . . mechanical is that focused practice [point to board]
Change of viewpoint		X		language/you
		X		we/grammar
		X		you/we
		X		it/you
			X	you/they
			X	you/they
			X	they/some
			X	you/we
Change of viewpoint			X	we/emphasis
Change of viewpoint + pause		X		grammar instruction/we . . .
		X		these/ . . . we
			X	this/ . . . you
Syntax		X		but
			X	there
			X	there
Syntax + blackboard		X		the model is something . . . the contrast is something [point to board]
Point to blackboard		X		this [point to board]
			X	this [point to board]
Point to blackboard + summary			X	this [refers to previous statement and board]
Summary			X	this [refers to previous sentences]
Pause			X	
			X	
			X	
			X	
			X	

Figure 1   Methods for obtaining learners' responses to listening material

remember it. This is something that we follow as a base or event for our grammar exercises in class.

L2S2: 3. Memory practicing the forms. ^rules^ till they get into mind not to be forgotten.

Notice that the student wrote terse notes on the information presented and put the information in his own propositions. Below is the speaker's text and the other student's notes showing the misinformation on minor points.

Speaker: Lots of students like to have a set of proverbs that will fit different situations . . . It's at once a tongue twister, something that's challenging to say but something that has this grammar point in it. She sells sea shells . . .

L2S1: solve problem in different situation, a grammar point in it. (She shall, sea shell)

Speaker: If they're adults, they'll want to hear the rule first. They are uncomfortable until they have the rule . . . till they have that rule, their minds are soaked.

L2S1: Until they attain the rule.

This student attempted to identify phrases that carried important information and write them down verbatim. However, the student had some sound discrimination problems and appears to have missed the intonation contours that give the speaker's remarks a different meaning from what was recorded in the notes.

It should be noted that all of the students wrote information in fragments of informational bullets rather than as a dictation of the lecture. Three students, one L1 and the two L2 students, related information presented in the lecture to their own experiences or background knowledge in their notes.

Conclusions

The discourse analysis method used proved to be an effective tool for identifying lecture topics and topic-shift markers. Dividing a monologue into smaller chunks based on the continued appearance of noun phrases across clauses is workable for identifying subtopics and minor points in a lecture. On the other hand, major topics are more readily found by identifying the signals that introduce these topics. Those signals are usually topic titling devices like meta-talk expressions, topic titles, summary statements and visual support.

Using a topic framework which looked at how and why information was encoded in the way that it was is the other tool needed for identifying topics. In lecture situations, the speaker often uses such devices as *we, you* and *us* to create a shared context with the listeners and to encourage the audience to interact with the material that is being presented. That was also the case in this lecture. The speaker presented information from the perspective of "we language teachers" and he often talked about "our students".

Comparing the analysis results to students' notes appears to be a viable method for measuring the quality of students' notes. It was possible to identify the major and minor points of the lecture that were represented in the students' notes. On the whole, there was not a great deal of difference in the number of points recorded in the L2 students' notes as compared to the L1 students' notes. Admittedly, the L2 students consistently recorded fewer points at all levels of the text than the L1 students, but there is not a dramatic contrast in numbers (see Table 1).

This analysis method made it possible to pinpoint wrong information in students' notes. As noted earlier, only the L2 students had written down wrong information. The ability to pinpoint such problems would be useful for helping students hone their notetaking skills. It would be interesting to see how the quality of students' notes, defined as the number of major topics and subtopics and the amount of supporting information written in their notes, correlates to their performance in the class. Especially since Kiewra, DuBois, Christian, McShane, Meyerhoffer, and Roskelley (1991) indicate that completeness of notes, that is, the number of major topics, subtopics and minor points that are contained in L1 students' notes, is the factor that they have identified as correlating positively with test performance.

Appendix A

Glossary of technical terms

Deixis The central reference point (usually the speaker) in a unit of talk for person, place or time. In the sentences, "Come here" and "Go away" the speaker is the point of reference for orienting the action to a place. In "Come here" the person being addressed is away from the speaker, whereas in "Go away" the person being addressed is near the speaker.

Discourse marker Organizational signal that appears at the beginning and/or end of a unit of talk and is used by the speaker to indicate how what is being said is related to what has already been said.

Discourse topic Semantically, what the talk or conversation is about.

Macroposition The major topic, main idea or theme of the text.

Macrostructure An overall structure of the text (van Dijk and Kintsch 1983).

Major topics The theme of the discourse, the main ideas of the discourse, the major points of the discourse.

Meta-linguistic operators Meta-talk markers that perform an evaluative function by indicating either the modification or the combination of propositions into more complex forms in ways that parallel logical operations (Schiffrin 1980).

Meta-linguistic referent Discourse marker that points to the language itself, entities in the text or an item in the text (Schiffrin 1980). "This" is used as a meta-linguistic referent in "This sentence is short." It points to an entity in the text, the word "sentence."

Meta-linguistic verb Discourse marker that fronts and names a speech act, speech event, or indicates what the speaker will do to a piece of talk. "I would argue that . . . " is an example of the use of a meta-linguistic verb. It indicates that the speaker is making an argument in the unit of talk that follows.

Meta-talk marker A class of discourse markers in which speakers specifically refer to aspects of the text itself: it is talk about the talk.

Minor points The less important details of the discourse. They modify the subtopic.

Referential distance How many noun phrases earlier the topic noun phrase last appeared.

Sentential topic What the sentence is about. In English it is usually assumed that the sentential topic is the first noun phrase in the sentence, a reflection of the subject–verb–object order.

Sequential topic A participant in the action which occurs in a series of sentences (van Dijk and Kintsch 1983).

Subtopics The supporting information for the major topic. They delineate the different facets of the major topic.

Topic framework Information from the physical context of the talk including time, place, participants and situation, and from what has already been covered in the talk, used by speakers and listeners to limit their interpretation and understanding of what is being referred to in the talk.

Topic persistence The number of consecutive clauses after the first appearance of a topic/noun phrase in which the topic continues to appear. To determine topic persistence, count the number of clauses that a noun phrase continues to appear in after its initial appearance.

Topic-shift marker Discourse marker that signals a change in topic.

References

Aiken, E.G., G. S. Thomas, and W. A. Shennum. 1975. Memory for a lecture: effects of notes, lecture rate, and informational density. *Journal of Educational Psychology* 67 (3): 439–444.

Brown, G., and G. Yule. 1983. *Discourse Analysis*. New York: Cambridge University Press.

Chafe, W. L. 1982. Integration and involvement in speaking, writing, and oral literature. In *Spoken and Written Language 9*, D. Tannen (Ed.), 35–54. Norwood, N.J.: Ablex.

Crawford, C. C. 1925. The correlation between college lecture notes and quiz papers. *Journal of Educational Research* 12: 282–291.

Dijk, T. A. van, and W. Kintsch. 1983. *Strategies of Discourse Comprehension*. New York: Academic Press.

Dunkel, P. 1988. The content of L1 and L2 students' lecture notes and its relation to test performance. *TESOL Quarterly* 22: 259–81.

Givon, T. 1979. *On Understanding Grammar. (Perspectives in Neurolinguistics and Psycholinguistics)*. New York: Academic Press.

Grimes, J. E. 1975. *The Thread of Discourse*. The Hague: Mouton.

Hansen, C. 1991. Topics in a lecture: how does a linguistic analysis compare to the professor's and students' notes? Unpublished Masters Thesis, University of Kansas, Lawrence, Kansas.

Hockett, C. F. 1958. *A Course in Modern Linguistics*. New York: Macmillan.

Keenan, E. O., and B. B. Schieffelin. 1976. Topics as a discourse notion: a study of topic in the conversation of children and adults. In *Subject and Topic*, C. N. Li (Ed.), 335–384. New York: Academic Press.

Kiewra, K. A., N. F. Dubois, D. Christian, A. McShane, M. Meyerhoffer, and D. Roskelley. 1991. Notetaking functions and techniques. *Journal of Educational Psychology* 83: 240–246.

Schiffrin, D. 1980. Meta-talk: organizational and evaluative brackets in discourse. *Sociological Inquiry* 50: 199–236.

1987. *Discourse Markers. (Studies in Interactional Sociolinguistics 5)*. New York: Cambridge University Press.

7 Variations in the discourse patterns favoured by different disciplines and their pedagogical implications

Tony Dudley-Evans

Abstract

In a recent paper Olsen and Huckin (1990) argue that a "point-driven" strategy rather than an "information-driven" one is required for comprehension of engineering lectures. They argue that students need to grasp the framework of main points provided by the lecturer as a means of organising the information in the lecture into a coherent "narrative" (Myers 1990) and that many of the non-native students in their study had failed to understand links between the various points of information presented by the lecturer. They show that the lecture used in their experiment was based on two main organising frameworks, a problem–solution pattern and the relationship between experimental data and theory.

Drawing on the author's experience in running team-taught sessions for M.Sc. courses in both Highway Engineering and Plant Biology, this chapter shows how the above two frameworks are typical of Highway Engineering lectures but less so of Plant Biology lectures. Plant Biology draws more heavily on a theoretical framework based on the work of various taxonomists who have developed systems of classification for plant genetic material. Thus the points made in many Plant Biology lectures are concerned with the classification and description of key crops.

The chapter accepts the argument for a point-driven approach to lecture comprehension but argues that students and ESP lecturers need to be aware of the different frameworks or narratives that different disciplines use.

Introduction

The literature on English for Academic Purposes (EAP) listening comprehension has concentrated on the analysis of the various strategies for listening and for note-taking considered to be needed by the non-native speaker who has to be able to follow lectures or seminars in English (Murphy and Candlin 1979; Montgomery 1977; Coulthard and

Montgomery 1981). The assumption seems to be that, if students control the relevant strategies, they will be able to apply them to the various lectures that they attend. While accepting the advantages of a generalised approach that can be followed by students of a variety of disciplines, we believe that more advanced students may need to be helped with more specific features of the actual lectures that they have to attend. This is the basis of the subject-specific approach to listening comprehension that we have adopted at the University of Birmingham. This involves recording subject lectures and running follow-up sessions based on the lectures team-taught by the language and subject lecturers (Johns and Dudley-Evans 1980; Dudley-Evans and Johns 1981).

The case that is made for the team-teaching approach mentioned above is usually a pedagogic one that stresses the advantages for the three sides of the triangle, i.e., the students, the subject lecturers and the language teachers. But the case can also be made from the point of view of discourse. The importance of an understanding of discourse features as one of the general strategies for listening comprehension is well established. Many researchers have, for example, suggested that an understanding of the role of discourse markers and relationships between different parts of the text is fundamental (e.g., Morrison 1974; Coulthard and Montgomery 1981; Chaudron and Richards 1986). Olsen and Huckin take this a stage further when they suggest that students in Engineering need to be taught appropriate strategies to understand the "discourse-level pragmatics of academic lectures" (Olsen and Huckin 1990: 42). They go on to argue that students need to be aware of the difference in the strategies needed to understand, on the one hand, a lecture that aims to present information and, on the other, a lecture that builds an argument based on a number of points. For the former, the students need an "information-driven listening strategy", while for the latter a "more context-sensitive point-driven strategy" is required.

Olsen and Huckin argue that the point-driven strategy that is required to understand the problem-solving lecture type will also be needed in other broad disciplinary areas such as the humanities and social sciences. They thus appear to be arguing that the point-driven strategy is another strategy that should be added to the list of general listening strategies that can be applied to any lecture in any discipline, as taught in various textbooks such as *Study Listening* (Lynch 1983) and *Listening Comprehension and Note Taking Course* (James et al. 1979).

It would not, however, be surprising if the discourse organisation of lectures in different subject areas revealed different patterns of organisation, or at least a different balance between the two basic lecture types described by Huckin and Olsen. Evidence for this can be found in the many studies of the rhetoric of different disciplines and the practices of different discourse communities (Hansen 1988; Dudley-Evans and Henderson 1990; Belcher 1992). These have revealed considerable variation in the patterns of argumentation favoured and there is growing evidence that students need to be made aware of the differences between disciplines (Johns 1988; Berkenkotter, Huckin, and Ackerman 1991). These studies are of written text, but the same arguments clearly apply to spoken text, particularly the relatively formalised genre of the lecture.

At one extreme it can be argued (Dudley-Evans and Johns 1981) that the key to the understanding of lectures is an appreciation of lecturers' individual styles. These can be divided into three broad categories, the *reading* style, in which lecturers either read the lecture or deliver it as if they were reading it, the *conversational* style, in which lecturers deliver the lecture from notes and in a relatively informal style with a certain amount of interaction with students, and the *rhetorical* style, in which the lecturers give a performance with jokes and digressions. The relative ease of the identification of these broad categories has been confirmed in studies both of the lexical phrases used in lectures (DeCarrico and Nattinger 1988) and the discourse intonation patterns prevalent in lectures (Samson 1984).

In this chapter I wish to argue for an approach that bridges the gap between the two extremes – on the one hand, an exclusive concentration on general strategies and, on the other, learning to listen to individual lecturers. This gap can be filled with a focus on the differences in the discourse structure of lectures in different subject areas and on how these differences reflect the disciplinary procedures and agendas of the subjects. I suggest that an awareness of these differences is just as important for listening comprehension courses as it is for courses in academic writing. In order to develop this argument, I shall refer to four postgraduate lectures, two given as part of the M.Sc. programme in Plant Biology and the other two given as part of the M.Sc. programme in International Highway Engineering.

The context

A short introduction to the context in which these lectures were recorded is necessary. For over ten years the English for Overseas Students Unit has been running classes in the two departments which are team-taught by a language teacher and subject lecturer (for a full description of these courses see Johns and Dudley-Evans 1980). In the first term of the programme the emphasis is on listening comprehension, and a lecture is recorded in each of the two departments in most weeks. The language teacher listens to the recording and prepares a handout that checks students' comprehension of the main points of the lecture and some of the language used in it. This handout forms the basis of a follow-up tutorial led by the language teacher and subject lecturer.

Although the courses lead to the same qualification – an M.Sc. from the University of Birmingham – there are marked differences in their respective procedures and views of the world. Using the classificatory system for disciplines developed by Biglan (1973) and Becher (1989),[1] I have classified (Dudley-Evans 1994) Plant Biology as being:

1. built around a strong research paradigm that is influenced by the work of a Russian botanist, Vavilov, and is concerned with concepts such as "centres of origin" and "centres of diversity". The original system developed by Vavilov has been extended by a number of scholars including a former head of the Plant Biology department. The course also includes an extensive introduction to genetics that underpins much of the theoretical work. The Plant Biology course should thus be placed towards the hard end of the hard vs. soft cline.
2. towards the centre of the pure vs. applied cline. Although the lectures make frequent mention of previous research and discuss the system of analysis set up by Vavilov and his followers, much of the emphasis of the course is on procedures for conservation of plant genetic material. This practical aspect of the course is, in fact, emphasized by its full title which is, "Conservation and Utilization of Plant Genetic Resources".
3. very largely concerned with life systems.

The International Highway Engineering course, on the other hand, should be classified as being:

1. more towards the soft end of the hard vs. soft continuum. Much of the emphasis in the course is on a set of empirically-derived models derived from tests such as the California Bearing Ratio test or the AASHO Road test. The research work reported in the lectures is frequently drawn from lecturers' own work as consultants to overseas governments. The discipline also draws on a number of other disciplines, such as soil mechanics, economics and management.
2. right at the end of the applied end of the pure vs. applied cline.
3. mostly concerned with non-life systems, such as materials, soils and climatic conditions, but also sometimes with life systems in the economic and management aspects of the course.

---

[1] Biglan suggests that the three dimensions to be considered are *hard* vs. *soft*, *pure* vs. *applied* and *life system* vs. *non-life system*. The hard vs. soft dichotomy relates to the presence or absence of a paradigm that underpins the discipline; a hard discipline has a dominant paradigm and is concerned with a clearly delineated set of phenomena while a soft discipline has no dominant paradigm and makes use of other sciences in developing its research. The pure vs. applied dichotomy refers to the extent to which the discipline is concerned with application, and the life vs. non-life dichotomy refers to the question of whether a discipline deals with living creatures or inanimate objects (Becher 1989).

The four lectures analysed below show the effect of the way that these disciplines see themselves. They have been chosen as typical of those we have recorded in both departments, and as providing evidence of the way in which the overall framework and procedures of the disciplines have an effect on the discourse patterns of lectures. They were delivered to groups of between ten and twenty students, and the lecturer adopted the "conversational" style referred to earlier. There was some limited interaction with the students during the lecture. Three lasted about 50 minutes each, the other lasted over 90 minutes.

The lectures

In this analysis I shall deal with two of the lectures, one from each department, in some detail. I shall also refer to two extracts from the other two lectures to confirm the points made in the detailed analysis.

The first Plant Biology lecture is concerned with adaptation of plants to different climatic conditions and reports a number of experiments on this subject; it does not report any of the lecturer's own research.[2] It is concerned with evaluating the various pieces of research reported in terms of whether their results tell a plausible and scientifically valid "story". It is to some extent concerned with what constitutes their validity. It assumes a knowledge of taxonomy, but, unlike many other lectures on the Plant Biology course that we have recorded, does not go into detail on taxonomy. The first International Highway Engineering lecture is on the topic of drainage, and is essentially concerned with the problems that rainfall creates for the road engineer. The lecturer presents a number of slides taken by himself on consultancy visits abroad to highlight the major problems of drainage, and then goes into a detailed analysis of each problem, drawing up a table on the blackboard with the headings: Defect; Cause; Design Comments. The lecture makes extensive use of the problem–solution pattern (Hoey 1983) with the defects and causes constituting the problem component and the design comments constituting the solution and evaluation components. The lecturer is clearly aware of the problem–solution pattern of the lecture and frequently makes use of negative evaluation as reconstituting the problem (Hoey 1983). To quote the lecturer's actual words in the lecture:

As you no doubt found in other highway design aspects, you design for one thing and you create a problem. It's like a vicious circle, solving one problem creates another. That's why I'm careful about this term "problem". So it's

---

[2] It is not suggested that the lecturer's exclusive use of reported research rather than his own work is totally typical; lecturers do of course refer to their own work. The point is that the lectures make extensive use of the reported literature in the field.

Defect–Cause–Remedy, the answer to the maiden's prayer . . . In many of the situations I've shown on the board there you're not going to get the optimal design, a maintenance-free design. You've got to lessen the problem, the most efficient economic option available.

Detailed analysis

The Plant Biology lecture is built around the presentation of five pieces of research reported in journal articles that make the point that species are not uniform and that different individuals and sub-species adapt to different climatic differences. It thus uses, in Olsen and Huckin's terms, a point-driven approach. The actual species themselves are not important, but merely serve to illustrate the theoretical point that is being made. As the lecturer says himself:

I'm going to give you several different examples illustrating different points. They're not about particular important species. They're just about things that happen to have been published. This is one of the problems of environmental ecology: most species in the world have not been studied. We simply have to take examples and expect that they apply to other species. My species don't matter; they are just examples of widespread principles.

The lecture does not, however, follow a problem–solution approach. It is concerned to make a number of theoretical points about adaptation and taxonomy that will have certain implications for the work of plant conservation. Those implications are not, in this lecture at least, made explicit. The structure of the lecture is dictated by the five papers reported and the discussion of the findings of those papers follows a pattern not dissimilar to the IMRD[3] pattern of an academic paper. In each case the lecturer mentions the species studied, the method and environmental conditions prevailing or set up for the experiment, and the main findings, and then provides an interpretation of the findings. For example, in the case of the first paper, the structure of the information presented is as follows:

Author of Paper:	Clausen
Species Studied:	Several, but particularly *Potentilla gladulosa*
Experimental Conditions:	3 experimental gardens at different altitudes
Main findings:	Sub-species did not survive if transplanted to gardens at other altitudes. Those grown at sea-level did not survive transplantation to higher altitudes and vice versa.
Interpretation:	Sub-species adapt to different ecological and geographical conditions. It was somewhat

---

[3] IMRAD refers to the following sections of an academic paper: Introduction, Method, Results, Discussion.

> surprising that the plants grown at higher and,
> therefore, colder altitudes did not survive at lower
> altitudes.

The lecture is clearly research driven and includes a considerable amount of reflection about the interpretation of results. The fifth paper discusses grasses growing in the North American prairies from the southern parts of the United States to Canada and reports that there is a relationship between the flowering date and latitude. The northern plants flower early while the southern plants flower late. The author of the paper suggests that the northern plants flower early to allow for the fact that there is in the north only a short growing season when it is warm enough to grow. In the south plants flower when the days are long. In discussing this lecture the lecturer suggests that it would be possible to make an equally plausible "story" if the results were exactly the opposite. The lecturer states:

The trouble is that it's easy to make a plausible story and there is a lot of this in ecology; there are a lot of plausible stories about. It's very hard to test experimentally and this seems to be one of those. I don't want to confuse you, but I think I could have made exactly the opposite argument. It's sometimes not easy to take experimental results and argue from those to the natural environment.

I wish to argue that the placing of the ideas presented in the lecture in the context of the ongoing research on the topic is typical of lectures on Plant Biology. This point is supported by the extract from the second Plant Biology lecture presented below. The lecture does not refer to the literature but is presenting generally accepted ideas in the field. The lecture presents them as uncontroversial and as an established system that the students need to learn as part of their course. The emphasis is on explanation of the system. The topic is *breeding* and the lecturer talks about *selfing, inbreeding in plants, mating systems*, and *sampling effects* in small populations. He begins the last topic in the way shown below. It is noteworthy that he introduces various methods without any particular evaluation of them; the purpose is just to outline and explain the procedures. I would not wish to argue that there is never any evaluation of procedures in the Plant Biology lectures, rather that the emphasis is on presenting the procedures without discussion of their advantages and disadvantages. The lecture is thus "information-driven" in Huckin and Olsen's terms.

Up to now we've been talking about everything on the assumption that we're dealing with a population that's infinitely large. Clearly, populations are not infinitely large. What I want to talk about now is the effect of population size. The first thing to say is that if the population is very large, effectively we can treat it as if it were an infinite population for many purposes. What I want to start off talking about is what happens when the population is very small. What are the genetic consequences of very small populations? The whole business about population relates to whether or not there is a chance for sampling effects to occur when we go from one generation to the next. Sampling effects occur when population size is small. There are a number of different ways we can look at sampling effects. We can give them an exact treatment, we can look at them in a statistical sense, or we can use computer simulation to look at the consequence of them.

The basic structure of the Highways lecture is as follows:

1. The lecturer begins by defining the two terms, an *unsealed* road and a *sealed* road. An unsealed road is an engineered road of earth or gravel, but does not have a sealed surface or an impermeable surface on the top. A sealed road, by contrast, has an impermeable top surface. The lecturer discusses the need to differentiate between the two types of road, and at this stage the problems that become the focus of the lecture are first mentioned. These are the problems of runoff, i.e., the problem of the movement of water (rainfall) on the road, and ravelling, the pulling out of stones from the road's surface.

2. The lecturer presents a number of slides of defects in roads, which are used to illustrate in greater detail some of the problems that have been introduced briefly in stage 1. The main problem is identified through the first slide as *seepage*, and the possible solutions of changing the type of material used for the surface and the longitudinal grade of the road are briefly discussed. The main option for remedying the problem is, however, identified as *sealing* the road. A possible problem with this is then introduced by the use of another slide. This shows a problem with the crossfall (the cross grade of the road) creating a build up of water on the road, which in turn leads to structural damage and the dangers of splash or spray on the road.

   The next slide shows the problems that result from the juxtaposition of an unsealed shoulder to a sealed road. This leads to ingress of moisture under the sealed surface and eventually to rutting in the outside wheel path on the road and edge-fretting at the side of the road (the breaking away of the edges of the road).

   The alternative of a maintained or grass shoulder is then discussed. A slide is shown and the problems are identified as the danger of trapping water on the road and the difficulty and cost of maintenance. One possible solution is to seal the shoulder, but the cost of doing this is again identified as a major problem. The final solution suggested is *kerbing*, the building of kerbs and a drainage system, which may be valid even in a country area despite the capital cost of construction.

3. This conclusion leads into the more philosophical part of the lecture, quoted above on p. 150. The lecturer concludes his discussion of the vicious circle of one solution leading inevitably to other problems by recommending that students take up accountancy, which has fewer problems and pays better!

4. This part of the lecture has introduced a number of problems and possible solutions through the use of slides. In the second half of the lecture the issues raised are summarised in a more systematic fashion through the use of the

TABLE I. PROBLEMS OF UNSEALED ROADS

Defects	Cause	Design comment
Erosion	High intensity rainfall High velocity runoff Erodible material (low Pi)	Use a more cohesive material. Seal and stabilise. Flatten the grade. Reduce the flow path. Use material with a higher Pi.
Seepage	Crossfall Longfall Permeability of material Low intensity rainfall (?)	Improve crossfall/longfall. Use material with a higher Pi.
Slippery	Students left to deduce	Reduce the permeability of the material. Seal the road.
Ravelling/ corrugation	Traffic Low Pi material	Not discussed.

table shown above (Table 1). This table was built up in discussion with the students. The table relates to unsealed roads only.
5. The lecturer concludes by asking the students to think about appropriate answers for a similar table for sealed roads.

The focus on problems and solutions is mirrored in the discourse by the frequent use of problem–solution patterns (Hoey 1983). Two examples are quoted below:

If it rains, then, as sure as night follows day, water will get in there somehow. And it depends on lots of factors that we're going to look at in a minute. Obviously, if it's very flat there, it's got a better chance of seeping into this layer here than if we have a very steep crossfall. So this is now something which may affect us for an unsealed road, and we have an option of possibly bringing that to the edge here to avoid that trap here. If K1 is greater than K2, I'm suggesting that's wrong there because it's going to form the bath-tub here. Water will trap in here because the permeability of this is greater than the permeability of that. So water can't get away as quickly as it can enter, and under certain circumstances one solution would be to change the permeability ratios of these, but also we could bring this right through to the edge as we've done there. So that is not such a critical situation then, as the water can move along this interface and out away. We've removed this trapped effect.

Another example comes when the lecturer discusses the problems of maintaining a shoulder:

So it's a very messy operation. So the answer is what? Seal the shoulders. Is that the answer? Think about it. Could be. It's money though, isn't it? It's money upfront. You've got capital costs.

The answer is, of course, to kerb the thing, get rid of the shoulder altogether, and we put a kerb at the edge of the seal. It does mean a lot more capital cost, but it does get rid of all the problems we've been talking about.

The second lecture from the International Highway Engineering course provides an excellent example of how advances in the subject are related to weaknesses in earlier models. The lecturer describes various models for pavement design and outlines the advantages and disadvantages of each model, and then shows how each new model solves a problem inherent in an earlier model. In doing this, the lecturer also makes extensive use of problem–solution models. The following passage is a good example:

We noted when we were looking at both the group index method and the CBR method that we weren't very happy about how the traffic damage was taken care of. With the group index method it was a bit vague, a bit vague and with the CBR method we saw coming from the Corps of Engineers it was probably slightly worse: it was just a single – it was going to take 6000 lbs wheel loads or 8000 lbs wheel loads or whatever. Well I suppose that's alright in a military area where you have a standard military lorry. It's not much good when we're trying to design a normal road. So we see the second great advance which we talked about was the AASHO road test. In the AASHO test what we were doing was trying to rationalise and standardise traffic damage. And we did that in terms of the Standard Axle. So the second big advance was to standardise and indeed quantify the amount of damage that is applied to a road. We did that with the Standard Axle, which we talked about the other day. And if we do that, then of course we can select the thickness of the pavement not only as a function of the subgrade strength but also as a function of the traffic in terms of the Standard Axle.

Discussion and pedagogical implications

The amount of data analysed in this chapter is clearly far too small for definitive statements to be made about the discourse patterns of the two subject areas. I would prefer to make the more limited claim that the differences noted in the four lectures are features that have frequently been observed in the lectures recorded for team-teaching purposes. They, therefore, merit some attention in the team-taught sessions, and various exercise types have been devised to make the discourse patterns explicit. The following exercise is a typical example. It was used in the follow-up session for the lecture on models for pavement design and aims to make overt the underlying structure of the argumentation used in the lecture.

When a lecturer discusses an empirical system used for an engineering purpose, he/she typically deals with the following points:

The disadvantages of the system;
The procedure for applying the system;
The situation/problems that the model deals with;
The advantages of the system.

In what order does he/she usually present these points?

In the handout accompanying the first of the Plant Biology lectures described here, the adaptation of plants to different climatic conditions, the following exercise was used.[4] Its aim was to draw students' attention to the scientific methodology that was underpinning the points made in the lecture.

The procedure for much scientific research may be crudely summarised as follows:

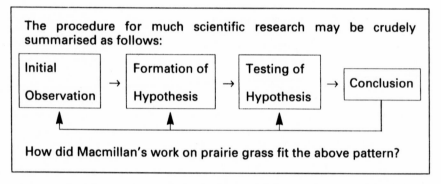

How did Macmillan's work on prairie grass fit the above pattern?

In other instances the exercises in the handout aimed to highlight the relationship between the points made in the lecture, as in the following example:

The table below lists various problems in pavement design and solutions to them. Match them up:

Problem	Solution
The moisture content in the subgrade will change when the road is on top of it.	Ensure that the total thickness is greater than 450 mm.
Failure associated with weak subgrade.	Build up knowledge by examining existing roads.
Frost heave.	Insert a capping layer.

[4] This exercise was devised by Tim Johns and I am grateful for his permission to use it here.

The exercise types have been found to be successful, both in alerting students to the patterns favoured by subject lecturers and also in sensitizing the lecturers themselves to some of the discourse patterns they use, often unconsciously, and to the unstated assumptions of their lectures. The discussion generated by the exercises is often very revealing to all participants in the sessions.

Conclusion

The claims made about the discourse structure in Plant Biology and International Highway Engineering lectures made in this chapter and the pedagogical points that arise from them have, I believe, various implications for the teaching of listening comprehension. The main one is that the concentration on common-core listening strategies, whether those be at the sentence level, the discourse level or based on a point-driven approach, may not be sufficient to prepare students for the listening comprehension tasks required on a lecture-based M.Sc. course. Students, as in the teaching of academic writing, will need to be made aware of the particular features that distinguish the practices of the discourse community they wish to become members of.

References

Becher, A. 1989. *Academic Tribes and Territories*. Milton Keynes: Open University Press.

Belcher, D. 1992. Writing in multi-paradigm disciplines: the social sciences and humanities. Paper given at the 26th Annual TESOL Convention, Vancouver, Canada.

Berkenkotter, C., T. Huckin, and J. Ackerman. 1991. Social context and socially constructed texts: the initiation of a graduate student into a writing research community. In *Textual Dynamics of the Professions: Historical and Contemporary Studies of Writing in Professional Communities*, C. Bazerman and J. Paradis (Eds.), 191–215. Madison: University of Wisconsin Press.

Biglan, A. 1973. The characteristics of subject matter in different scientific areas. *Journal of Applied Psychology* 57 (3): 195–203.

Chaudron, C., and J. R. Richards. 1986. The effect of discourse markers on the comprehension of lectures. *Applied Linguistics* 7 (2): 113–127.

Coulthard, M., and M. Montgomery. 1981. The structure of monologue. In *Studies in Discourse Analysis*, M. Coulthard and M. Montgomery (Eds.), 31–38. London: Routledge and Kegan Paul.

DeCarrico, J., and J. R. Nattinger. 1988. Lexical phrases for the comprehension of academic lectures. *English for Specific Purposes* 7: 91–102.

Dudley-Evans, A. 1994. Variation in communication patterns between discourse communities: the case of Highway Engineering and Plant Biology. In *Language, Learning and Success: Studying through English* (Developments in ELT), G. Blue (Ed.). London: Macmillan, Modern English Publications and the British Council.

Dudley-Evans, A., and W. Henderson (Eds.). 1990. *The Language of Economics: the Analysis of Economics Discourse* (*ELT Documents* 134). Modern English Publications in association with the British Council.

Dudley-Evans, A., and T. F. Johns. 1981. A team teaching approach to lecture comprehension for overseas students. In *The Teaching of Listening Comprehension* (ELT Documents Special: 30–46). London: The British Council.

Hansen, K. 1988. Rhetoric and epistemology in the social sciences: a contrast of two representative texts. In *Writing in Academic Disciplines: Advances in Writing Research*, D. A. Joliffe (Ed.). Norwood, N.J.: Ablex.

Hoey, M. 1983. *On the Surface of Discourse*. London: George Allen and Unwin.

James, K., R. R. Jordan, and A. Matthews. 1979. *Listening Comprehension and Note-Taking Course*. Glasgow: Collins.

Johns, A. 1988. The discourse communities' dilemma: identifying transferable skills for the academic milieu. *English for Specific Purposes* 7: 55–59.

Johns, T. F., and A. Dudley-Evans. 1980. An experiment in team-teaching of overseas postgraduate students of transportation and plant biology. In *Team Teaching in ESP* (*ELT Documents* 106: 6–23). London: The British Council.

Lynch, T. 1983. *Study Listening*. Cambridge: Cambridge University Press.

Montgomery, M. 1977. The structure of lectures. Unpublished M.A. thesis. The University of Birmingham.

Morrison, J. W. 1974. An investigation of problems in listening comprehension encountered by overseas students in the first year of postgraduate studies in science in the University of Newcastle Upon Tyne. Unpublished M.Ed. thesis, University of Newcastle Upon Tyne.

Murphy, D., and C. N. Candlin. 1979. Engineering lecture discourse and listening comprehension. *Practical Papers in English Language Education* 2: 1–79. Lancaster: University of Lancaster.

Myers, G. 1990. *Writing Biology: Texts in the Social Construction of Scientific Knowledge*. Madison: University of Wisconsin Press.

Olsen, L.A., and T. N. Huckin. 1990. Point-driven understanding in engineering lecture comprehension. *English for Specific Purposes* 9: 33–47.

Samson, L. 1984. An experimental study of the discourse intonation categories in monologue. Unpublished M.A. dissertation, The University of Birmingham.

8 University lectures – macro-structure and micro-features

Lynne Young

Abstract

This chapter presents a different way of examining the macro-structure of university lectures which results in a reconfigured schema for this generic type. The discussion begins with a brief description of the corpus used in the analysis and then outlines the model of analysis. This is followed by a discussion of the different strands of which lectures are composed. After summarizing some of the main features of the strands that contribute to the macro-structure of lectures, the chapter identifies some of the pedagogical implications that result from a re-configuration of the schema of lectures. The focus in this section is on the reasons why students should be presented with an accurate representation of the formal schema of lectures.

The purpose of the research and the new proposed macro-structure for monologic discourse at the tertiary level is to offer teachers of ESL and EFL (and their students) a more realistic representation of the schematic patterning of lectures to facilitate students' processing of information transmitted in this mode.

Introduction

The intention of this chapter is both to describe the macro-structure of university lectures and to identify some of the more prominent micro-features that contribute to this structure. My purpose is to propose a new schema for this generic type based on my analyses of many lectures. My research into this language variety has been motivated by my experience of teaching English as a Second Language to foreign students coming to study in Canadian universities. During the course of such teaching it became increasingly evident that these students experienced great difficulty in processing spoken academic discourse. It seemed important, therefore, to investigate the nature of this genre in terms of its form and content in order to be able to acquaint students with the spoken language of academia, especially since so much of what students are required to learn is transmitted through lectures.

While it has been the case that written discourse, in particular narrative structure, has received considerable attention, that of the macro-structure of spoken monologic discourse has scarcely been examined. Studies on narrative discourse frequently indicate the importance of form to comprehension. This is particularly evident in the work of Carrell (1984, 1987) who maintains that

> ... rhetorical form is a significant factor, more important than content, in the comprehension of the top-level episodic structure of a text and in the comprehension of the event sequences and temporal relations among events. (1987: 476)

If a knowledge of macro-structure is as significant as suggested for narrative discourse, then presumably it is equally so for expository discourse – written and spoken. It may be of even greater importance in terms of the spoken mode given its timed nature. My assumption has been that such is the case and that if we can characterize the formal schema of university lectures for foreign students, their processing of information will be greatly facilitated. Providing an accurate schematic pattern of this generic type will be particularly relevant then to teachers of English for Academic Purposes.

Description of corpus

The research I am reporting on in this chapter is based on the analysis of seven two-hour university lectures from third and fourth year courses. Three are from a Western European university in which non-native speakers of English delivered lectures in English in Soil Physics, Sociology and Economics; four are from two North American universities, in Geology, Sociology, Economics and Engineering. The corpus was selected for two reasons. First, native and non-native speakers were chosen to determine whether the macro-structure of both would be similar, given similar fields of discourse. If such proved to be the case, and if it proved to be a schema that resembled earlier studies in which first year university lectures from similar disciplines were analyzed (see Young 1990), it would strongly suggest that there was, in fact, an identifiable macro-structure across disciplines and across levels. Second, most, if not all, students to whom I have been teaching English for Academic Purposes take other university courses concurrently; it therefore seemed appropriate to select a corpus that reflected disciplines in which a majority of ESL students were also studying. The lectures selected for analysis then reflect the fields of study in which most students are engaged: Pure and Applied Science, Economics/Business and Social Science.

Model of analysis

Having identified the need to study and describe university lectures and having selected the corpus for analysis, it then was necessary to choose a model that would not only reveal the macro-structure of this language variety but would also identify some of its most significant micro-features.

I have been working with the model of Systemic Functional Grammar for several years, for two reasons. First, it explicitly indicates the connection between situational factors, or contextual constructs, and language choices. This is to say, it shows how different contexts engender different language varieties. If we are interested in describing particular language events, it is important to be able to explain both how they result from different contextual factors, and how each language variety differs from others because of situational influences. The second reason for selecting this model is that it allows a researcher not only to identify the macro-structure of a language variety, but also, to greater or lesser degrees of detail, to identify the micro-features that make up this structure. With such identification available, teachers of English can then acquaint students with the distinctive features of different varieties of language. Teachers can also select appropriate teaching material based on a knowledge of characteristic features of such varieties.

Having suggested that situational factors generate linguistic choices, it is important to understand just what they are. In order to facilitate understanding of the following brief sketch of the model of analysis, I have included a diagram of this model in Appendix A. The upper left side of the diagram consists of a box labelled "Situation". Situations consist of three main constructs. The first is *field* which accounts for the activity in which speakers and listeners are engaged in a specific situation. It is, in other words, what is going on through language in a particular time and place. In contexts in which the language activity constitutes the whole of the activity, that is, in situations which are constituted of nothing other than language (for example, in lectures, in sermons or news reports), we can equate field with subject matter. In the corpus being reported on here, consisting as it does of university lectures, the fields are easy to identify: Engineering, Economics, Sociology, etc.

Another determining factor of language choices is the situational construct of *tenor*. This concerns the relationship between speakers and listeners or between writers and readers, a relationship that can be sub-divided into two categories. The first is *personal tenor* which refers to the degree of formality between the participants in an instance of language. It accounts for the ways in which different relationships, for example, those which pertain between lecturers and students, between employers and employees, and between husbands and wives, influence language choices. Equally evident is the influence of another aspect of this relationship which is covered by the concept of *functional tenor*; this relates to the purpose for which language is being used. That is to say that the language choices a speaker makes are also determined by the purpose of a person's speech, such as lecturing to an audience, giving a sermon to a congregation, persuading someone to buy a car. The idea again here is that people make different linguistic choices depending on the reason for which they are communicating. In writing this chapter, my linguistic choices, the words and syntax I choose to use, are influenced by my purpose, which is to inform you, the reader, about a particular schema of university lectures that has emerged out of a particular type of analysis. Rather obviously, if I were giving a recipe to a friend, I would make very different language choices.

In addition to these influences, there is a third, that of *mode*, which refers to the channel of communication. In the least delicate sense it accounts for the differences that arise between spoken and written language; a more detailed description of this construct might seek to account for differences that arise in spontaneous versus planned speech, or between spoken monologues and dialogues.

Each of these factors influences not only what we say but how we say things in different situations. Now, having maintained such an influence, it remains to indicate explicitly the nature of the connection between a situation and the language that results from and responds to that context. Referring to the Appendix A diagram again, we see that situational factors influence the linguistic code – the language we select in any given context – with each of the constructs of the situation generating different types of language choices that we make (as indicated in the middle of the diagram).

It will be easier to show the connection between situational factors and linguistic choices once some of the main aspects of the language code have been outlined. It is to that discussion that I now turn.

When we communicate, we choose not only what to say but how to say it; we decide what meanings we want to convey, what our evaluations or judgments of these meanings are, and how to connect these meanings to what has gone before in a particular utterance. All of these decisions influence the lexis and the syntactic choices we select, that is, the actual linguistic code. This code consists of two levels, the semantic and the syntactic strata; the former is seen as generating the latter. The semantic stratum is composed of three different general functions for which we use language, referred to in the literature as metafunctions. To explore this idea a bit further, when we communicate, we do so about some event, some activity, or some experience, and, furthermore, about those who participate in these events and the circumstances in which they take place. For example, we might say something like "Did Tom hit the boy last night?" Here, there is an event, "hit", and the participants in this event, "Tom", "the boy", as well as the time of the event, "last night". These elements express the content of our ideas and it is for this reason that this general function is called the *ideational* one. It is the component at the semantic level that accounts for the experience we are communicating. It reflects the *what*, the *who*, and the *where* and *how* of our activities. Putting it another way, it accounts for the processes – which are anything that can be expressed by a verb, an event (physical or not), a state or a relation – and the participants in that event or state or relation, along with the circumstances in which it occurs. Our ideas, of course, need not always be about activities such as in the example above, but could instead be about mental states, as in the following examples: "They have to know the answer." "Think about the problem." Our utterances are also just as often about relations between things or people, as in: "She is the president." "Obviously, he is handsome." "She is a singer." This metafunction, as we note from the examples, generates specific structures at the syntactic level: the nominal groups realizing subjects and objects; and the verbal groups realizing transitive or intransitive verbs, those taking objects or not, as in the following two sentences: "She hit *the dog*." "He thinks." This ideational metafunction, then, accounts for processes, participants and circumstances at the semantic stratum, and these are realized in the syntactic level by nominal and verbal groups.

In addition to communicating about something, speakers and writers also express their stance or attitude towards the content; that is, they decide whether to ask questions, or state information, or express their opinion towards the content. The metafunctional component that accounts for an addressor's assessments, choices of speech function, etc., is the *interpersonal* one. And so when we look at the above sentences, we note that the interpersonal metafunction generates choices such as the use of modals, and whether or not a question is selected, or what attitude the speaker adopts to the utterance. In the above examples, in addition to the verbs and subjects and objects, we have other elements in the utterance that are generated by this interpersonal metafunction. And so in the sentence, "They have to know the answer", we have a modal element "have to" which reflects not the experience of the speaker, but his attitude towards it, expressed in a modal of necessity; in another sentence the speaker has selected a command instead of a statement or a question in the sentence, "Think about the problem." In yet a third way a speaker has expressed attitude towards the content by his choice of the word "obviously" in, "Obviously, he is handsome." All of these are reflections of the interpersonal metafunction which generates mood choices, the use of modals and other attitudinal elements which are distinct from the features which realize ideational choices.

The last metafunction that language serves is the *textual* one, which accounts for cohesive features such as ellipsis, reference, collocation, etc. Cohesive features show how we connect our ideas to each other through, for example, reference, where a pronoun refers back to a previous object or event in the discourse, as in the following, "Tom didn't know the answer. *He* should have known *it.*" These are the kinds of choices that are governed by the textual metafunction.

The language code, then, is composed of the semantic or meaning stratum which generates particular structures and lexis at the syntactic level.

Having briefly examined the elements of the code, we can now return to the question of the connection between it and situational factors. In the model I have been sketching, the field generates the content of our ideas, fashioning the ideational metafunction, which in turn generates the verbal and nominal groups of utterances, the syntax. Tenor, the second situational factor, influences the interpersonal metafunction which engenders choices of modality and other attitudinal elements as well as mood selections at the syntactic level. The final situational construct, mode, leads to the textual metafunction which at the syntactic level is reflected in different cohesive devices.

To summarize, language takes place in situations which influence the different meanings that we choose to convey in language; furthermore, these meanings generate distinct syntactic selections. What follows from this is that different situations generate different choices. The advantage of using the model of Systemic Functional Grammar is that it helps us better understand how and why language varieties resemble or differ from each other because we can characterize the nature of the situations which engender choices made when we communicate.

When we look at language in terms of metafunctional choices, we also come to realize that they form definite patterns in different discourse types. During any language event, in other words, there are different activities going on – in lectures, there are explanations, exemplifications, metadiscoursal (Lemke 1990: 118) strands such as summarizing, evaluating and announcing of new directions – and each is identifiable in terms of the language choices made by an addressor. One way by which we can better see this is through the concept of *phase*, which is designed to reveal similarities in different strands of a particular discourse in terms of what is being selected ideationally, interpersonally, and textually (Gregory 1983: 127). With phasal analysis we can configure different patterns, different threads of a discourse. Phasal analysis seems to reveal a more accurate configuration of the discourse structure of university lectures than alternatives which characterize lectures in terms of a beginning, or introduction, a middle or body, and a conclusion. As we shall see in the description that follows, phasal analysis suggests that there are many beginnings, many middles and many ends.

Phases, then, are strands of discourse that recur discontinuously throughout a particular language event and, taken together, structure that event. These strands recur and are interspersed with others resulting in an interweaving of threads as the discourse progresses. What this suggests is that in speaking or writing one doesn't just begin a topic, discuss it and then conclude it before going on to a new one; rather, one's discourse is composed of different topics which are introduced, described, summarized, returned to and are interspersed with other sub-topics which are themselves announced, discussed and exemplified. Through analyzing texts such as university lectures it becomes evident that there are different strands because there are different activities taking place, activities in which language serves metadiscoursal purposes, among others. We see good examples of this when lecturers indicate to their audiences what will follow in the discourse, when they summarize information already given, and when they evaluate this information. All of these strands, along with others, form the macro-structure of lectures. Each is distinct in terms of different meanings being conveyed and different realizations of these meanings. In the sections headed "Discourse Structuring phase", "Conclusion phase" and "Evaluation phase" in this chapter we will see the distinct characteristics of each of the phases, those that distinguish one from the other. We will also recognize a schematic patterning of lectures different from one which configures lectures in terms of an introduction, a body and a conclusion.

In order to identify phases in a piece of discourse it is necessary to analyze each line of a particular corpus in terms of semantic and syntactic choices. This completed, one reviews the analyzed lines to identify the distinct configurations of language choices which reveal the characteristics of each strand. Once these strands or phases have been identified, the analyst must then find a means of distinguishing each of them. One approach is to number phases; another is to label them in order to show where they recur in a discourse. A phase could be numbered I, a, b, c, d. The letters, with line references, show the recurrence of the phase in different parts of the text. The second possibility is to label phases and then list all of the lines that together constitute a phase. The advantage of the latter approach, especially with the type of corpus being described here, is that labels can be chosen to reveal the purpose that each phase serves in the discourse. The names that I have selected for the phases (to be described in the section "Phasal description") do just that, identify the uses to which language is being put in different parts of the discourse.

In different registerial varieties the labels would change, but not the existence of the phases themselves. In other words, each variety will have its own phasal signature, as it were. Since my concern is with academic discourse I will focus only on the phasal macro-structure of one specific type of such discourse, namely university lectures at the third and fourth year levels, but the descriptive tool of phase can be, and has been, applied to other registerial varieties (Gregory 1984; Malcolm 1982; Stillar 1992) to reflect the different patterning of different types of language events.

Phasal description

Having discussed the model and descriptive concept of phase, I now turn to the description of the macro-structure of lectures in terms of the phases that have surfaced in this and former corpora. There are six strands or phases, three of which are metadiscoursal, that is, strands which comment on the discourse itself. After briefly describing these and the other three strands, I will return to the metadiscoursal ones for a more detailed treatment in order to show the role they play in university lectures.

Once again, the purpose of the description, as will become particularly evident in the section "Pedagogical implications", is to offer accurate descriptions of one language variety so that language teachers can acquaint foreign students with the schema of monologic discourse at the tertiary level.

Of the three metadiscoursal phases that occur in all of the corpora, the first is that of the *Discourse Structuring* phase in which addressors indicate the direction that they will take in the lecture. Thus we see such strands recurring with great frequency throughout the lecture as the speaker proceeds to new points. It is, as I have described elsewhere (Young 1990: 85), an announcing phase in which a lecturer indicates to listeners new directions of the lecture. When taken together, they form a distinctive pattern of codal choices. Examples of this phase will be provided in the section "Discourse Structuring phase".

The second and equally important metadiscoursal phase is one labelled *Conclusion*, where lecturers summarize points they have made throughout the discourse. The frequency with which this and the Discourse Structuring phase occur is to a large extent determined by the number of new points made in any particular discourse. That is, if the speaker introduces only three new points in a lecture, then there will tend to be three Discourse Structuring and three Conclusion strands discontinuously occurring throughout the lecture. We will look at examples of this latter phase in the section "Conclusion phase".

The third phase that serves metadiscoursal purposes is that of *Evaluation*, which is not always as frequent as the two former metadiscoursal phases, but is still significant. Here, the lecturer reinforces each of the other strands by evaluating information which is about to be, or has already been transmitted. Lecturers do so by indicating to the audience how to weigh such information by giving their personal endorsement of or disagreement with various aspects of the content, which represents a further structuring of the substance of the lecture. Examples which reflect the nature of this phase will be given in the section "Evaluation phase".

These three phases seem to be the direct result of the influence of the situational factor of tenor in the sense that, because of the relationship between lecturers and students, the former explicitly structure their discourse by indicating how they will proceed (the Discourse Structuring phase), following this with a summation of what has been said (the Conclusion phase), and reinforcing both with an appraisal of material (the Evaluation phase), to facilitate the processing of information by the students. These three occur across disciplines and levels, indicating that the relationship between addressors and addressees in this situation fashions a particularly consistent macro-structure.

Three other phases mark university lectures. The first, *Interaction*, indicates an important feature of this registerial variety, namely the extent to which these lecturers maintain contact with their audience in order both to reduce the distance between themselves and their listeners and to ensure that what has been taught is in fact understood. This they accomplish by entering into a dialogue with the addressees by posing and answering questions. Whereas, as we shall see in the section "Discourse Structuring phase", the Discourse Structuring phase is peppered with *wh* interrogatives, realizing rhetorical questions posed by the speaker in order to focus attention, here there are many polar interrogative questions intended to be answered by someone other than the speaker. A few lines from this phase in an Economics lecture will illustrate the nature of these questions and of this phase:

353. Does anyone have an idea?
354. Think about it.
356. Yes?
357. *Student answer:* Where they intercept.
       Lecturer responds: Yah.

The two other phases that compose the macro-structure of university lectures constitute the actual content of these discourses. The first may be alternatively labelled *Theory* or *Content*, to reflect the lecturer's purpose, which is to transmit theoretical information. It is in this phase that theories, models, and definitions are presented to students. This phase is interspersed with the metadiscoursal ones, and with that of Interaction, as lecturers indicate what they are about to say, summarize different elements of the content, evaluate it and then check, in the Interaction phase, to ensure that students have understood various points. The phase is further interspersed with strands of the last phase that structures lectures, that of *Examples*. It is in this last, a very significant phase in all of the lectures, that the speakers illustrate theoretical concepts through concrete examples familiar to students in the audience. It is interesting to note that in several of the lectures, strands of this phase are more numerous than the theoretical ones, suggesting how important the role of exemplification is in monologic discourse in universities. Having briefly discussed the different phases of lectures, I want now to elaborate on the three metadiscoursal ones in more detail because they play such a significant role in structuring lectures and as such have implications for teaching the schematic patterning of lectures.

Discourse Structuring phase

The Discourse Structuring phase, as already mentioned, is one in which speakers announce the direction they will take, telling the audience what will come next in the discourse. Here the speakers identify topics that are about to be covered to facilitate processing by the students. The addressors, in predicting content, ease the burden of comprehension of new information. As Frank Smith suggested about reading:

Prediction means asking questions – and comprehension means getting those questions answered. (1978: 66)

Looking at a few lines from one of the lectures will indicate the types of features that characterize this phase and that are evident across disciplines.

(*Note:* in all of the examples, the following notation system will indicate the discipline and show whether the speakers are from Europe or North America: E = Engineering, Ec = Economics, S = Sociology, P = Physics, G = Geography; N.A. = North America, Eu = Europe; each of these will be followed by a number, indicating the line(s) in which they occur in different discourses.)

S–Eu–130:   Let me give an example from Belgium
S–Eu–374:   I just give you a list of words, terms, notions you will find in many of the articles, books . . .
E–N.A.–147: Now, at this point we're going to make another assumption . . .
Ec–Eu–86:   Now, a second assumption that I'm gonna use here, is that there are no . . .
Ec–Eu–148:   So what I will do now first is to give you some description . . .

What is particularly noteworthy here, in terms of ideational choices (those that involve the processes, the participants and the circumstances), are two types of selections. First, we see that the speakers consistently use very similar verbal groups such as "give an example", "give a list of words," "give a description," all forms of verbalization, a type of mental process, followed by nominal groups that tell the listener what will follow. That is to say that, over and over again, lecturers explicitly indicate with such choices what they intend to focus on in the lecture so that students are alerted to the nature of the ensuing material – whether it be "examples", a "list of words," or a "description." Second, evident to some extent in the examples above and in many others in the corpus, are particular choices of pronouns selected to involve the audience in the lecture: first person plural, and second person pronouns. In other words, selections such as "we," and "you," are designed to engage the students in the unfolding of the lectures. The speakers continually switch from "I," to "you," to "we," in order to include the audience in the activity going on here.

In terms of mood, there is significant variation, with that of *wh* interrogatives alternating with imperatives and declarative statements. Almost all of the realizations of the interrogative are rhetorical questions posed and answered by the addressors. They function as a focusing device, further alerting students about what is to come. Some examples of this will indicate the extent to which the speakers use this technique to point out information to follow:

Ec–N.A.–113: And so *who* bears (*lecturer points to graph while speaking*) the brunt or the effect or the impact of this increase in wage costs?

In the very next sentence, the addressor answers the question:

Ec–N.A.–114: And the answer is . . .

In another lecture the same focusing is evident:

P–Eu–211: So the question now is *what* is the volume water content and *what* is the volume water percentage?

Once again the answer comes immediately from the lecturer:

212: So the volume water content . . .

Other examples are:

Ec–Eu–93:   Now *what* is a tariff?
Ec–Eu–205: *What* is trade creation?

In each of these cases, the lecturer is alerting students about what is to come through rhetorical questions, a purpose also served by commands:

E–N.A.–122:   Now uh *let's look* at this uh simple code again (*lecturer points
               to diagram and draws box around material*)
Ec–N.A.–38:   *Let's construct* now the marginal revenue curves . . .
Ec–N.A.–413:   So now *let's look* back and see what's happening.
P–Eu–319:   So *let's talk* a little about bulk density . . .

This focusing strategy is reinforced in choices of modality where the
majority of modals indicate intention and prediction:

Ec–N.A.–54:   I'*ll* draw it in (*lecturer erases area on graph while speaking*) and
               then I'*ll* explain the reason . . .
E–N.A.–32:   What we're *going to* start to look at today . . . so today we're
               going to start to look at a box . . . which is called a coder.
E–N.A.–52:   . . . we *will* be looking at block codes . . .

What we see then in this phase are several features which consistently
mark it (a fact which foreign students could be taught), that is, that
lecturers explicitly indicate what they are about to talk about through
the choice of particular verbal groups, that lecturers alert students about
what is coming next in the lecture by asking rhetorical questions and
using commands to focus on the information, and that they further
indicate the topics to follow by modals of prediction and intention.

Conclusion phase

Turning to the Conclusion phase, a different pattern is evident in terms
of processes, participant chains and in interpersonal choices of mood
and modality. Here we see significant evidence of another type of
process, that of *relations*, in which lecturers identify and classify what
has already been discussed to ensure that the information is grasped by
the students. In other words, the focus here is on relations between
elements already raised in the Content strands. In addition, the participant roles are filled by the key terms and ideas of the theories presented
throughout the lecture. What we see here is a repetition of key aspects
forming a chain of elements.

Let's examine a few examples that illustrate the focus in this phase:

E–N.A.–89:   So this (*lecturer points to material written on the board*) is an
               example of a rate one third code.
E–N.A.–153:   So, the outcome is that we get what's called the maximum
               likelihood decoding rule.
E–N.A.–232:   And that's another general statement that you can make about
               codes and decoding.

Here we find a predominance of relational processes as signalled by
the verbal group "is", with participant roles filled by terms such as:
"code", and "decoding rule".

In a Physics lecture the same type of activity takes place with the lecturer summarizing by identifying and classifying what has been discussed, thereby creating a participant chain that emphasizes the main topics of the lecture:

P–Eu–33:   So there are two different approaches of the same subject, namely the water in the soil.
P–Eu–103:   So there are different ways of expressing that soil water content.
P–Eu–210:   So that's the way how a volumetric water content is measured.

The chain formed here is composed of nominal groups such as "water in the soil", "soil water content", and "volumetric water content", all focussing on the main topic of the lecture.

Another marker of this phase, which clearly distinguishes it from the Discourse Structuring one, is in interpersonal choices. As is evident in the few examples above, there is no mood variation, with almost all of the utterances being realized by the indicative declarative mood.

In terms of modals, there are a few of different kinds but none plays a particularly important role here. This is a neutral phase, one in which lecturers don't offer evaluative commentary on the material; it is a "factual" strand focussing on key aspects of the lecture. The most recognizable features then are in the type of process here and the participant chain formed by the repetition of terms.

Evaluation phase

When we turn to the Evaluation phase, what is immediately noticeable are the ways in which lecturers do evaluate material, not by attitudinal elements such as modals or other interpersonal choices, but through the selection of one type of predominating process, that of attributive relations. Here, it will be remembered, lecturers primarily evaluate points they have already made, which acts as a reinforcement to the strands of the Conclusion phase by indicating judgement on information already given to students. Examples from the same two lectures chosen for the Conclusion phase – Engineering and Physics – illustrate not only the nature and purpose of this phase, but also the way in which it reinforces points already summarized by repeating and evaluating key terms or theories.

E–N.A.–47:   ... obviously error detection is a very important function ...
E–N.A.–71:   There are advantages and disadvantages of each.
E–N.A.–91:   It's not a very efficient code but it ...
E–N.A.–230: So this (*lecturer points to information on the board*) is in effect a more efficient code than this one.
E–N.A.–233: The larger the code the more efficient the code can be.

Again we see the same sort of reiteration of key terms that we saw in the Conclusion phase; here, however, they are being evaluated so that students will know how to weigh each of them. The same sort of reinforcement is also found in the Physics lecture:

P–Eu–69: Now this ability of the soil to store water is very important . . .
P–Eu–364: But the easiest and simplest way and the most exact way is of course the soil sample.
P–Eu–424: So there is of course also a more direct way to calculate the mass water content.

Even in these few examples we see a participant chain similar to the one of the Conclusion phase; similar as well is the lack of mood variation and marked modality. What is evident here are explicit judgements reflected in selections such as: "very important", "very efficient code", "easiest and simplest way", "most exact way", and "more direct way". In other words, lecturers are revisiting the same points touched on in the Conclusion phase and evaluating them so that students will know how to weigh each of them, will know which are the best and, by implication, which are less satisfactory approaches to issues raised in the lecture.

Summary

This description of the metadiscoursal phases shows that each phase recurs discontinuously throughout different lectures. Each strand is interspersed with others, so that what emerges is a continual inter-weaving of threads of discourse which forms a macro-structure very different from one configured in terms of a simple beginning, middle and end, a point that we shall explore further in the next section. Further-more, we have seen that each phase is different from the other, and that each has features that distinctively characterize it. The Discourse Structuring phase is marked by processes of verbalization, with participant roles realized by first and second person pronouns, by rhetorical questions alternating with statements and imperatives, and by a type of modality that indicates the purpose of the phase, to announce future directions, namely that of intentionality and prediction. The Conclusion phase is mainly identifiable in terms of two types of relational processes in which key terms and elements of the lecture are identified and classified. Further, participant roles are filled with these terms which are repeated with morphological variation, forming a chain of related items to ensure that students realize just what were the most important terms and concepts in the lecture. In the Evaluation phase, the lecturers emphasize these concepts and approaches by evaluating each, by passing judgements on various aspects of the lecture, further ensuring that students know which approaches and which views to adopt and, by implication, which to reject.

This view of lectures as being configured in terms of phases has clear pedagogical implications beyond those briefly referred to in the preceding discussion. It is to these that I now turn.

Pedagogical implications

I would like to focus the discussion on the pedagogical implications that relate to a reconfiguration of the macro-structure of university lectures resulting from phasal analysis. Phases reveal the schema of university lectures in terms more accurate than descriptions exemplified in note-taking outlines provided in study skills books (such as that of Woods 1978: 42), where the macro-structure suggested by outlines is one of a beginning, middle and end configuration. As we have seen from the brief description of phases, what actually happens in the unfolding of the discourse is that introductory or predicting strands are interspersed throughout a lecture, precisely because there are several information strands in which different content is transmitted. Similarly, there are several concluding strands that follow each discussion of new information. If one of the purposes of study skills books and courses is to familiarize students with the structure of lectures in order to facilitate their notetaking, it is imperative that an accurate macro-structure be presented to them. My point here is that phasal analysis seems to offer a more realistic portrayal of the nature of this particular genre. If it is the case that university spoken discourse is composed of different structuring strands, in addition to content and exemplification phases, then this is what students need to be told. Only an accurate representation of macro-structure will facilitate their processing of information.

My assumption has been and remains that an acquaintance with the correct schematic patterning of lectures will greatly assist students. The connection between the understanding of form and content has clearly been established in schema theory and related areas of research:

A relationship exists between an individual's psychological conception of a form and his or her ability to comprehend and utilize it. (Crookes 1986: 59)

The literature on schema theory suggests that readers have a narrative schema in mind when approaching narratives, and that understanding involves filling in the empty slots of the schema with appropriate information from the text (van Dijk and Kintsch 1978). While schema theory has largely been concerned with narrative structure, I think it is appropriate to extend the theory to expository structure (see Flowerdew, this volume). Students need such a schema for expository spoken discourse; without it they cannot accurately predict, which hampers their ability to understand. One way to help them anticipate what will follow is to provide them with a schematic pattern of lectures, a point related to Carrell's, mentioned earlier in the paper, that

> ... rhetorical form is a significant factor, more important than content, in the comprehension of the top-level episodic structure of a text and in the comprehension of the event sequences and temporal relations among events (1987: 476).

Given this insight into narrative structure, it seems particularly important to acquaint teachers of ESL and ESP courses, particularly those in post-secondary institutions, with an accurate macro-structure of university lectures so that they can present students with a schema that fully reflects what is going on in this generic situation. Foreign students, particularly those from non-Western cultures, whose educational and cultural backgrounds may differ widely and whose schemata correspondingly may also differ, particularly need this assistance.

It is important to identify for foreign students, who have great difficulty in taking notes that, first, lecturers often explicitly announce all new topics, and to acquaint them with the more common ways in which they do so; second, that information is imparted in several ways, through theoretical discussion, through exemplification, and through summarization. If students know that the same information is revisited in a number of ways, and that if they miss it the first time they will be able to capture it later, they will be better able to cope with the information transmitted in lectures. If language teachers can equip students with an appreciation of macro-structure that accurately reflects what goes on in university discourse, their comprehension of information will be made easier. Furthermore, with the knowledge of the ways in which lecturers pattern their discourse, teachers will be able to select appropriate features which indicate, for instance, how speakers signal their summaries or their introductions to new points. With such information, students' processing of lectures should be greatly facilitated.

Conclusion

My analysis of university lectures indicates first, that there is consistency of codal choice across disciplines in terms of macro-structure, and between native and non-native speakers' discourse in this registerial variety – university spoken discourse. Second, it suggests the structure of lectures be reconsidered on the basis of phasal analysis in order to reflect more accurately the macro-structure of this genre.

Although much more research into this and other language varieties is needed, the model of analysis offers a new approach to the typing of genres. Descriptions which reveal the macro-structure and distinctive micro-features of language varieties, as well as the situations which engender them, should not only facilitate the selection of appropriate teaching materials but also provide teachers with the necessary tools for acquainting students with the basic characteristics of different generic types.

Appendix A
Model of analysis
The relationship between situation and linguistic code

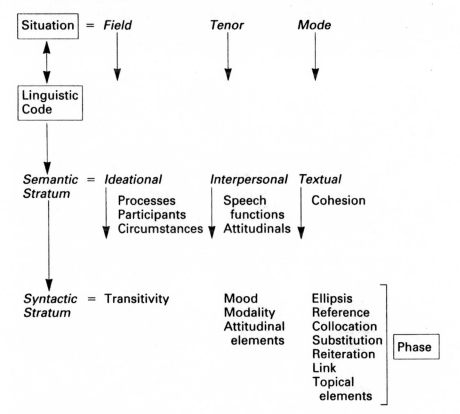

References

Carrell, P. L. 1984. Facilitating reading comprehension by teaching text structure: what the research shows. Paper presented at the 18th Annual TESOL Convention, Houston, Texas, March.

1987. Content and formal schemata in ESL reading. *TESOL Quarterly* 21: 461–481.

Crookes, G. 1986. Towards a validated analysis of scientific text structure. *Applied Linguistics* 1: 57–70.

Dijk, T. A. van, and W. Kintsch. 1978. Cognitive psychology and discourse recalling and summarizing stories. In *Current Trends in Text Linguistics*, W. V. Dressler (Ed.), 61–81. Berlin, New York: Walter de Gruyter.

Gregory, M. 1983. Towards communication linguistics: a framework. In *Linguistics in a Systemic Perspective*, J. D. Benson and W. S. Greaves (Eds.), Volume 1 (1985), 119–134. Amsterdam; Philadelphia: John Benjamins.

1984. Discourse as the instantiation of message exchange. In Hall (Ed.), 243–254.

Hall, R. A. (Ed.). 1984. *The Eleventh LACUS Forum*. Columbia, South Carolina: Hornbeam Press.

Lemke, J. 1990. *Talking Science: Language, Learning and Values*. Norwood, New Jersey: Ablex Publishing Corporation.

Malcolm, K. 1982. Communication linguistics: a sample analysis. Mimeo. Toronto: York University.

Smith, F. 1978. *Understanding Reading: a Psycholinguistic Analysis of Reading and Learning to Read*, 2nd ed. New York: Holt, Rinehart and Winston.

Stillar, G. 1992. Phasal analysis and multiple inheritance: an appeal for clarity. *Carlton Papers in Applied Language Studies* IX: 103–128.

Woods, N. 1978. *College Reading and Study Skills*, 3rd ed. New York: Holt, Rinehart and Winston.

Young, L. 1990. *Language as Behaviour, Language as Code: a Study of Academic English*. Amsterdam; Philadelphia: John Benjamins.

PART IV:
ETHNOGRAPHY OF SECOND LANGUAGE
LECTURES

Editor's introduction to Part IV

The three chapters in this section offer a broader view of the lecture comprehension process than do those of the previous two sections. An ethnographic approach to lecture comprehension, as Benson, in the first chapter in this section, points out, views this process as part of a wider "culture of learning" in which "structures, contexts, rituals, universals, significant symbols, roles, status markers, patterns of behavior, beliefs, values, assumptions, attitudes, and even the allocation of praise and blame" all have a role to play. Benson's chapter analyzes nine features of lectures from such an ethnographic perspective. The analysis leads Benson to argue that preparation for L2 lecture listening is best conducted by offering the students the experience in miniature, i.e., some form of content-based language instruction. Only in this way are learners exposed to something approximating to the authentic "culture of learning" associated with lecture listening.

The second chapter in this section, that of Mason, further develops the idea of lecture listening as part of the wider culture of learning. Mason uses one of the many research tools available to the ethnographer, the interview, to examine learner and lecturer perceptions of L2 lecture strategies. Mason's analysis goes beyond the content of what is normally considered to be a part of academic listening to demonstrate how closely listening is tied in with speaking, noting that in her body of interviews there is a growing expectation of oral participation in the lecture theatre. Mason also discovers that while the standard 600+ score on the TOEFL for independent post-graduate study does not ensure comprehension of lectures that deviate from a straight talk-and-chalk style (reinforcing a point made by Dunkel and Davis, this volume), students are able to make up for this deficiency by greater efforts in reading.

The third chapter in this section, by King, uses two other tools available to the ethnographer, direct observation of lecture listening in a naturalistic setting and analysis of the product of this activity in the form of student notes. In particular, King studies the relation between student notes and visual information presented by means of slides, overhead projection and on the blackboard, an important element in the post-graduate engineering lectures King is concerned with. In general, student notes capture most of the important information in the visuals and at least some of the comments which accompany them. However, where comment is not supported by visuals, typically in "evaluative" parts of the discourse, student notes are less effective.

Two points in King's chapter are worth highlighting here in relation to other chapters in the collection. First, it is interesting to compare the approach to note-taking research adopted by King to that of Chaudron, Loschky, and Cook, on the one hand, and by Hansen, on the other. Chaudron, Loschky, and Cook adopt an experimental procedure, asking subjects to make notes on carefully prepared pre-audio-recorded lectures. Recall is then measured and compared, by means of psycho-metric tests, for subjects who were allowed to refer to their notes and subjects who were not. Because Chaudron, Loschky and Cook were interested in one particular variable in the lecture comprehension process, that of the effect of referring to or not referring to notes made during a lecture, it was important that all other possible variables were controlled as rigorously as possible. King, on the other hand, is concerned with more naturalistic behaviour, and how note-taking relates to other aspects of academic listening comprehension as an "event", as part of what Benson calls "the culture of learning". An *in vivo* methodology is thus more appropriate. Regarding Hansen's chapter, it would be interesting to know how her method of evaluating notes based on her topical analysis would cope with lectures such as those investigated by King in which the visual element was so important.

The second point from King's chapter worth relating to another chapter in the collection concerns the question of the discourse function of evaluation. In his conclusion, King calls for more research into the role of this discourse function in lectures and the problems it might pose for L2 comprehension. The focus of Tauroza and Allison's chapter, earlier in the collection, is this very question. Evaluation was indeed a problem for the students in their study. However, the explanation put forward for this difficulty was that this discourse function is relatively unusual in the lectures the subjects were familiar with and thus did not fit in with their existing schematic knowledge. The type of lectures with which King's subjects were familiar, in contrast to those of Tauroza and Allison, did typically contain evaluation. King tentatively relates the problem to the fact that evaluation is not accompanied by visual support, whereas most of the other stages of the lecture are. However, it could be that prior to the course in question, students had not been accustomed to either evaluation or the use of visual support. Either lack of familiarity with the communicative function of evaluation or absence of visual support (or both) could, therefore, account for the problem of evaluation among King's subjects. Clearly, this is an area for further research into both the role of visuals and the discourse function of evaluation in lectures.

The three chapters in this section offer some interesting, if not disturbing (for some), challenges for L2 listening comprehension research. If listening needs to be viewed as an integral part of a wider culture of learning, where does that leave research which is purposefully focussed on but one small part of the phenomenon, whether that be the processes of comprehension, as measured by tests of understanding and recall of the information content of recorded lectures (viz the chapters in Part II of this collection, *The L2 Academic Listening Process*), or whether it be the object of comprehension, as manifested in transcripts of lectures (viz the chapters in Part III of this collection, *Discourse of Academic Lectures*)? There is an answer to this question, but it is an issue that will be taken up again in the concluding chapter to this volume.

9 Lecture listening in an ethnographic perspective

Malcolm J. Benson

Abstract

The premise of this chapter is that "learning", particularly learning in terms of students and universities, is capable of being seen as a specific and developed culture. In universities, the central ritual of this culture is the lecture. Nine features of the lecture are discussed here: its performative nature, its organization, its relation to other learning channels, the contexts in which it takes place, the norms on which it relies, the principles and goals it activates, the demands it makes, how it is patterned, and the range of learning events it promotes. A number of these features touch on points which have implications for ESL students, for example, the effect of hierarchical administrative planning on lecture content, the connection between student motivation and strategies used, the coding of values in speech acts, and the domination of classroom activities by broad cultural norms.

Introduction: on the nature of ethnographic understanding

There is a culture of learning which everyone who has ever been a student has experienced. Once we think of learning as a culture, it is clear that it has its own structures, contexts, rituals, universals, significant symbols, roles, status markers, patterns of behavior, beliefs, values, assumptions, attitudes, and even the allocation of praise and blame (together with their consequent rewards and punishments) just like the larger entities we call cultures. And as with fully-grown cultures, it is open to ethnographic description ("establishing rapport, selecting informants, transcribing texts, taking genealogies, mapping fields, keeping a diary, and so on." Geertz 1973: 6) and analysis ("sorting out the structures of signification . . . and determining their social ground and import." p. 9).

Given the above view that learning is a culture, this chapter is a contribution to the ethnography of that learning, in much the same spirit as earlier writers (Bauman and Sherzer 1974, 1989; Hymes 1962) have approached the ethnography of speaking. The general aim, now as then, is to produce a descriptive theory of learning as a cultural system, or what Watson-Gegeo (1988) has called a "descriptive and interpretive-explanatory theory" (p. 577). Such a theory, working from grounded "thick description" (Geertz 1973), would reveal how a student – ESL or native speaker – is part of the culture: how he or she takes part in its rituals, adopts a suitable role, merges personal values into the general structure, and derives meaning from the whole. The explanation would show the patterns of structure and behavior that dominate the culture of learning.

In this chapter I shall focus on one specific learning channel – the lecture – since it has achieved what has been called "paradigmatic stature" (Waggoner 1984: 7) as the teaching–learning activity of higher education worldwide. Even more particularly, since an increasing number of students are from an "international" background, I shall attempt to bring out the role that listening to lectures plays in their learning.

The lecture: some critical features

Listening to lectures is a major part of the culture of learning, as any student will attest. It is one of the learning channels available to students, some others being reading, interaction with other students, and discussions with the teacher. The sociolinguistic features of a lecture consist of some or all of the following: (a) it is a "performance," one usually given special status by attendance being "compulsory"; (b) it is organized along two axes: the first is the structural one of the university, the department, and the lecturer; the second is that of its relationship to the rest of the course; (c) it is also organized vis à vis the other learning channels, and students are usually clear about their personal preferences among these channels; (d) it takes place in specific contexts of time and place; (e) it relies on the norms and rules of the temporary speaking and listening community that is called the "class"; (f) it activates the principles and values and goals which guide the members of the speech community; (g) it makes linguistic and cognitive demands on the listener; (h) it is patterned into certain classes of communication acts which are recognized by the participants and are capable of being described; and (i) it allows for a specific range of events to occur.

In the following section, the descriptors (a) to (i) above will be illustrated. The interested reader might wish to consult two earlier studies that were based on the same research project (Benson 1989, 1991).

(a) A lecture is a "performance," one usually given special status by attendance being "compulsory"

Aspects of performance have attracted considerable attention from ethnographers (for a review of current positions see Bauman and Sherzer 1989: Introduction). There are two important ways in which speech may be a performance, and one of these, the "artistic" side, is seen as:

a specially marked way of speaking, one that sets up or represents a special interpretive frame within which the act of speaking is understood. In this sense of performance, the act of speaking is put on display, objectified, lifted out to a degree from its contextual surroundings, and opened up to scrutiny by an audience. (Bauman and Sherzer 1989: xix)

Now, while all of the above applies to performances whose main aim may be to entertain, amuse or persuade, at least some applies to the giving of lectures. Within the lecture hall, the words used become the material of the proceedings, they take on "public" attributes, no longer being the words of a private individual. If circumstances allow, they can be called into question. The extract in Figure 1 is from a lecture in a course called "Education and Development" (for the full context, see Benson, 1989).

This leads on to number three on the board here, to Functionalism and Structuralism. These are terms that are hinted at in here, but are not exactly completely developed, so I'd like to . . . just develop it for a second here . . .

[*Writes on board*]
FUNCTIONALIST	STRUCTURALIST
PROCESSES	FORM
FUNCTIONS	STRUCTURE
	THE "SET-UP"

Functionalists are interested in the way things work, in the processes [*writes and underlines "PROCESSES"*] . . . Structuralists are interested in how things are set up, they're interested in form [*writes "FORM"*], the structure [*writes "STRUCTURE"*], the set-up [*writes "THE SET-UP"*]. When there's a problem in education, or anything else, the functionalist says, "Let's find out what the problem is so we can fix it." For example, many children drop out of school: "How can we interest them more in school? How can we keep them in school for a longer period of time?"

Figure 1   Lecture extract: functionalism and structuralism

This is recognizably the special public language of the lecture hall, with its mistakes, its repetitions, its pauses for writing the main ideas, and even its dramatic flourishes. Importantly, it is accountable language.

The second aspect, that attendance at lectures is compulsory, is related to their being performances. Not merely does a performance require an audience, but the ethnographer soon realizes that factors other than the transmission of information must be at work; this is evident from the fact that the same body of knowledge could far more easily be given to students in the form of a reading assignment or a handout. So what is the real reason for attendance at lectures being compulsory? One possible answer is that the lecturer by his or her performance is proof that the problems confronting the class are solvable, that the ideas are graspable; the audience literally gain access both to the speaker and to his/her ideas:

in consequence of the way he handles himself, he can render his subject matter something that his listeners feel they can handle. (Goffman 1981: 192)

Order and knowledge replace chaos and bewilderment. In sum, what the ethnographer sees is a performance where the main goal is to establish contact with students who are being initiated into a world in which problems are solvable, and where relations can be established with a person who has "been there."

Several points relevant to ESL arise from this realization. The first is that the performance requires the listeners to grapple with the semantics of the material: what does a passage of lecture monologue mean in the context in which it is uttered? Asides, for example, far from being irrelevant parts of a lecture, may serve to "increase global semantic and pragmatic unity and to introduce a variety of mutually reinforcing interpretive frames" (Strodt-Lopez 1991: 117). The lecturer's example of the children who drop out of school (see Figure 1) calls up certain familiar frames; it provides the required "pragmatic unity."

A second point is that the lecturer overtly or covertly reveals attitudes towards the content. In Figure 1 the dropouts are presented to clarify the structuralist–functionalist dichotomy. But the personal interpretation by the lecturer, through the immediate choice of that particular example, is of at least equal importance. It reveals attitudes of concern for children and for the future of education – concerns, incidentally, which are by no means cultural universals.

A third, related, point is that the lecturer also indicates the level of detail at which the material should be viewed by the students. The passage quoted above, most would agree, shows a lecturer offering broad definitions of the structuralist–functionalist dichotomy, but content to leave it at that. By doing so, the lecturer has made assumptions regarding both the students' knowledge of the terms involved, and their needs for this particular course. These assumptions and needs lead directly to the next point.

(b) A lecture is organized along two axes: the first is the structural one of the university, the department, and the lecturer; the second is that of its relationship to the rest of the course

Any one lecture is the product of an immense amount of "vertical" planning and organization, so that it fits in with the whole elaborate university structure. We may usefully look at three levels of administrative goals, those of the department, the course, and the teacher. The highest meaningful one is that of the department involved, which in the present case was stated as follows:

The focus of graduate study and research is Educational Policy Studies with the goal of improving the quality of educational policy making and educational practice. (University Bulletin)

The Department offered some 26 graduate-level courses under this rubric, including the course being described here. Course level goals, the second level, bring matters into slightly sharper focus:

Overview of the roles of education in national development and in promoting social, economic, and cultural improvement. Emphasis given to less developed countries and Third World communities at home. (University Bulletin)

Nevertheless, it is notable that neither the departmental level goals nor the course level goals give the student (particularly the international student) much clear guidance. At the third level, the teacher's Course Outline did not specify any goals, but (a) named the books to be used, (b) outlined her "Expectations" of the students (seven points in all), and (c) gave the topic and readings for each session. The topic and required readings for the 11th session – "Education and the State" – were given as shown in Figure 2.

Session 11: Education and the State
Paradoxes and Unanswered Questions. The Role of Research.
Reading: Fägerlind and Saha, Chapter 9, pp. 234–254.
(TERM PAPER DUE NEXT SESSION)

Figure 2   Formal description of a lecture theme (from Course Outline)

The ethnographer notes the strong session-by-session structure implicit in this Course Outline extract, together with the lecturer's own

1 Papers and announcements, etc.
2 Education and the State – "Finale"
3 On "functionalism" and "structuralism" [see Figure 1]
4 Bibliography – Things to note
5 Background re Botkin and the Book
6 A new approach: the 3 kinds of learning
7 Next time

Figure 3   Session Objectives [on blackboard]

personal goals for the session. These goals were translated into specific teaching objectives at the outset of each session, and were written on the board (see Figure 3).

What finally occurred in the class (and the lecturer did keep to her outline in Figure 3) was, therefore, the product of elaborate structural planning, and in a very specific sense the information, attitudes, views, and so forth that constituted the lecture content were "delivered" (Gagné and Driscoll 1988: 151). This initially alarming term captures the important idea of the vertical structure inherent in higher education.

When we look at the "horizontal" axis of a lecture course, we see that each lecture (a) builds on the previous one(s), (b) is a "free-standing" speech event with its own interior structure, and (c) anticipates the next. In this sense, learning is additive, moving on from lecture to lecture, often keeping pace with a book or books, and with written work proceeding in the background (note Figure 2: TERM PAPER DUE NEXT SESSION). In another sense it is not additive, as information, attitudes, and views are all recycled, sometimes consciously, sometimes unconsciously. The moral here, as far as listening is concerned, is that to place too much stress on one specific passage of lecture listening is to ask the discourse to do more than it is asked to do in real life.

(c) A lecture is also organized vis à vis the other learning channels, and students usually have personal preferences among these channels

Figure 2 showed that for this session the students were asked to read some 20 pages. The original instructions regarding the readings for each session were clear (see Figure 4).

Figure 4 shows that regarding the readings, the instructions were for the students to read the material before the session, not necessarily in order to understand the lecture, but to create a "common basis for further discussion". The students were, therefore, placed under a double obligation: not merely to read the material, but also to be prepared to discuss it.

1 This is a seminar. As such *active participation* in class is expected and will play a part in the final evaluation. Discussion in class will be based on presentations, on the required readings, and on the personal experience of seminar participants.

2 The required readings provide a common basis for further discussion. You are expected to be conscientious in keeping current with the readings.

Figure 4   Classroom Expectations (from Course Outline)

NNS Group (n = 7) Responses

Student No.	R	W	L	S	Int	Least favorite
2	Yes				Yes	Being lectured
5		Yes				Nil
13					Yes	Exams
18		Yes	Yes			Reading
19	Yes					Interaction
20					Yes	Listening
22		Yes				Nil

Note: R = Reading; W = Writing; L = Listening; S = Speaking; Int = Interaction. Least = Least preferred way; Yes = strong preference.

Figure 5   Question: "Tell me about your favorite way to learn."

Bilingual Group (n = 4) Responses

Student No.	R	W	L	S	Int	Least favorite
1 (Eng/Spanish)					Yes	Being lectured
7 (Eng/Afrikaans)			Yes	Yes		Rote learning
10 (Eng/Spanish)	Yes	Yes			Yes	No interaction
15 (Eng/French)					Yes	Being lectured

Figure 6   Question: "Tell me about your favorite way to learn."

When the class under observation for this study (Benson 1989, 1991) were interviewed about their preferred learning styles, the answers were as seen in Figure 5.

With the bilingual group the results showed much the same pattern (see Figure 6).

In the monolingual group (n = 11), learning from listening received five endorsements, two of which were "strong" ones; learning from interaction was only selected by three students, although the record shows that they did most of the talking! Several balked at the idea of identifying just one learning channel:

I think my favorite way would be to read and listen, 'cause reading, if your ears don't grab it your eyes might catch it, but to rely on one solely you're kind of out of luck, I think, you need to depend on your other senses too, to help you along the way. (U.S. monolingual student)

From Figures 5 and 6, we see that regardless of language background, listening was as evenly distributed as the other learning channels. Interestingly, interaction (which often gets little or no attention in ESL preparatory courses) was popular in the ESL/Bilingual group. Did these international students learn from what the monolingual group took to be just "business as usual" classroom interaction? Is this a genuine case of cultural preferences, or a happenstance of this particular group? No answer is available from this data, but ethnographic studies in this way open up thought-provoking possibilities which perhaps deserve larger and more comprehensive investigation.

(d) A lecture takes place in specific contexts of time and place

In the ethnographic view, the historical period in which a lecture, or course of lectures, is given is of great importance. So too is the location (country, state, institution). These may have determining influences on what occurs, not only in terms of the behavioral norms and the relative status of the participants, but also in terms of expectations, attitudes, learning styles, and the outcomes of learning. The ethnographer quickly becomes aware that what is occurring in the class under observation would be unlikely to occur in any other context: should one factor change, everything would change. This lack of generalizability about education leads the ethnographer to distrust, at the research level, those findings which claim to have found general rules for specific teaching methods, texts, study habits, or indeed any other factor treated in isolation. The learning preferences indicated above (Figures 5 and 6) are products, above all, of particular time and place considerations; they reflect an era when the "lecture" class is changing (Waggoner 1984), when interactive methods of learning are available alongside traditional ones, and when both teachers and students feel the influence of a greater egalitarianism than in periods past.

(e) A lecture relies on the norms and rules of the temporary speaking and listening community that is called the "class"

The social norms of a lecture class specify:

who can take part, what the role relationships are, what kind of content is admissible, in what order information can be introduced, and what speech etiquette applies. (Gumperz 1982: 155)

These behavioral norms work on both general and particular levels, with the latter being indicated in the form of "class rules" which are very quickly apparent to the students. For example, in the class being described here the teacher soon made plain that interaction, particularly in the form of relevant questions, was always welcome. Later in the same session, following the structuralist–functionalist extract (Figure 1), the interaction shown in Figure 7 took place. What is evident here is a dynamic relationship between the readings, the interaction, and the lecturer's input.

DR. WHITE: . . . but that you also have harmony in mind, and that the two can be combined in some kind of dynamic system that produces betterment for children in school, or betterment for whoever is involved. Yes?
STUDENT: Is this the structural–functionalism that we learned about on page 14?
DR. WHITE: Page 14 . . . [*Gets out book and opens it*] 14? OK. Yes. So in a sense we do have here the same . . . the idea that we expressed is expressed on page 14. [*Long pause*] OK, Let's move on, to, page 245, at the bottom . . .

Figure 7   Classroom Interaction

Other norms refer to the status or roles of the participants. In university classes, the roles "teacher" and "student" provide powerful behavioral frameworks which both constrain and liberate those involved. The teacher is constrained in terms of language (e.g., levels of formality, see Joos 1962), presentation of content, and in a variety of sociolinguistic ways. However, generally speaking the teacher is free to treat the topic in any preferred manner, using any appropriate methodology, and relinquishing the floor only at will. The student role, while constraining certain behaviors, such as taking the floor, also liberates by removing a variety of intellectual and social obligations. There is a great sense of freedom in being a student!

Norms such as these are by no means the same across cultures. In some Asian countries, for example, attendance is regarded as more important than interaction, but in the U.S. the "bright" student who interacts whenever allowed is generally esteemed. Figure 8 shows interaction from an ESL student who is perfectly at ease with the behavioral and interactional norms of a U.S. class.

STUDENT: This [*points to Structuralist side*] is Marxist. What's the name of this side?
DR. WHITE: This would be liberal, liberal democracy . . .
STUDENT: Could we have some capitalist-structuralists?
DR. WHITE: Yes . . . yes, there are capitalist-structuralists too, for example? [*Offers it back to student*]
STUDENT: Raymond Aron, and Jean-Jacques Shriver.
DR. WHITE: Yes, or Ivan Illich. Très bien!

Figure 8   Interaction: Teacher–ESL Student (W. Africa)

The turn-taking follows English discourse norms, as well as the local rules of this class. It also comfortably incorporates the Western interpretation of the roles "teacher" and "student," an interpretation in which this student would certainly have been earmarked by the teacher as "bright" and "involved." Many international students, however, are at a loss when faced with such discourse and behavioral "norms," which to them are not normal at all.

(f) A lecture activates the principles and values and goals which guide the members of the speech community

The norms of classroom behavior indicated above (e) are the product of a variety of principles and values held by each participating member, and in practice translated into goals. These values may be investigated in several ways (e.g., by interview), and in general the ethnographer is likely to be impressed by the variety that exists even in a relatively small and homogeneous group.

Let us look at two examples from this research, one of which focuses on the teacher, the other on the students. In the first, the conceptions that the participants had of the teacher's role were examined, as reflecting a social aspect of cognition. The relevance to ESL may be noted from the very first finding, which was that almost half the class ($n = 22$) said that in their view the teacher's role was that of "facilitator," while a further six saw her as a "guide." Only one or two felt she was "teaching" in the traditional sense of the word. Further probing showed that the role of facilitator was seen as enabling students to study by providing them with an adequate framework (for example, a reading list), stimulating lectures, objectives, requirements and deadlines, plus the opportunity for classroom interaction. The idea of freedom within a solid framework was implicit in many responses, as in the student who said the teacher had a "tight structure" but ran a "loose operation."

The notion of "guide" focused on the teacher's experience and the fact that both in terms of the course, and of her practical experience in development education, she "had been there before." One student said, "I don't think she's a disseminator of information, more as a stimulator of thought." The varied roles of the teacher were summed up by another student as follows:

I see her playing two roles, you know, the first role is that of guidance, you know she's trying to guide us to key issues that we have to look at, and so on, in other words a role of a facilitator in a learning process which is essentially the responsibility of the individual, and then secondly there is also an element of the teaching role in the sense that there are certain things that she feels are so important that these have to be put across, so there is the question of supplementing what is in the b—, enriching really what is in the book, and again, you know, a lot comes through from her own personal experience and so on, so I see these roles. (Zimbabwean student)

For international students the egalitarian concepts of "facilitator" and "guide" may well be alarming. Often holding a more traditional view, students from a number of societies (e.g., Japan – see Nakane 1970: 59) may well expect a teacher to be first of all one who teaches, a stern, authoritative, and demanding person. Such a view, when carried over into discourse terms, leads to the belief that every word uttered by the teacher is significant. The "facilitator/guide" approach, on the contrary, works by suggestion and consensus, the value of words and ideas being contingent upon their acceptance by the class.

The second example of principles and values focuses on the students themselves, and may be exemplified through the varied viewpoints that they held regarding learning (see Figure 9).

1 Learning is getting the knowledge about a given area. This makes one capable of understanding a situation and/or taking decisions. It makes one able to apply the knowledge in some way to real life. (Saudi student)
2 Learning is a change of focus in the conceptualization process of the learner. It's a very complex process involving, you know, recognition, familiarity, recall, putting things together, you know, but I think if I had to define learning I'd say learning's a transfer to new situations, you can manipulate it, adapt it to another aspect of life. (Caribbean student)

Figure 9   Question: "How would you define learning?"

The implications of diverse views of learning, such as those seen in Figure 9, have particular impact on two areas: motivation and strategies. Hodgson (1984) has looked at the way L1 students experience lectures, finding three different kinds of motivation: "extrinsic," "intrinsic," and "vicarious." A comparison with ESL data shows a student (Figure 9 No. 1) who appears to view learning in terms of what it can do for him, and how it may be used ("apply the knowledge to real life"), a largely extrinsic viewpoint. The other (No. 2) offers a version closer in spirit to Hodgson's idea of the intrinsically-motivated student, one for whom the desire to know outweighs considerations of personal advantage or applicability. Although no ESL student approached Hodgson's vicarious type (motivated towards a subject based on the "lecturer's perceived interest or enthusiasm for the material" 1984: 99), the idea remains that motivation varies among ESL students just as much as among their native-speaking classmates.

When talking to students in the course of data collection, the ethnographer also becomes aware that motivation and strategies are intimately linked, and that there is a causal link between the two. To know that a student is deeply interested in a subject helps to explain occurrences of question-asking, extensive reading in the area, careful note-taking during lectures, and so forth. Such strategies have been described by O'Malley et al. (1989) as conscious learning decisions that students make, or "social/affective" (p. 423) strategies. The observation of such strategies in action is fundamental to a thorough understanding of the student, though at times observed behaviors may be inconsistent with proclaimed attitudes. Considerable "triangulation" may be needed to cross-check the truth of incoming data. For example, in this research a student who indicated in interview that he did not usually learn much from listening did in fact make use of various social/affective strategies, and clearly did learn from them (Benson 1989).

(g) A lecture makes linguistic and cognitive demands on the listener

Ethnography, with its focus on socialization rather than cognitive psychology (Watson-Gegeo 1988), is inclined to see the ESL student as becoming socialized or acculturated (Schumann 1986) into the learning culture of an English-speaking university. In this view, the student discovers through interaction the structures, values, norms, and procedures of that culture, which may or may not have parallels in his or her own educational system.

However, this bypasses the question of "learning from listening," which is surely central to any discussion about lectures. Not merely are there purely linguistic aspects to be considered (such as the speaker's vocabulary, syntax, voice and intonation, indeed anything that can be subsumed under the general term "discourse"), but there is also the cognitive aspect as well. Freedle (1972: 205) separates the learning of "simple facts" from the learning of "complex systems of ideas," and then states that the latter "cannot be handled by such limited conceptions as short- and long-term memory . . . " He then goes on to argue for an apparatus that will "select those parts of the old knowledge system which need alteration (substitution, addition, or subtraction of semantic relations) in the light of . . . semantic and pragmatic decisions." The cognitive side of listening to lectures, therefore, becomes one in which alterations are made to existing constructs, rather than one in which totally new ideas must be comprehended in toto. In this view, strategies (linguistic, cognitive, social) can be used to cope with the learning culture. Strategies thus represent the upper, often observable and sometimes teachable layer of a learning culture which also contains a lower, hidden layer of unspoken values, assumptions and beliefs.

For the ESL student, prior exposure both to the skills and strategies aspect, the observable and teachable side, and to the learning culture, the hidden dimension, are vital. Regarding listening, the skills and strategies that come from intensive training are a necessary but not sufficient part of that exposure. Consequently, a possible way that language teachers can help is by providing adequate opportunities for content learning through English. This gives exposure to the learning culture by providing an introduction to the way knowledge is made available, how it is to be selected, recorded, and integrated with existing knowledge.

(h) A lecture is patterned into certain classes of communication acts which are recognized by the participants and are capable of being described

A major part of the descriptive and analytical work that the ethnographer does is on the language itself, in particular the act sequences, instrumentalities, and keys employed by the teacher. While these are all closely connected with the other components of speech (Hymes 1972), they represent specifically linguistic forms which are of particular interest to listening researchers. Work here has taken the form of a focus by discourse analysts on asides (Strodt-Lopez 1991), on discourse markers (Chaudron and Richards 1986), on main and subsidiary discourse (Coulthard and Montgomery 1981), and on phrasal analysis (Young 1990). Other studies have dealt with the registers of particular lecture types (e.g., engineering lecture discourse: Murphy and Candlin 1979; see also various contributions to this volume). Such analyses of the classes of communication acts are an excellent beginning to an ethnographic study of a lecture class.

By way of example, let us look at how the idea of Structuralist and Functionalist approaches to education was presented (see Figure 10).

The extract (Figure 10) is structured as follows: the two approaches (ll. 1–2); the Structuralist viewpoint (ll. 3–11); the Functionalist viewpoint (ll. 12–17); the Structuralist viewpoint clarified (ll. 18–23); conclusion (ll. 24–26). An apparently even-handed treatment of each side is seen, reflecting both the lecturer's pedagogic concern to present

1 And in this way // these two approaches // are –
2 divide a lot of people a lot of writers on education /
3 Some people are structuralists /
4 usually this is a Marxist approach /
5 that is from a Marxist point of view /
6 what's wrong with education in society is not that the
7 things don't work right /
8 it's just that the basic structure is all wrong /
9 you have too man– few people controlling too many resources
10 and that the people aren't really able to /
11 do what they want to do //
12 If you / are a functionalist /
13 then you look at society and say /
14 look / nothing is perfect / but we can make it better //
15 and here are some simple steps that we can carry out /
16 to make it better / and /
17 still play within the rules of the game /
18 Over here //
19 no one wants to play within the rules of the game /
20 they say the rules have shown you that you can't win and
21 that er – // according to the way schools are set up some
22 people will always fail / and if you look at who fails /
23 you can see how the rules are written //
24 So these are two different approaches / to government /
25 two different approaches / to education //
26 and it is implicit in this work on the state and education.

Figure 10   The presentation of Structuralist and Functionalist

the two sides equally, and the more cultural value of disinterested academic inquiry. One specific linguistic feature by which this impartial approach is achieved is the use of the "timeless" Present Simple, which is both dramatic and enhances the truth-value of each side.

However, closer analysis of the extract in Figure 10 leads to the conclusion that the speaker was not altogether impartial. To start with, there are two specific examples of Structuralist thought ("few people controlling too many resources" and "some people will always fail"), but none to convey Functionalist thought. Further, the Functionalist segment (ll. 12–17) is presented in a key ("tone, manner, spirit" Hymes 1972: 62) which in a variety of ways casts doubt upon the speaker's belief in what she is saying. For example, the use of "look / nothing is perfect" (l. 14) brings the discussion down to bar-room level, and the sequence "we can make it better // and here are some simple steps' (ll. 14–15) invokes the language of childhood and the solving of trivial problems. Lastly, the image of education as a "game" (l. 17) confirms the idea of Functionalist thought as essentially non-serious.

Even such a sketchy analysis of a segment of lecture monologue reinforces the idea that a lecture (or series of lectures) is a culturally organized form of discourse aimed at the production of culturally constituted meaning. In Figure 10 that meaning is, in fact, essentially structuralist itself, but is only retrievable through listeners being aware of the cultural implications of certain words and phrases. Put differently, all students need cultural knowledge and access to the necessary interpretive strategies. In the case of ESL students, not only the language forms (vocabulary, syntax, etc.) but also the underlying cultural grammar and interpretive strategies may be initially unknown.

(i) A lecture allows for a specific range of events to occur

Lastly, a lecture, or course of lectures, is made up of a range of specific events which themselves are part of the culture of learning. In this class such macro events as lecturing itself and concomitant listening, note-taking, extensive/intensive reading, writing, and interaction (both inside and outside the classroom) were seen, but not group or project work, or role-playing. Nevertheless, each event is part of the repertoire of modern Western education, and each is capable of producing learning, either alone or in conjunction with one or more of the others. Each is capable of micro analysis, but it is the contention of this chapter that any one should not be treated in isolation from the others. Learning is assumed to be polysemic.

The relationship between such learning channels and their learning outcomes for both L1 and ESL students is a large area that has not yet been explored. Such exploration is of prime interest to university teachers, for example, in helping them decide when to make use of one channel and not another, when to lecture and when to engage in interaction, when to use visuals and when to use handouts, and so forth. The findings would also be of interest to ESL practitioners, who need to give their students practice not only in listening, but also in related and complementary learning methods. While ethnographic research is not the only means of investigating such questions, it nevertheless remains a very viable one.

Conclusion: Ethnography and ESL

The ethnographic viewpoint certainly casts the ethnographer in the role of explorer and very possibly in the role of revolutionary as well. Explorer, because the process of doing ethnography may necessitate the description of previously undocumented areas of experience; moreover, it may involve the ethnographer in a variety of disciplines which purists would argue are unconnected. For example, in this research attention has been drawn to the differing administrative and conceptual structures under which teacher and students labor; to the persistent connection between motivation and employed strategies; to the pattern of values and goals implicit in the class structure and explicit in speech acts; and to the way in which the cultural norms of the wider framework dominate the class. Further, we have noted the dynamic relationship between learning channels, particularly listening, and how they combine (in ways unexplored here) to produce learning. Specifically regarding learning conceptions, ESL students were seen to have preferences as sharp as those of L1 students. Similarly, interactional norms such as turn-taking were seen to be perfectly accessible to ESL students.

And possibly revolutionary, because ethnographic findings may not lend support to conventional wisdom. For example, what students learn from lectures, at least in the social sciences, may best be described using constructs such as the lecture as performance, student viewpoints on the teaching role, approaches to learning, and required levels of detail regarding the material. Listening to lectures constitutes a central and symbolic act in the culture of learning – students at the feet of the master – but detailed information is almost certainly not what is being absorbed, if it ever was. Consequently, preparation for listening to lectures is perhaps best encouraged by offering students the experience of lectures in miniature; hence the idea that preparatory ESL language training should include "English through content."

What ethnographic research can contribute to our understanding of the culture of learning may be summed up as follows:

1. *Accurate grounded description of what is occurring in lecture classes.* This would provide other researchers, text book writers, and teachers of specific skills such as listening with data which is a permanent and factual record of events that took place. Regarding ESL listening, transcriptions showing how lecturers present content across different subject areas would be a beginning, as would detailed accounts of communication acts; also useful would be descriptions of how a single lecturer presents differing types of content, and the teaching strategies used. The creation of a corpus of such data is a worthy research goal.

2. *Analysis of the described events.* The patterns existing in relevant areas (motivation, classroom interaction, roles either adopted or conferred, organizational structure, etc.) would thus be brought out and ranked for importance. For ESL listening, the cultural patterns that help to determine learning preferences are a point of departure. So too are the patterns that associate learning preferences with specific strategies, and that relate learning preferences to content.

As Geertz (1973) says, such ethnographic description would not be "predictive" (p. 26); rather, it would produce retrospective analysis in the hope of drawing "large conclusions from small, but very densely textured facts" (p. 28). Such an achievement may represent as Geertz elsewhere suggests, an unattainable ideal; nevertheless, the densely-textured facts about ESL lecture listening *do* fit into the overall culture of learning in higher education; they *are* part of a pattern. Ethnographic research, by examining the minute but interlocking elements of the listening experience, opens up the possibility that the grander pattern may soon become apparent.

References

Bauman, R., and J. Sherzer. 1974, 1989. *Explorations in the Ethnography of Speaking.* Cambridge: Cambridge University Press.

Benson, M. J. 1989. The academic listening task: a case study. *TESOL Quarterly* 23 (3): 421–445.

1991. University ESL reading: a content analysis. *English for Specific Purposes* 10: 75–88.

Chaudron, C., and J. C. Richards. 1986. The effect of discourse markers on the comprehension of lectures. *Applied Linguistics* 7: 113–127.

Coulthard, M., and M. Montgomery. 1981. The structure of monologue. In *Studies in Discourse Analysis*, R. M. Coulthard and M. Montgomery (Eds.), 31–39. London: Routledge and Kegan Paul.

Fägerlind, I., and L. J. Saha. 1983. *Education and National Development: A Comparative Perspective.* Oxford: Pergamon Press.

Freedle, R. O. 1972. Language users as fallible information-processors: implications for measuring and modeling comprehension. In *Language Comprehension and the Acquisition of Knowledge*, J. B. Carroll and R. O. Freedle (Eds.), 169–209. New York: John Wiley and Sons.

Gagné, R. M., and M. P. Driscoll. 1988. *Essentials of Learning for Instruction.* Englewood Cliffs, N.J.: Prentice Hall.

Geertz, C. 1973. *The Interpretation of Cultures.* New York, N.Y.: Basic Books.

Goffman, E. 1981. *Forms of Talk.* Philadelphia, P.A.: University of Philadelphia Press.

Gumperz, J. J. 1982. *Discourse Strategies.* Cambridge: Cambridge University Press.

Hodgson, V. 1984. Learning from lectures. In *The Experience of Learning*, F. Marton, D. Hounsell, and N. Entwistle (Eds.), 103–123. Edinburgh: Scottish Academic Press.

Hymes, D. 1962. The ethnography of speaking. In *Anthropology and Human Behavior*, T. Gladwin, and W. C. Sturtevant (Eds.), 13–53. Washington, D.C.: Anthropological Society of Washington.

1972. Models of the interaction of language and social life. In *Directions in Sociolinguistics: The Ethnography of Communication*, J. J. Gumperz and D. Hymes (Eds.), 35–71. New York: Holt, Rinehart and Winston.

Joos, M. 1962. *The Five Clocks.* (Publication No. 22). Bloomington, Indiana: Indiana University Research Center in Anthropology, Folklore and Linguistics.

Murphy, D., and C. N. Candlin. 1979. Engineering lecture discourse and listening comprehension. *Practical Papers in English Language Education* 2: 1–79. Lancaster: University of Lancaster.

Nakane, C. 1970. *Japanese Society*, Berkeley: University of California Press.

O'Malley, J. M., A. U. Chamot, and L. Kupper. 1989. Listening comprehension strategies in second language acquisition. *Applied Linguistics* 10 (4): 418–437.

Schumann, J. H. 1986. Research on the acculturation model for second language acquisition. *Journal of Multilingual and Multicultural Development* 7: 379–392.

Strodt-Lopez, B. 1991. Tying it all in: asides in university lectures. *Applied Linguistics* 12 (2): 117–140.

Waggoner, M. 1984. The new technologies versus the lecture tradition in higher education: is change possible? *Educational Technology* 24 (3): 7–12.

Watson-Gegeo, K. A. 1988. Ethnography in ESL: defining the essentials. *TESOL Quarterly* 22: 575–592.

Young, L. 1990. *Language as Behavior, Language as Code: a Study of Academic English*. Amsterdam: John Benjamins.

10 By dint of: Student and lecturer perceptions of lecture comprehension strategies in first-term graduate study

Abelle Mason

Abstract

Lecture comprehension strategies of 26 foreign graduate students (FGSs) studying in English or in an English-speaking environment for the first time are examined through their own perceptions and those of graduate school lecturers. A description of current lecture styles and discussion of related comprehension issues follow. Findings include the common and distinctive approaches to comprehension of the group. Common findings include: 1. the importance of oral participation in lectures is growing; 2. 600+ on the TOEFL does not assure comprehension of a lecture that deviates from a straight "talk-and-chalk" style delivered in standard academic speech; 3. students with 600+ on the TOEFL, however, do have the requisite tools and knowledge of the language to acquire necessary proficiency; 4. in order to clarify understanding, the majority of students relied on background knowledge of their subject and were willing to spend long hours on reading assignments; 5. the majority of students did not engage in questioning in class to clarify understanding.

Introduction

First-term graduate students using English as a medium of instruction and/or studying in an English-speaking environment for the first time enter a critical period in their academic life. The successful ones single-mindedly pursue an understanding of the subject matter. They do not pretend to know more than they do. In fact, they work knowing that their comprehension is limited. Like the good adult language learner posited by Naiman et al. (1978: 17), foreign graduate students (FGSs) find "ways to overcome obstacles, whether linguistic, affective or environmental." This study seeks to identify both the common and distinctive ways that these students handle their strengths and compensate for their weaknesses in English to acquire the necessary knowledge in their fields. The focal point is their course lectures.

For this purpose, 26 first-term FGSs in eight graduate programs at Georgetown University agreed to be interviewed twice during the Fall '91 Semester. The graduate programs included business administration (MBA), chemistry (CHEM), demography (DMOG), economics (ECON), foreign service (SFS), government (GOV), linguistics (LING) and public policy (PBPL). To gain perspective about the various fields and the FGSs in them, 18 lecturers from the represented programs were also interviewed. For each field of concentration, at least two FGSs and two lecturers were interviewed. In the case of the MBA program, eight FGSs and four lecturers were interviewed.[1]

The personal interview as a research tool

In the study of strategies of second language learning, the well-constructed personal interview as a research tool affording "verbal report data" (Cohen 1987: 35) has gained credence in recent years (see Chamot, Cohen, Rubin, and Wendin in Wendin 1987). As Chamot says (1987: 87), "What emerges is the fact that the best way to get at what strategies lecturers actually use . . . is to ask them." While earlier studies focus on strategies used in learning a second language, this study looks at those strategies used in handling academic disciplines in a second language. Personal interviews here were particularly suitable because the focus was the perceptions of respondents.

The student subjects

Having met the entrance requirements for their various degree programs, the FGSs in this study came from a pool of entering graduate students deemed well-qualified in their fields and in their English language proficiency. From Table 1 we see the composition of the 26 foreign graduate students.Of the 26 FGSs, 21, or about 80%, were men; 20 were Asian; and 21 were between the ages of 24 and 34 years. Of their native languages, 9 were speakers of Chinese; 8, Japanese; 4, Spanish; and of the others, 1 speaker each of Arabic, Indonesian, Korean, Russian and Thai. Japan was represented by 8 FGSs; next was the PRC with 5; then the ROC with 4, Mexico with 3, and 1 each from the other nations. Nine were Ph.D. candidates and 22 scored 600 or above on the TOEFL.

From Table 2, we see the composition of the 18 lecturers. Of the 18 lecturers, 4 were women, 5 were born outside the United States and for

---

[1] The MBA program is the largest of those included in the study; hence, it provided the greatest number of FGS participants.

3, English was a second language. The majority, 15, were professors or associate professors. Of these, 5, or 33%, held or had held the top administrative post in their programs.

TABLE 1. COMPOSITION OF THE 26 FOREIGN GRADUATE STUDENTS

Programs	Sex M	F	Ph.D. Candidates	TOEFL 600+	Languages		Countries		Age range
8	21	5	9	22	8		10		21–40
MBA					*Language*	#	*Country*	#	21 FGSs
CHEM					Arabic	1	Chile	1	were
DMOG					Chinese	9	CIS	1	between
ECON					Indonesian	1	Indonesia	1	23 and 45
SFS					Japanese	8	Japan	8	years of
GOV					Korean	1	Jordan	1	age
LING					Russian	1	Korea	1	
PBPL					Spanish	4	Mexico	3	
					Thai	1	PRC	5	
							ROC	4	
							Thailand	1	

TABLE 2. COMPOSITION OF THE 18 LECTURERS

Programs Same as Table 1	Sex M	F	Born outside the U.S.	English Second Language	Dean or Chair or Former	Prof. or Assoc. Prof.	Asst. Prof.	New to GU Fall '91
8	14	4	5	3	5	15	3	2

The foreign graduate student interviews

The interviews of the FGSs were designed to find out their perceived degree of lecture comprehension; what they attributed that to; how they were feeling about it; and what they were doing about it. The first interview took place early in the semester, and the second, a short time before or after final exams. The interviews followed a "flexible questioning format" to allow the interviewer to modify the phrasing of questions and permit "the respondents to provide information along lines that they [could] themselves determine.' (Cohen 1987). The interviews were taped and transcribed.

The first student interview

As a warm-up, the FGSs were asked about their background and academic and English language training. The interviewer also restated the purpose of the study and reaffirmed the commitment to confidentiality.

Then, the interview would turn to the courses that the FGS was taking. The FGS was asked how each course was organized; how many students were in the class; whether and when the lecturer asked or took questions; whether there was a discussion period; and whether any small-group work was required. Further information was sought about the syllabus, the hand-outs, the reading and other types of assignments.

The next questions dealt with lecture comprehension. How well did the FGS feel she or he understood the lectures? How did the FGS account for this perceived level of comprehension? Did the FGS understand the questions or comments of the other students in class or in academic group discussions outside of class? Could the FGS give any examples? What did the FGS do, if necessary, to improve her or his comprehension or participation?

Toward the end of the interview, the conversation broadened to other issues of language, communication or culture in terms of how the university system in the United States compared to that in the FGS's own country.

The second student interview

The second interview led with the tone of "How's it been going since we talked last?" The review of courses would start with "Which was your most difficult course?" and then a discussion of the reasons. Next, "Which did you rate as the best course?" and "Why?" After that, a new line of questioning began with: "Was there a point in the semester when you began to feel more comfortable studying in English? Have you become used to the set-up of your program – that is, the way that faculty and students and students among themselves relate?"

The interview became flexible at this point but always seemed to go to the language-culture area, or to a reevaluation of performance over the semester. The last planned question was, "How do you rate your relative English language proficiency in listening comprehension, speaking, reading and writing?"

The faculty interviews

The purpose of the faculty interviews was to provide a context in which to consider the student perceptions. They were scheduled in midsemester between the two series of student interviews, and discussion lasted 30–45 minutes. The lecturers described the organization of their programs and the make-up of their graduate student population.

More particularly, the lecturers were asked how they organized their courses and what they expected of students in terms of outside work and class participation. While they were asked to give their impressions of FGSs generally, individual identities were kept confidential. They were also asked what they did, if anything, to integrate FGSs into the culture of the lecture class group. The final questions concerned the qualities, as they saw it, that make for an outstanding student and future professional in their field; that is, what they look for in graduate students and their impression of FGSs in that regard.

Nature of the lecture

The lecture will be considered as the setting where the subject matter of a course is explained, discussed or otherwise taken up in a meeting between lecturers and students. The largest graduate lecture class reported in the study had about 40 and the smallest, 5 students.

In descriptions by the lecturers and the FGSs of actual classroom practice – as opposed to catalog nomenclature – three main styles of lectures emerged: first, what Bereday has described as the "talk-and-chalk" lecture where the lecturer expounds the material using the blackboard as the prime visual aid; second, the "give-and-take" lecture (Bereday in Mason 1983a: 175) where the lecturer presents material in order to encourage discussion, questions and comments between students and lecturer; and third, a more recent format which I will call the "report-and-discuss" style.[2]

In the report-and-discuss mode, the lecturer initiates topics for small groups to study and present for discussion in the class. The lecturer frames the issues and intervenes when appropriate to ensure that all the important issues are raised and all important contributions are noted. In short, the oral participation of students becomes an integral part of the lecture. In some cases, the report-and-discuss style is a seminar, but the style is also used in management courses of 40 students and law courses of 120. Hence, class size seems not to dictate the style or combination of styles that a lecturer might employ. However, it is the nature of a lecture that the lecturer is always directing the agenda.

---

[2] The direction of lectures styles accords with a comment of Bereday, made where he compares the Continental and US lecture styles:

> In American society there is, as we know, a much stronger tradition of participation and interaction. In fact, an absence of give-and-take in a lecture room would ... be considered an adverse qualification of a professor. (George Z. F. Bereday in Mason 1983a p. 29)

Lecture comprehension problems

The body of research into second language (L2) lecture comprehension dealing with the level of effectiveness of notetaking, rhetoric, recall, memory reinforcement and so on – as exemplified by many of us writing in this volume – has focused on receiving and processing information from traditional academic lectures in the talk-and-chalk style. Indeed, mastery of such a process is essential for academic listening as tested in the TOEFL.

Another level of problems, however, involves processing the lecturer's manner of speaking – speed, pronunciation and style of discourse; understanding the lecturer's references, which may be culturally specific; and catching the "in-talk" comments of fellow students who are native speakers. Another level of problems involves accommodating to the educational system: learning how faculty and students interact; knowing when student apprenticeship should give way to independent expression; and understanding how reporting and discussion reflect these educational values. A last level of problems involves lecture formats: the traditional talk-and-chalk style of lectures is giving way to the more give-and-take or report-and-discuss styles described above. Therefore, in discussing the lecture comprehension problems and strategies of FGSs, accommodation to these varied factors is key.

Ease of comprehension

According to the FGSs, the talk-and-chalk lecture was generally the easiest to comprehend when these conditions held:

1. *The lecturer spoke in clear standard academic English at a normal pace.*
   A strong regional or foreign accent increased the difficulty (unless the native language of the speaker was the same as that of the listener. A Mexican FGS reported no trouble understanding a lecturer from Argentina.)[3]
2. *The course of lectures was clearly organized.*
   Well-organized lectures and good syllabi detailed in hand-outs or on the blackboard increased comprehensibility.
3. *The students had some background in the subject matter.*
   Previous study of a subject often served as "a second language," that is, a means of communication of itself.

The FGSs felt that the talk-and-chalk lecture style was "normal," something that they were used to from their own educational systems. This type of lecture was present in all the eight programs.

---

[3] Two FGSs said they understood certain non-native speakers of English who spoke slowly and with few idioms better than many native speakers.

The difficulty of lecture comprehension increased when the lecture style required the oral participation of FGSs and their aural comprehension of other students' speech. Thus, the give-and-take style of lecture where lecturers asked and took questions was more difficult to comprehend. For some FGSs, a lecture with a short question period at the end seemed easier to understand than one where questions were taken at random.

Variations of the report-and-discuss style of lecture were described by lecturers in the SFS, MBA, PBPL and LING programs. The 14 FGSs enrolled in such courses deemed them the most difficult since the greatest amount of aural/oral participation was required. Again, when 25–30% of the grade depended on class participation, as was the case for nine FGSs, poor aural/oral skills would weigh still more heavily.

The nature of course assignments bore heavily on lecture comprehension. The volume of reading assigned seemed overwhelming to 14 FGSs. Again, some FGSs had never been expected in their countries to read a number of experts in a field and then deal with the diversity of views. Half of the above FGSs spoke of this point. For 11 others, there were new techniques of study requiring long periods of small group work such as with the case method.

Finally, lecture comprehension depended on how the lecturer approached and conceptualized his or her material. Five FGSs reported that they had previously studied a certain subject in a theoretical way and now were being asked to study it in a very practical way. A lecturer in management confirmed this perception: when FGSs request a more theoretical framework, he indicates his readiness to discuss theory, but reminds them that the course is "really practically based." With five others, it was just the reverse. A FGS in CHEM had studied biochemistry in his country as it applied to medical practice. Here, the approach was through that of molecular structure.

Aural comprehension of lectures: issues and strategies

This section starts with eight individual accounts sequenced to show the range of aural comprehension problems and the steps taken to deal with them. The overall FGS data regarding aural comprehension are then examined with Tables 3a and 3b.

ZZ (individual FGSs are designated by a doubled letter of the alphabet) is a Chinese student in CHEM. In the first interview, he reported great difficulty in lecture comprehension. In one class, the lecturer had a strong foreign accent; in another, he could not understand the new terms; but there was another class which gave him the greatest difficulty. Although the lecturer spoke clearly, ZZ could "not catch the deep meaning." The reasons became clear in our second interview. ZZ reported that he did well in all his courses but that the most troubling class mentioned above remained "very tough." ZZ said that he found two-thirds of the material unfamiliar mainly because the approach was entirely new to him. ZZ learned this subject by taking up to ten hours reading each assignment. It was almost as if for ZZ what the lecturer provided was the sequencing of material, the study plan and a verification center. That is, on a particular day when he "understood" the lecturer, ZZ knew he had "caught" the deep meaning of the assignment.

Whereas some background knowledge, some aural comprehension and a lot of study did the trick for ZZ, EE from the ROC in the SFS program could not overcome his weak background in one subject so easily. He understood the lecturer's English, but that was not the issue. "If the lecturer says, 'Okay, the income increases, the interest rate declines', I know what he is saying, but I don't understand the theories and this is the problem." EE and two other FGSs mentioned that they got outside help from individuals speaking their native language.

Conversely, a strong background in the subject matter could make up for certain deficiencies in aural comprehension. 12 FGSs attested to that. For example, QQ from Japan had a good background in statistics, the subject he was taking. He reported that the lecturer liked to tell jokes, use slang and make references to things QQ knew nothing about: "So sometimes it's hard to understand." However, he was not worried because he is good at the subject.

When the jokes, slang or cultural references a lecturer uses are intended mainly to liven the lecture, that is one thing. However, when these references serve to illustrate the larger points that the lecturer is trying to make, then their comprehension is very important. For example, OO, an MBA student from Japan, reported that one of his lecturers used topical material such as clips from American movies to explain certain types of business behavior. While the native speakers in the class laughed hilariously and at the same time could underscore points in their notes, OO was at a loss. However, OO and an American MBA student struck up a friendship. Sometimes after this lecture hour, OO's friend "would explain all the stories and also say how these things relate to the theme and issues."[4]

DD from Taiwan also had problems with the cultural references even though he knew the culture better than OO did. In the GOV program, DD said that he understood about 90% of his lectures. Nonetheless, current references – particularly in a course involving the media in America – often eluded him. "After the second class, I spoke to the

---

[4] The 12 FGSs who got to know Americans over the semester seemed to profit in terms of language learning. However, there were many mixed reactions regarding interactions between FGSs and American peers. Analysis of this issue goes beyond the scope here.

lecturer for one minute because I know he is very busy. I said, 'You know, I'm very glad that I found out that [the person you were talking about] Bernard Shaw is a news reporter on CNN and not the playwright.' We both laughed and the lecturer said, 'Okay, we must make allowance for that.'"

Besides the strategy of speaking with the lecturer, DD spent time listening to TV and reading newspapers. By the second interview, DD still had trouble with cultural references. Nonetheless, he said he had come to know the various academic approaches that the lecturer followed – historical, legal and so on. This was perhaps more important than DD realized. As one government lecturer described it, understanding the theoretical and comparative approaches to the subject was basic to the study of his discipline.

Cultural comprehension of the educational system

Lecture comprehension involves the culture of the educational system as well. A LING student from Japan, JJ, explained that along with understanding lectures, getting used to the style of lecturing was very difficult for her: "When I got here, I found that American university scholars are very 'performative.' That is, you see them walking down the classroom, sitting on the desk, using their hands and making facial expressions when they talk. Also they ask students to respond and give their opinions. So students interrupt and the teacher talks and students interrupt over and over. Such a combination really makes it difficult for me to understand."

Fortunately, JJ was also a Teaching Assistant (TA) drill instructor in Japanese. She got to know about American students and their usual classroom behavior by teaching them. She felt that American students "are so honest in their reactions. I know that Japanese students just listen even if the lecture is really boring. But [when] American students . . . are bored, they show it. They ask me lots of questions and try to argue with me if they find that a language form is irrational." In the second interview, she said about her American students: "Sometimes when I am trying to explain Japanese grammar in English, they will help me and say, 'is that the word you are looking for?'" Regarding the lectures she attends, JJ remarked: "I've come to realize it is a very enjoyable thing just to participate in the discussion and share knowledge and ideas."

As a Chilean student in the PBPL program, CC also noted a difference in educational practices. The educational system she was used to was "not so based on bibliography as it is here." She found the wealth of research and publication that FGSs in her field were expected to process almost overwhelming. "I know I could be very 'down' because of all that's happening to me. But I know it's not a problem of my abilities. It's just that I don't have the resources, the 'instrumentale' in my head. So I guess it's a matter of time."

Cultural comprehension of the subject matter

AA, a Russian MBA student, had a problem associated with the culture of the subject matter. While a course in statistics was not hard because he had a good math background, the one in managerial accounting struck him as an "artificial subject", having little to do with the world he had known. The course in marketing management, however, was intriguing but difficult. In style, the course was "really talking and discussion which of themselves was not so difficult. But it was very deeply associated with psychology – going into people's psychology and applying that to business was something I had never done before and that was quite difficult." It was especially difficult "because we had a very good instructor and he really motivated us: he put the task as high as possible and you know we just tried to reach [that level]." So the difficulty for AA was understanding the culture of the business corporation.

Fourteen FGSs mentioned courses that would *not* be a subject of study in their own culture. For example, organizational behavior is rarely viewed as a subject for study in cultures where such behavior is a matter of traditional relationships. This issue was also mentioned by faculty members in both the PBPL and MBA programs. The five FGSs in GOV and ECON also mentioned subject matter that either in terms of political content or theoretical approach represented something culturally novel to them.

Overall FGS responses regarding aural comprehension

In the foregoing examples and discussion of FGS aural comprehension, the relevance of academic and cultural background in the subject matter was explored. Table 3A, "Comprehension issues reported for talk-and-chalk and give-and-take lectures", matches the overall responses to two lecture styles. Discussion of the comprehension strategies will follow.

The 25 FGSs are placed into four groups, roughly corresponding to their reported degree of listening–speaking proficiency and the interviewer's impressions. Eight issues were identified for the talk-and-chalk lectures and two more for give-and-take lectures. For the talk-and-chalk lectures, 17 FGSs reported problems with issue 1: "Aural comprehension – academic language" and issue 2: "Questions of students – native speakers." Fourteen FGSs reported difficulty with issue 3: "Cultural references – the lecturer," issue 4: "Cultural background – one subject" and

TABLE 3A. COMPREHENSION ISSUES REPORTED FOR TALK-AND-CHALK AND GIVE-AND-TAKE LECTURES

Proficiency Listening–Speaking				Issues: Talk-and-chalk								Give-and-take	
Group	Student	Country	Program	[1]	[2]	[3]	[4]	[5]	[6]	[7]	[8]	[9]	[10]
I	AA	CIS	MBA				X			−			
	BB	MEX	GOV			X	X	X		−			
	CC	CHIL	PBPL				X	X	X	−			
	DD	ROC	GOV		X	X	X					X	
	EE	JORD	CHEM			X					+		
	FF	ROC	SFS		X	X				−			
II	GG	ROC	SFS	X	X			X	X	−		X	
	HH	ROC	PBPL	X				X	X	−	+		
	II	MEX	MBA									X	
	JJ	JAP	LING	X		X		X		−		X	
	KK	JAP	SFS	X	X			X	X		+	X	
	LL	JAP	MBA	X	X	X	X					X	
	MM	MEX	GOV		X			X	X			X	
III	NN	PRC	CHEM	X			X	X		−		X	
	OO	JAP	MBA	X	X	X	X				+	X	
	PP	JAP	MBA	X	X	X	X	X	X	−	+		
	QQ	JAP	MBA	X	X	X	X			−	+	X	X
	RR	JAP	MBA	X	X	X		X	X			X	
	SS	JAP	MBA	X			X				+	X	X
	TT	PRC	ECON	X	X	X	X	X	X	−	+	X	X
IV	UU	THAI	LING	X	X	X					+	X	X
	VV	INDON	DMOG		X			X			+	X	X
	WW	PRC	ECON	X	X	X	X	X		−	+	X	X
	XX	PRC	DMDG	X	X							X	X
	YY	KOR	PBPL	X	X	X	X	X			+	X	X
	ZZ	PRC	CHEM	X	X		X			−		X	X
										(5−/+)			
Totals:				17	17	14	14	14	8	13−	12+	19	9

Note: X = Reported Difficulty   − = Background Lack   + = Prior Background
For talk-and chalk lectures
    [1] = Aural comprehension – academic language
    [2] = Questions of students – native speakers
    [3] = Cultural references – of lecturer
    [4] = Cultural background – one subject
    [5] = Reading – volume of
    [6] = Reading – diversity of views
    [7] = Background lack – one subject
    [8] = Academic background – one subject
For give-and-take add:
    [9] = Asking and discussion substantive questions
    [10] = Asking mechanical questions

issue 5: "Reading – volume of," and of these, eight found problems with issue 6: "Reading – diversity of views." As for issue 7: "Background lack – one subject", 13 mentioned such an academic background lack while 12 reported having 8: "Academic background – one subject." Five of the FGSs noted having a prior background in one subject and a lack in another.

Regarding the give-and-take lectures, 19 FGSs had difficulty with issue 9: "Asking and discussing substantive questions", while nine also had trouble with issue 10: "Asking mechanical questions."

Overall FGS responses regarding strategies

A look at Table 3B below, "Strategies reported for talk-and-chalk and give-and-take lectures", shows that FGSs relied on ten strategies to deal with the comprehension issues reported.

Sixteen FGSs followed strategy 1: "Rely on previous background in subject matter"; 15 FGSs noted strategy 2: "Compensate with concentrated study of reading materials." Thirteen did initially follow strategy 3: "Begin with reduced course load or include EFL or other support course." Eleven followed strategy 4: "Listen to or seek out American peers"; and ten undertook strategy 5: "Follow TV and print media regularly." In general, FGSs followed three or four strategies: twelve reporting three, and nine reporting four.

Participation in report-and-discuss lectures

In Table 4, "Oral/aural contexts and strategies reported for report-and-discuss lectures," five contexts were found.

Eleven FGSs participated in some version of A: "Study group discussion." Of these, five did well while four reported real difficulty. Of the eleven FGSs involved in C: "Group oral reports in class," seven reported difficulty. Eleven also had to give D: "Individual oral report in class; take questions." Eight reported difficulty. Finally, of the thirteen involved in E: "In class, defend or oppose a position, change direction of discussion," nine found this very difficult.

Basically, for contexts C, D and E, three strategies were added to those mentioned in Table 3B: strategy 11: "Memorizing or reading from notes," strategy 12: "Pre-planning of subject matter and phrasing to enable speaking from cards" and strategy 13: "Having another individual explain one's work." Four FGSs did strategy 12; another four did strategy 11 mostly but tried strategy 12 once; two did strategy 11 solely and two sometimes followed strategy 13. The three TAs referred to in B "As a TA in class with familiar subject matter" reported that they were able to communicate well in this setting.

TABLE 3B. COMPREHENSION STRATEGIES REPORTED FOR TALK-AND-CHALK AND GIVE-AND-TAKE LECTURES

Proficiency Listening–Speaking				Strategies: talk-and-chalk give-and-take	Strategies key:
Group	Student	Country	Program		
I	AA	CIS	MBA	[2] [4] [7]	[1] = Rely on previous
	BB	MEX	GOV	[4] [5] [6]	background in subject
	CC	CHIL	PBPL	[4] [6] [8] [10]	matter
	DD	ROC	GOV	[2] [3] [4] [5] [6]	[2] = Compensate with
	EE	JORD	CHEM	[1] [4] [5] [9]	concentrated study of
	FF	ROC	SFS	[1] [2] [3] [5] [8]	reading materials
II	GG	ROC	SFS	[1] [2] [3]	[3] = Begin with reduced
	HH	ROC	PBPL	[3] [5] [6] [8]	course load or include EFL
	II	MEX	MBA	[1] [4] [7]	or other support course
	JJ	JAP	LING	[1] [2] [4] [6] [9]	[4] = Listen to or seek out
	KK	JAP	SFS	[1] [2] [4] [9]	American peers
	LL	JAP	MBA	[1] [7]	[5] = Follow TV and print
	MM	MEX	GOV	[2] [4] [6]	media regularly
III	NN	PRC	CHEM	[1] [2] [8] [9]	[6] = Speak to professor or
	OO	JAP	MBA	[1] [3] [4] [7]	advisor
	PP	JAP	MBA	[3] [4] [7] [9]	[7] = Learn about culture
	QQ	JAP	MBA	[1] [2] [7]	through courses such as
	RR	JAP	MBA	[2] [3] [7]	accounting, career
	SS	JAP	MBA	[4] [6] [7]	management
	TT	PRC	ECON	[2] [4] [5] [6] [8] [9]	[8] = Seek outside help in
IV	UU	THAI	LING	[1] [3]	subject matter in own
	VV	INDON	DMOG	[1] [3] [5] [6]	language
	WW	PRC	ECON	[1] [2] [5] [9]	[9] = Use TA class or
	XX	PRC	DMOG	[1] [2] [3]	course with familiar subject
	YY	KOR	PBPL	[2] [3] [5] [8]	matter to gain confidence
	ZZ	PRC	CHEM	[1] [2] [3]	to speak
					[10] = Drop a course
					during semester

Number of strategies used per FCS

No. of FGSs		No. of strategies
12	used	3
10	used	4
3	used	5
1	used	6
1	used	2

Total numbers of FGSs using each strategy

No. of FGSs	No. of strategies
16	[1]
15	[2]
13	[3]
12	[4]
10	[5]
8	[6]
8	[7]
6	[8]
4	[9]
1	[10]

TABLE 4. ORAL/AURAL CONTEXTS AND STRATEGIES REPORTED FOR
REPORT-AND-DISCUSS LECTURES

Proficiency Listening/Speaking				Contexts: report-and-discuss					Strategies added:	
Group	Student	Country	Program	[A]	[B]	[C]	[D]	[E]		
I	AA	CIS	MBA	+		0	0	0	[12]	[12]
	BB	MEX	GOV					0		
	CC	CHIL	PBPL							
	DD	ROC	GOV							
	EE	JORD	CHEM		+					
	FF	ROC	SFS							
II	GG	ROC	SFS	0		X	X	X	[12]	
	HH	ROC	PBPL							
	II	MEX	MBA	+		0	0	0	[12]	
	JJ	JAP	LING		+					
	KK	JAP	SFS	X		X	X	X	[12]	
	LL	JAP	MBA	X		X	X	X	[11]	[12]
	MM	MEX	GOV			0		0	[12]	
III	NN	PRC	CHEM	0	+	X			[13]	
	OO	JAP	MBA	+			X	X	[11]	[12]
	PP	JAP	MBA	+		0	0	X	[11]	[12]
	QQ	JAP	MBA	X		X	X	X	[11]	[12]
	RR	JAP	MBA	+		X	X	X	[11]	
	SS	JAP	MBA	X		X	X	X	[11]	
	TT	PRC	ECON							
IV	UU	THAI	LING				X	X	[11]	[13]
	VV	INDON	DMOG							
	WW	PRC	ECON							
	XX	PRC	DMOG							
	YY	KOR	PBPL							
	ZZ	PRC	CHEM							
FGS Totals:		16	11	3	11	11	13			
FGS Experience:		5+	4−	3+	7X	8X	9X			

Note: X = Reported difficulty   + = Strength   0 = No special comment
For report and discuss add:
[A]   Study group discussion
[B]   As TA in class with familiar subject matter
[C]   Group oral reports in class
[D]   Individual oral report in class; with response to questions
[E]   In class, defend or oppose a position, change of direction of discussion
Strategies key:
[11]   Memorizing or reading from notes
[12]   Pre-planning of subject matter and phrasing to enable speaking from cards
[13]   Having another individual explain one's work

Moving towards oral participation

This section presents eight examples of FGSs involved in making an oral report, engaging in class discussion, influencing the course of discussion and functioning in a study group.

Making an oral report

While at least six FGSs were orally proficient, for others, presenting one's own work or ideas in class even as part of a group could be a daunting experience. These examples from three programs show increasing levels of participation:

1. Chemistry. NN, a student from the PRC, participated in problem sessions conducted by the lecturer. A week in advance, the lecturer assigned questions to groups of three students. The groups met during the week and then presented their solutions to the class. NN was placed in group with two Americans. In the discussions of the three, NN always participated fully; but during class presentation, NN "always" felt extremely nervous. "So I said to them 'You please explain; not me.'"[5]
2. Business Administration. SS is a Japanese student who found herself in a five-member study group with four American men. She said that the group members were "aggressive and they speak a lot so I cannot get into their conversation. But they know I cannot speak, so sometimes they say, 'What do you think, SS?' They ask me so that is helpful." When the group had to make a presentation, SS said a few words that she had memorized.
3. Linguistics. UU is a Thai student in computational linguistics. In the section meeting consisting of about fourteen people, students display their program work on a monitor, explain it to the class and answer any questions. UU rarely asked questions when other students reported because "I can see the work and I understand what they have done." As for explaining his own work, UU reported in the second interview that "it was very hard to do in the beginning . . . Right now . . . [he had given 5 reports] . . . I'm still nervous, too, but I think it is better . . . If I can't explain it clearly, the TA (a native speaker) will help me to explain it because he has seen my program and he can understand what I have done."

Of the three FGSs, SS was the most disadvantaged because of the importance of oral participation in the MBA program. In one course, where SS had never spoken in class, the lecturer explained in private that class participation would account for 30% of the final grade.

---

[5] Despite performing well as a TA, NN found the presentation of her own work daunting.

First attempts at class discussion in two programs

These examples show first attempts at class discussion.

1. Government. At the first interview, MM, a Mexican student, talked about his initial contribution to a report-and-discuss class of 15 students. At first, he experienced some frustration in this encounter. He spoke only after he had managed to pull together his ideas and the requisite language. As a result, MM felt that he had not presented his argument at "the very precise moment that was required." However, his point was not lost because near the end of the hour, the lecturer spoke and incorporated what MM had said.
2. The Foreign Service Program. KK is a Japanese student who found his bearings in a course of 15 students which included undergraduates. The lectures were in a give-and-take style and therefore "the main part was the discussion." While understanding other students was the key difficulty for him, KK found that the "content of the course was very familiar" because of his previous professional experience. The other students did not have his first-hand experience "so they could learn from my comments."

Influencing the direction of the discourse

Implicit in the self-reports of a number of FGSs was their frustration in not being able to hold their own in class discussion. As FF, a student from the ROC in the SFS program, put it, "It would be very interesting if I could discuss a number of international issues with my American classmates because I want to know what they are thinking . . . This is especially true because I have a certain understanding of these issues and I have work experience in these areas." However, FF felt great pressure when in a serious discussion with Americans: "I have many points to argue, but I cannot express these points in the right way – so it is not so convincing." Furthermore, he continued, the native speaker will always be "conducting the conversation."

Late in the semester, II, a Mexican MBA student, reported "pulling his own weight" in a management communication course. Paired students took turns interviewing each other on previously prepared topics. When it was II's turn to be interviewed, the first two questions to him were irrelevant to the topic. II's task, as he saw it, was to refocus the discussion:

So in one of my answers I had to bring him back . . . [to the topic] . . . I was feeling a kind of shock in the first two questions because they were so general and so easy and I didn't expect that. So in the second question I decided to answer it very . . . [briefly] . . . and then start talking about my [prepared] topic; and then the rest of the interview was O.K. In the end, it was a nice experience.

This experience contrasts with II's description of himself at the beginning of the semester when he had to explain what he meant to a lecturer "three times because he didn't get it."

Functioning in a study group: the MBA program

Several programs form, or encourage students to form, small groups for study.[6] In the MBA program, the study groups are an essential part of the first-semester curriculum. In the groups, students learn to work cooperatively to analyze problems and formulate positions. An important task of the groups is to study cases. A case, as one lecturer defined it, is "an incomplete description of a complicated situation or dilemma. Students must make sense of it and give . . . advice."

LL and OO are two FGSs who have had several years' experience working in their companies in Japan. The most difficult cultural issue for them was working in a group – American style. LL was used to group work in Japan where the goal was to reach a consensus which would bring a strong commitment by group members to the final decision. LL noted that such a process requires a great deal of time and patience, qualities, he felt, that an American-style group seems to lack. In fact, it was some time before he could get attention for his ideas. However, the group finally accepted an idea of his when those of others did not seem to work out.

It happened that LL's proposal "produced very good results" for that particular group project. Thereafter, the group trusted LL and even sought his views. LL felt that he would have to be very careful when he returned to Japan because such persuasion by results would never work in his company.

The first interview with OO took place in the latter part of October. He reviewed his experience over the first few weeks in one group. In the beginning, his American classmates spoke quickly and used language that he did not understand. OO said he followed the Japanese behavior whereby "I listened very carefully to what everyone said, trying to pick out the major ideas and then trying to put them all together." This method, he said, also afforded him the time to improve his listening comprehension and summon up the courage to speak.

After a couple of weeks, he spoke up and gave a short summation of the discussion near the end of the group meeting. He began to do this more. Some students told him afterwards that his opinions were "always clear and well-organized." Later in the semester, OO felt sufficiently comfortable to state his views candidly in the group. OO also commented that American-style "brainstorming" is very difficult for Japanese students.

---

[6] In varying degrees, the MBA, SFS, CHEM and ECON programs are so directed.

Perceptions of lecturers and lecture practices

In general, lecturers were quite aware of the difficulties FGSs may have in the lecture hall. A lecturer in the foreign service program said he tried to "create conducive conditions" for classroom participation by his choice of subject matter and personal encouragement. He recognized that it takes several months for certain students – particularly Asians – to feel comfortable asking and answering questions in class. He also noted that some students can remain silent during lectures and absorb everything. On the other hand, he had seen the opposite, where certain FGSs stand up and speak but don't follow through with analytical thought, for instance, in written assignments.

Other lecturers mentioned making their outlines and notes available in print-outs or on diskettes. A lecturer in the public policy program has students fax him a "one-page distillation" of his reading packet a day before the lecture. He uses these distillations as a basis for engaging students in discussion. A lecturer in the government department is careful to mention all student contributions in his end-of-class wrap-up. A lecturer in the demography program said she tried to use illustrations that were universally understandable and to explain those that were culturally specific. A lecturer in the economics department found that the mix of specific and open-ended questions gave students with differing speaking proficiency an opportunity to participate. Those lecturers who involve their students in small group study mentioned their efforts to mix FGSs with Americans. Two lecturers commented that lecture techniques that were intended at first to integrate women, FGSs or others into the group as a whole proved finally to be beneficial to all.

Addressing the importance of language skills in the MBA program, one management lecturer stated that a student's influence is limited by language facility. "When others realize it's worth the time to listen to FGSs," their influence increases. She felt that students were supportive of FGS participation. She also asserted that FGSs were smart and well-prepared, but "until they participate, Americans cannot determine this." This idea was echoed by other lecturers in the SFS, GOV, PBPL and DMOG programs.

The long road to the Ph.D. degree allows some FGSs time to become proficient in English before the critical undertaking of presenting their own work. For example, lecturers in the economics and chemistry departments spoke of the apprenticeship and careful mentoring that they take their students through. TAs receive a lot of faculty support: in economics, in the first term one is an Apprentice TA, and in the second term, a Formal TA; in chemistry, the lecturer-in-charge meets with TAs once a week. Again in chemistry, a recitation in one's research group is not scheduled until the second term. Thus, while participation is desirable from the beginning, it is necessary down the road.

Other perceptions of the lecturers had to do with the development of professionals in their field and the qualities of mind that were called for. A linguistics lecturer spoke of the importance of students coming to the subject with "an objective view of the nature of language and 'a' or 'many' languages" and an ability to "deal with abstract theories which may or may not be conducive to study." A government lecturer spoke of the importance of being interested in "exploring and interpreting ideas relating to political theory and history and being able to structure them in an 'architectonic' way." An economics lecturer defined creativity in his field as an "ability to blend the highly rigorous techniques of the discipline with basic intuition." A chemistry lecturer saw the qualities that make for a "star" in this field as 40% ability and 60% curiosity, venturesomeness and strong motivation to know the answers. Thus, the lecturers, particularly in the Ph.D. programs, stressed the fact that lecture comprehension involves understanding the fundamental thrust of the subject matter. Furthermore, as lecturers and mentors they saw it as their job to guide the study to this level of comprehension.

Conclusions

The whole body of interviews makes clear that there is a growing expectation of oral participation in the lecture hall. For graduate students, that includes the lectures, the small group study for the lectures, oral reports and discussion in the lectures and for some, the role of lecturers, as TAs themselves. For FGSs, it means that greater attention must be paid toward enhancing aural *and* oral skills.

The data also show that the aural proficiency level measured by a score of 600+ on the TOEFL does *not* assure comprehension of a lecture that deviates from a straight talk-and-chalk lecture delivered in standard academic speech. More than half of the FGSs said that they understood less than 50% of the lectures during the first month. On the other hand, with such a TOEFL score the FGSs have the tools and knowledge of the language to acquire the necessary proficiency. We see that the majority relied on their previous background in the subject matter and a willingness to spend long hours on reading assignments. And while the FGSs adopted a variety of other strategies as well, the give and take of questions and responses in class as a way of clarifying one's comprehension of lectures was *not* one of them.

The expectation of greater oral participation in lectures presents a challenge to FGSs and is an issue for lecturers and professionals in English for Academic Purposes to address. This is not meant to indicate that requirements for FGSs should be any different than for other graduate students. FGSs are prepared to meet high standards. In fact, the group interviewed here gained proficiency of a high order by hard work and by dint of the various strategies they have reported here.

Acknowledgments

I wish to thank Carol J. Kreidler, Director of the Division of English as a Foreign Language, Georgetown University, for her support and encouragement; also of Georgetown University, Frederick J. Bosco, Mary Coit and William E. Norris, and Robert S. Mason, my husband, for their excellent suggestions regarding the chapter. I also give special thanks to the foreign graduate students and to those faculty members who contributed their time and perceptions.

References

Chamot, A. U. 1987. Learner strategies of ESL students. In Wendin and Rubin (Eds.), 71–83.

Cohen, A. D. 1987. Studying learner strategies: how we get the information. In Wendin and Rubin (Eds.), 31–40.

Mason, A. 1983a. *Understanding Academic Lectures*. Englewood Cliffs, N.J.: Prentice Hall.

  1983b. *Understanding Academic Lectures. Transcripts.* Englewood Cliffs, N.J.: Prentice Hall.

Naiman, N., M. Frohlich, H. H. Stern, and A. Todesco. 1978. *The Good Language Learner*. Research in Education Series, 7. Toronto: Ontario Institute for Studies in Education.

Oxford, R. 1990. *Language Learning Strategies: What Every Teacher Should Know*. N.Y.: Newbury House.

Rubin, J. 1987. Learner strategies: theoretical assumptions, research history and typology. In Wendin and Rubin (Eds.), 15–30.

Wendin, A. L. 1987. How to be a successful language learner. In Wendin and Rubin (Eds.), 103–118.

Wendin, A. L., and J. Rubin (Eds.). 1987. *Learner Strategies in Language Learning*. Englewood Cliffs, N.J.: Prentice Hall.

11 Visual and verbal messages in the engineering lecture: notetaking by postgraduate L2 students

Philip King

Abstract

This chapter presents a brief review of previous work on lectures and notetaking, including work which investigated L1 students. It then goes on to report research carried out by the author into notetaking by overseas postgraduate students on Transportation and Highway Engineering courses at the University of Birmingham. This research has a dual focus: the relationship between the visual and verbal aspects of the lecture; and the notes made by overseas students with reference to the visual–verbal distinction. The lecture event is described and analysed. It was found that there is regularly a complementary relationship between the visuals and the accompanying speech: evaluation is frequent in the spoken lecture (and is regarded as important by the lecturers), but is not often provided visually. Student notes all capture at least some of the lecturer's comments, in addition to most of the visuals. There is some indication that better students capture more of the verbal message, and categorisation of the ways in which they do this may give a basis for a quality of notes measure. These findings are related to other research and implications for EAP teaching are discussed.

Previous research: a brief review

As various contributors to this volume point out, empirical research on academic lectures and notetaking has been characterised by its relative paucity. This is in marked contrast to the central part such activities play in the lives of students. What research there has been has approached notetaking and lectures from three angles: educational psychology, academic staff training, and linguistics (sociolinguistics and discourse analysis), and these areas will be reviewed briefly in turn. There is also a body of work in the form of materials aimed at EAP students (see Hamp-Lyons 1983 for a review of earlier materials) which present lecture notetaking simulations, and may include notetaking techniques; this will not be further considered here.

Work in educational psychology has tended to concentrate on the effectiveness of notes in helping students to recall a lecture, but has not been concerned with L2 students as such. It has had little to say about the lecture itself, largely because it has mostly been laboratory-type research with lectures specially set up for the investigator, with post-lecture testing with or without students being allowed to review the notes taken. The approach to students' notes has been quantitative, relating the number of words or "information units" in their notes measured to the number of words or ideas in the lecture. Hartley and Davies (1978) review previous work and note a number of shortcomings associated with this approach. They point out that if the lecture has little value for the students, they may well take few notes, so a criterion such as proportion of the lecture captured, often used for judging "successful" notes, can be meaningless. This is an argument for "naturalistic situations, replications with different lectures and lecturers, and students unaware that they are taking part in experiments" (Hartley and Davies 1978: 218), although the difficulty then is that "it is hard to be precise about what is going on". Nonetheless, as they point out, to provide findings of help to practitioners, direct observation and case histories are needed to supplement the experimental approach.

In this approach, the lecture was conceived of in a narrow sense, as a one-off event on a self-contained topic, which was strictly controlled for manner of presentation. Visuals (anything from writing on the blackboard to a film presentation) caused problems for the experimenters: if you are counting words or information units, then a graph is a hindrance, and if your test requires a verbal response, then it may be a poor probe of non-verbal information presented on a slide (try verbalising a city street plan). Problems could also be caused for the students: having a visual displayed while the lecturer was talking could, it was claimed, cause student overload. There was also an unspoken assumption that all academic disciplines could be brought under the same presentational criteria, presumably as those operating in a humanities or social science environment, and to the extent that the lectures were specially constructed for the experimental event, it is likely that discipline-related topics were not treated as they would be by the appropriate department; one investigation of an astronomy lecture in which slides were used concludes curiously that:

The criterion for the use of a slide by the lecturer often seems to be that it is a quick way of showing material that is too complicated to write or draw on the board . . . Such a criterion ignores the fact that if it is too complicated for the lecturer, then it will also be too complicated for the student. (Hartley and Fuller 1971: 41)

Hartley and Fuller's finding, however, that students tend not to record visually presented material is supported by McDonald and Taylor

(1980) who found that students in veterinary medical education (arguably a more visually-dependent discipline) do not often draw diagrams.

As I shall elaborate below, the postgraduate engineering lectures which I investigated show a strong reliance on visually presented material in the form of slides, overhead projector transparencies and blackboard work. One might expect this to be generally true of science and engineering departments.

More recently, there has been a growing EFL/ESL-based concern with L2 students' notetaking behaviour. Dunkel (1988) undertook a cross-cultural investigation into the notes of 129 L1 and L2 students and their relationship to immediate retention of lecture concepts and details. Among her findings was that "terseness" of notetaking (the compacting of spoken discourse into propositions) related more closely to good postlecture quiz scores than did the total number of words written down. L2 students who performed less well had written more structure words and made less use of symbols, drawings and abbreviations. She concludes, however, that a single general model of notetaking is unlikely to be of value and that researchers still need to seek for an L2 "quality of notes" measure.

Lecturer-training has concentrated on advice to lecturers; in particular as far as our concerns go, on how to organise lecture behaviour so as to help students to take effective notes. Structuring the presentation and maintaining student interest are seen as ways of getting students to take "good notes", while showing a complicated diagram and talking at the same time poses the problem for students of whether to note what they see or what they hear (Brown and Tomlinson 1979). This latter point will be discussed below in the context of my own research.

Lecturers are advised to be aware that successful students may not follow a single path to success (Gibbs 1981) so a plurality of approaches to notetaking has to be recognised. Main's (1980) tutorial approach to students with notetaking problems agrees:

It is always my aim to allow the student to shape his own notetaking style . . . rather than to encourage him to model himself on someone else's style . . . The student himself remains the judge of when his notetaking practice and shaping is complete. (p. 47)

A similar, pluralistic approach is advocated by Gibbs (1981).

Linguistic approaches to lectures and notetaking have in the main been discourse analysis of the structure of lectures in particular, often motivated by a consideration of the problems for the overseas student (see, for example, Holes 1972; Montgomery 1977; Murphy and Candlin 1979). Murphy and Candlin's paper is especially germane, looking as it does at an engineering lecture to undergraduate students, but considering the implications for teaching the foreign student. Firstly, they are positive about the visual element in the lecture:

The visual element has an important role to play in increasing the potential avenues of interpretation open to the student in the discipline as much as to the foreign language student. (p. 65)

They also consider what constitutes a good set of notes:

A satisfactory set of notes from the lecturer's point of view was, when we asked, an accurate record of what he had noted on the blackboard. Points worthy of correction were, for example, incorrect copying of a graph slope, making it too steep, or careless reproduction of a diagram. The need for accurate notes was paramount since they provided the information content for the practical tasks elsewhere on the course. Hence the comparatively slow, meticulous presentation of information in comparison with an Arts course. On the basis of a small sample we found that native British students did not seem to expect (in their first year anyway) to supplement what they copied from the board with notes of what was said but not written down by the lecturer. (p. 65)

The authors recognise that differences in presentational style are appropriate to different disciplines, and the importance of diagrams and their accurate reproduction in notes is stressed.

More recently, perspectives have broadened. Janda (1985) is interested in the textual features of the notes themselves. He argues from the evidence of sets of notes by L1 students that notetaking English can be regarded as a simplified register; he identifies particular characteristic features as abbreviation and symbolisation, omission of form words, amalgamation of two or more sentences into a single topic-comment structure, and various syntactic reorganisations including passivisation.

Benson (1989) is a longitudinal, naturalistic, *in vivo* study of one L2 student on a master's course. The extracts from the student's notes are compared with a transcript of a segment of a lecture and with the notes of an L1 student. The L2 student makes use of abbreviation and reformulation, but what comes out most clearly is that he is selecting what to put down, leaving out much subsidiary (Coulthard and Montgomery 1981) discourse; and in relating the lecture to his own interests he notes down a different set of points with different emphases from the L1 student. It is difficult to see how this sort of behaviour could be captured by a set-piece experiment, which may be thought likely to engender a greater degree of conformity. Dunkel speaks of test-wise students employing particular notetaking strategies, and even in the uncontrolled situation, Benson notes that some of his subjects' behaviour may have been prompted by test-wiseness and says that the use of lists by lecturers stimulates notetaking by students because they recognise the list as being something testable.

That certain types of lecturer behaviour may prompt notetaking is also pointed out by Fisk (1982), reviewing earlier work. She notes that verbal signposting ("This is important"), walking away from a podium, and writing on the blackboard all made it more likely that students would take notes, while they were less likely to do so when visual aids were displayed. Olsen and Huckin (1990) also support this last point. They note that engineering lectures rely heavily on visual materials (p. 35), but that "typically, science and engineering students take notes by copying what is on the blackboard; they often minimize the role of . . . audio-visual materials . . . " (p. 41)

Student perceptions of notetaking and cultural differences have been explored by Hartley and Davies (1978), and Dunkel and Davy (1989). Hartley and Davies note that there are some significant differences between the way British and U.S. students view notetaking, with British students showing much less exam awareness or exam orientation in their notetaking. Dunkel and Davy compare L1 and L2 students in the United States, and note that the perceptions of these two groups are broadly similar, although most of the L2 students felt that lecturers do not give them enough time to take notes in English.

This short survey gives an idea of the broad range of concerns and approaches which have been brought to bear on the lecture notetaking situation. There seems to be convergence on the idea that students tend not to note down visuals that are non-linguistic (graphs, diagrams, etc.), while lecturers may regard these as important. Problems relating to the use of visuals seem to some extent to have been created by the expectations of researchers or the difficulties of handling them in certain types of analytical framework; sometimes it seems as if insufficient allowance is made for different presentational preferences in different subject cultures. As Dunkel says: "a naturalistic investigation of notes students take during actual classroom lectures and their relationship to performance on actual classroom exams is sorely needed" (Dunkel 1988: 277).

The present research

The present writer's research was undertaken with the limited aim of comparing the notes taken by L2 students with each other and with a record of each lecture to see what were the systematic relationships between the notes and the visual and verbal aspects of the lecture. A naturalistic approach investigating real lectures was preferred; lecturers in the department concerned had been accustomed over a number of years to cooperating with tutors from the English for Overseas Students Unit, by allowing their lectures to be recorded for team-teaching purposes (Johns and Dudley-Evans 1980). Additionally, the notes that students took should be those they needed for their own purposes on the course. The scale of the research – 14 lectures spread over a large part of one term – made it unlikely that students or lecturers would consistently modify their behaviour in any way on account of the presence of the researcher. At the same time, limits had to be placed on the extent of the intrusion, which precluded the use of video equipment, or interviews with students.

The lectures were all of 90 or 120 minutes' duration and were delivered to students on the M.Sc. course in Highway Engineering at the University of Birmingham in 1984. The core research data consists of the notes of four students over fourteen lectures (consecutive parts of three courses in maintenance, highway capacity and transport economics) given by three different lecturers in the department. In each case the record of the lecture consists of an audio recording, and copies of the overhead transparencies used and of any handouts distributed and used in the lectures; notes of the slides indicating type, caption, and salient features; and a note of everything written on the blackboard. This gave a complete record of everything that was made available by the lecturer to the students. The first step was to transcribe the lecture and then to map onto the transcript the exposure of each visual. The transcript was then marked up with the points on it which corresponded to notes taken by the four students being followed.

Student characteristics

Four students on the course were identified with the help of one of the subject lecturers. One was effectively bilingual and was regarded by the lecturers as a very good notetaker. One was relatively weak, but not so weak as to be put at risk by the intervention of the researcher. The other two fell in between. The same four students were followed through the lectures, although occasional absences meant that for some lectures only three sets of notes were collected. Their notes were collected after each lecture and photocopied. The students were from Hong Kong, Greece, Indonesia and Cameroon. They were aware of the presence of the researcher in the lectures, and agreed for their notes to be photocopied for research, although they were not aware of the researcher's precise purposes.

Lecture characteristics

Engineering lectures are characterised by heavy use of visual aids in the form of slides, overhead transparencies, and blackboard work, sometimes with handouts as well, although there was considerable variation from one lecture to another: in one lecture, for instance, only a single word was written on the blackboard, while in at least one lecture the extensive blackboard was covered twice over. Handouts containing worked problems were also distributed in more than one lecture and gone through by lecturer and students together. The centrality of the visual element is shown by Table 1.

TABLE I. USE OF SLIDES AND TRANSPARENCIES IN LECTURES

Lecturer A			*Lecturer B*			*Lecturer C*		
lecture no:	*slides*	*trans-parencies*	*lecture no:*	*slides*	*trans-parencies*	*lecture no:*	*slides*	*trans-parencies*
1	6	8	1	21	2	1	13	4
2	0	5	2	41	0	2	23	2
3	0	5	3	37	2	3	10	2
4	0	8	4	34	0	4	9	8
5	5	4				5	7	6
Total:	11	30		133	4		62	22

The fourteen lectures contained 206 slides and 56 transparencies. (If the same slide or transparency was shown more than once in the same lecture, it is only counted once for that lecture. If the same slide was shown in different lectures, it is counted once in each lecture.) Although there was considerable variation from lecturer to lecturer, and some variation across lectures by the same lecturer, even the lecturer who relied least on visuals still had an average of eight visuals per lecture, apart from any use made of the blackboard and handouts. If it is true that visuals cause problems for notetakers by competing with a simultaneous verbal message, the problems here could be horrendous. However, such an assessment needs to look more closely into the nature of the interplay between the visual and the verbal messages.

It is clear that since the visuals are mostly prepared in advance, they have a major role in structuring the lecture. There is thus a parallel between this aspect of the lecture and the practical demonstration (Hutchinson 1978), where the presence of the display item imposes a logic on the development of the spoken discourse.

The type of material displayed varied from notes and headings structuring the main lecture sections through mathematical working to non-linguistic charts, graphs and photographs. Clearly these would all require different treatment by students intent on capturing and retaining the information. Material presented on the blackboard was not always linguistic: formulae, calculations, and simple graphs and grids were also put up on the board. In principle these were easier to note down, taking roughly as long for students to get down as for the lecturer to put up, although because the information was sometimes built up piecemeal or because the lecturer could modify the blackboard work, for instance, by erasing part of it and substituting something else, there were potential problems for notetakers of running out of horizontal or vertical space, or having to cross out and redraw something. These points are illustrated below. In the natural lecturing situation, lecturers are sensitive to their audience, and often provide clues as to what they expect the students to do with the visuals. Thus, they may be encouraged to take notes:

. . . I want you to use this in your revision of these notes, which of course you'll be doing tonight . . .

. . . I'll leave this overhead up for you to make notes from . . .

or be told that something is not worth noting:

. . . you'll find this overhead just a summary of what's in McCullum's work . . .

. . . I don't think there's any need to take this down . . .

. . . we've lost a bit at the top, I think you can probably read it, but it doesn't really matter . . .

. . . beyond that you have a column headed beta; you can ignore that for present purposes . . .

. . . you don't need to jot this down in any way, but, the SPSS results are summarised there . . .

Or indeed the lecturer can change her or his mind about the slide she or he wants to show; one slide flashed up evoked only this comment:

. . . I don't think I want to talk about that; you'll find that in the back of l r eight three three . . .

We can regard this as interactive evaluation; the lecturers are providing for the students their assessment of the importance of what they are presenting, for the purposes of notetaking. The underlying question can be formulated as: is this something the detail of which in the lecturer's estimation needs to be retrieved for the purposes of this course and its exams or for the knowledge of the subject? The students appear on the whole to follow the advice.

The clues the lecturer gives are not always linguistically explicit; non-linguistic behaviour such as Fisk notes (above) was not part of this research, but at many points in the lectures there are long pauses of up to 60 seconds. During some the lecturers are occupied with their notes or writing on the board, but during others they are clearly just giving students time to note down information from a visual. At least once, a lecturer asked:

. . . have you all finished with this?

Although this seems an easy enough way to get around the problem of simultaneous visual and aural input for students, and although all lecturers did it, there was a fair degree of variation between them. In a lecture with many visuals no lecturer is going to pause for long during all of them.

The relationship between the verbal and visual elements of the lecture

We have said (with Hutchinson), that visuals can provide a sequence, and therefore structure, to the lecture. But the simultaneity of visual and verbal information has until now been considered only with regard to its potential for interfering with the students' ability to retrieve the overall message. A question to be asked is whether the two modes are in conflict, whether one of them is simply redundant, or whether they complement each other in some systematic way or ways.

In fact, the last of these three alternatives appears to be the case: it is indeed possible to see a pattern in the relationship between the visuals and the verbal message, which can be illustrated by the lecture excerpt below (from lecture B4). In this, the lecturer is pulling together the threads of one or more previous lectures, creating a list on the board as he speaks. In the following transcript, capital letters represent what was written on the board; punctuation is solely to aid readability.

. . . so we have this idea of DIAGNOSTICS. well, let's see what we can do with it. well, let's see first of all, what have we got? and i think we put up a list of all the things that we have. let's say we had CRACKING, RUTTING, Bump Integrator readings, SCRIM reading, DEFLECTOGRAPH reading, CURVATURE if we believed it, and as i say, you see, we're right on the – , i'm stressing the fact that we're right on the edge of knowledge at the moment, because we don't know a great deal about curvature – that's the sort of thing we shall be looking at – and then if you've gone through all of those, then you think about CORING and TRENCHING. let me hasten to add that there are other variants on all of these – not all of them, but i mean you could have the PCA ROAD METER here, you could have the PENDULUM tester here, you could have the Falling Weight Deflectometer here but essentially what you're doing is, you're building, you're bringing in all these ideas, squashing them together and saying now what is wrong with this patient? sometimes we may have to probe a little deeper, so we can almost say we have an idea of PRIMARY STUDY, – write this up – primary study, leading where necessary, we'll write WHERE NECESSARY to FURTHER STUDY. in fact we could say, we could say well now there's a problem here because we might want to divide this up a bit, because you see we know the deflectograph is quite slow, we know the deflectograph is quite slow so we might even want to divide up this.
[*The lecturer then recounts his old solution to the problem of the deflectograph being slow.*]

. . . but that isn't really the solution. the solution is to use the cheap forms of
investigation, plus the rapid forms of investigation, to have a primary
screening. we'll call this now, primary, we'll call this the PRIMARY SURVEY.

The lecturer's remark "write this up" is delivered sotto voce to himself
rather than to the students. On the words "divide up this" he drew the
horizontal lines. The result by this point was a board diagram with
roughly the following spatial relations:

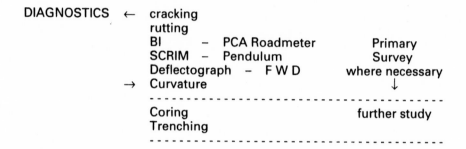

Figure 1   Lecturer's boardwork

The word "Study" had originally been written below "Primary", but
this was erased and the word "Survey" written in. More modification
and extension of the diagram followed, but is not part of the present
analysis. The arrows represent the position and direction of arrows
chalked up on the board.

This description of the build-up process is enough to show that the
creation of the diagram is not a simple left-to-right, top-to-bottom
procedure; lines are inserted, a word is replaced, arrows drawn in later.
This is more complex than presenting a photograph or a diagram, where
the information, whether revealed in one go or gradually, is not
subsequently modified.

Viewed as a product, however, the boardwork consists, in language
terms, of noun phrases (except for the proviso "where necessary") that
represent procedures. Propositionally, these can be viewed as statements
of fact or possibility – "we (can) use coring", and so on. What is present
in the lecturer's verbal account but not in the notes he creates is any of
the cautionary aspect – curvature is problematic, the deflectograph is
slow, etc. Following Hoey (1983) we can say that what is present
visually may be regarded as a representation of a situation, but what is
conveyed only orally is the statement of some kind of problem related to
or arising from the situation, and the evaluation of possible solutions as
successful or unsuccessful.

The same relationship in simpler form can be seen in the next extract (from lecture A3), where the lecturer is working through a multiple regression example. He says (conventions as before):

. . . doing the arithmetic one finds that R SQUARED IS EQUAL TO POINT NINE NINE SEVEN, very high indeed, which implies that ninety nine point seven per cent of the variation is explained by the regression plane, in other words that almost one hundred per cent, ninety nine point seven per cent of the variation in y, independent variable y, is explained statistically by the variation of the independent variables x and w. it's a very high r squared. perhaps too high, for reasons i shall be indicating to you in a moment. but there's no problem in the sense that we haven't got a relationship; there is definitely a relationship there . . .

What goes on the board is simply the proposition $r^2 = 0.997$. The lecturer speaks of an implication of this, and evaluates the value as so high as to be perhaps too high. He also interprets the result as proving that a relationship does exist, so the question whether one exists or not has been given a definite answer, and in this sense it has been successfully answered.

Though such a relationship does not occur with every instance of a visual being presented, it is quite pervasive throughout all the lectures investigated. The lecture task of transmission of information and ideas, it can be argued, is shared out between the modes of presentation available to the lecturer, and thus the notion that the visual is doing no more than make up for a lecturing deficiency, implied in some of the research noted above, is wide of the mark. Rather, there is a complex pattern to the message that is coming across, and if this does overload students, as reported in some research, we might expect their notes to reflect this. What we see then in these illustrative extracts is that one of the functions of the lecturer's oral discourse is to evaluate the content of the lecture which is presented in the visuals.

The relationship of students' notes to the visual and verbal elements

For L2 students, lectures are often seen as a problem of listening comprehension, to the extent that most lecture-comprehension-related EAP materials are based on audio-taped lectures. The lectures investigated here each contain between 7,700 and 17,700 spoken words. Student notes were generally about four or five pages long, including many of the visuals. The seven sets of notes (one student was absent from one of the lectures) for the two lectures extracted above cover 28 pages of A4 paper, but are made up largely of reproductions of the visual displays, and do not utilise every line. Thus, a very low proportion of the word total was being captured, although this in itself did not appear to be a problem.

The starting hypothesis for this research was that L2 students would tend to note all the visually available information in a lecture and none of the verbal information, the argument being that noting the visual information is copying, while writing down what is heard requires real-time processing, and, therefore, more attention and effort. Clearly the hypothesis is a statement of an extreme position, but it was useful in requiring analysis and interpretation of any deviation from this. A refinement of it would be that L2 students would tend to get down exactly what was said, without reformulation (this requiring less effort again than recasting the ideas). And *ceteris paribus*, better students would tend to note down more of the verbal message as a proportion of their notes.

However, this position in turn needs modification. In particular, this research has not yet addressed the question of what the "better" student does do. The first hypothesis also has had to be modified since many of the visuals are clearly not presented with any expectation that they should be noted down – photographs being an obvious case in point. This leaves a modified hypothesis that students will tend to note down what is visually available, especially if time and its perceived importance allow, and will tend not to note down what is said; and that this will be more true of L2 students, who experience more difficulty in the listening comprehension aspect of the lecture. This in turn, however, still rests on the assumption that all other things are equal; given the possible cultural differences, and differences between and within individuals, one is unlikely to be able to give overwhelming evidence in support or refutation of the hypothesis. What can be done here is to investigate the weaker case, and ask to what extent students get down the verbal message, and what it is that they do capture.

We now turn, therefore, to a consideration of the notes which students took of the points covered in the lecture extracts above. One of the students (the one rated as good in advance by the lecturers) was absent from the second lecture, so comments are based on four sets of notes for the first, and three for the second lecture.

All students noted the information presented on the board, though not necessarily in the same way as it was presented. The student rated as good captured the diagram as presented in Figure 1 above, though with the right-hand column ("Primary Survey" and the words below it) changed to a left-hand column, and with the following evaluations: against cracking and rutting, he added "cheap and quick"; against bump integrator and scrim he added "quick" and against deflectograph, he added "slow". Thus the evaluations were clearly captured and noted down.

Another student noted the diagram as in Figure 1, and added the evaluation as a piece of text:

rutting, cracking   BI, SCRIM

Generally use the <u>cheap</u> ↑ types of investigation and the <u>quick</u> ↑ of them and make a primary survey . . .

we have	cracking		
	rutting		
slow test	BI	–	PCA Roadmeter
	SCRIM	–	Pendulum test
further study — ↓ —			
	deflectograph	–	F. W. D.
fast test	curvatura [*sic*]		

All that are as primary study, and if it is necessary, do further study, such as:

coring
trenching

Figure 2   Student's notes relating to Figure 1

The third student similarly broke up the diagram with running text, but unfortunately got the evaluations attributed to the wrong diagnostic items, the faster ones being designated "slow" and vice versa (Figure 2).

The fourth student simply reproduced the blackboard diagram without adding any of the evaluation.

The notes taken during the second lecture extract show similar inter-student variation in the capture of the evaluations, two of them noting simply what was on the board, the third adding a bracketed evaluation after the figure 0.997: "(it means that the correlation is very good)".

These snapshots represent about five minutes' activity taken from something like twenty-three hours of lecturing. While more of the data has been analysed, amounting to about a quarter of the total, any extrapolation must be done with care and caution. Nonetheless they present a variety of features which gives us a more sophisticated view of the complexity of notetaking itself. One of the reasons for not investigating the recall of information from these notes is that as the first extract suggests, over a series of lectures the lecturer himself will cross-refer to earlier lectures and sometimes engage in dialogue with students to see what they do remember; cumulatively over a series of lectures, recall will be assisted within the framework of the lectures themselves, and reformulations or extensions of earlier notes may be captured in new notes. Recall thus cannot be uniquely related to one point in the lectures or in the notes.

A complementary and more extensive bird's-eye view can be obtained if we look at student notetaking through the course of an entire lecture. Table 2 is a quantitative overview of four sets of student notes for lecture A1 (see Table 1). It notes whether the slide or transparency was reproduced by the student in his notes or not, and if so, whether the student has made any modification to the item as presented, or added anything from the verbal message ("comment"). The student identified as relatively weak is represented in the left-hand column; the student regarded as very good is in the last column. The lecture topic was elasticity of supply, demand and cost, and the visuals were both linguistic, consisting of definitions and lists, and non-linguistic, consisting of ratios, equations, graphs and the relevant arithmetic operations. They are listed in the order in which they were put up. Slides and transparencies generally overlapped; that is, a transparency was not taken off until the next transparency was put up, and similarly for slides. A "Y" or "N" denotes whether the visual was noted down or not (generally where a visual was noted, it was taken down in its entirety); all other items relate to information which was not available visually or to reworkings where the visual was represented by the student in a different form. Minor deviations such as failure to label the graph axes are ignored. The term "comments" is used as a catch-all, and includes framing remarks, evaluation and exemplification.

Some brief detail discussion is called for here on two points: (1) more on the annotations of Table 2 themselves, and (2) some sort of comparison between students. The introductory material in some notes (indicated as "intro") relates to the lecturer's verbal introduction of the topic of elasticity and captures some of his scene-setting remarks about its broader relation to supply and demand of a commodity, or his structuring remarks about what he is going to deal with today ("in making a start today I intend to cover three main points: first how elasticity is defined, secondly how in principle it might be measured, and thirdly how in practice we might have to estimate it"). There is variation in what different students note, but this is not considered further here.

The gloss "comments" refers to anything noted by students which was not available visually. An important first question is whether the comment is simply a noting down of part of the verbal message or whether it represents the student's own reaction or attitude to what is said or presented. Overwhelmingly, the comments seem to be a capture of what the lecturer has said, often with a degree of reformulation. For example, student 1's "comment" at transparency 6 is a framing remark picked up from the lecturer. Four lines of the transparency show four labels for different types of elasticity, with four equations next to the labels. One of the lecturer's framing remarks on putting the transparency up is: "there's four main price elasticities of demand which we will be interested in in the transport sector". Student 1 captures this as "The

TABLE 2. NOTES OF FOUR STUDENTS IN ONE LECTURE

	Student 1	Student 2	Student 3	Student 4
Trans. 1		8 lines intro	10 lines intro	6 lines intro
	Y	Y	Y	Y
Trans. 2	Y	Y	Y	Y; comment
Slide 1	Y	Y	Y; comments	Y; comment
Trans. 3	Y	Y; slight rework	Y; comments	Y; comments
Slide 2	Y	Y	Y; comment	Y
Trans. 4	Y	Y	Y; comment	Y
Slide 3	caption only	N	N noted; some reworking	only graphs
Trans. 5	Y	Y; comment	Y; 3 comments	Y
Slide 4	Y	Y; some condensing	Y; graphs only	N
Trans. 6	comment	Y	Y; comments	Y; with minor changes and comments
	Y			
Trans. 7	Y	Y; comments	Y; comments reworking	Y; one
Slide 5	N	N	·N	N
Slide 6	Y	Y	Y; cross ref. added	N
Trans. 8	Y	Y	Y	Y

four main factors in the transport field are:", and then reproduces the labels and their corresponding equations.

Another type of comment is the gloss. To illustrate again from transparency 6, student 3 notes down the four types of elasticity, and against the third (income elasticity) glosses the term as: "change to pass demand with increase in incomes". ("Pass" is an abbreviation for "passenger".) The lecturer put this in the form of a question: "what will happen to passenger demand if, if their incomes increase?"

A third type of comment is the evaluation. This has already been discussed above, but a further example will help to establish the pervasiveness of this type of comment. Transparency 3 is a worked example demonstrating the concept of arc elasticity, and showing all the algebra and arithmetic. Against one of the final values, student 3 has written: "10% change in price > 20% change in Q (very sensitive)". The lecturer at this point said: " . . . the elasticity magnitude turns out to be minus two. This implies that a ten per cent change in price will induce a twenty per cent change in quantity. Quantity appears very sensitive to the price of the vehicle." The evaluation again comes only in the verbal message. This is, in fact, a complex example, because as well as the evaluation, we are dealing with an implication (what does the value minus two imply?).

Further analysis along these lines may make it possible to relate quantity of such things occurring in notes with a notion of quality. Certainly there is a rough correlation here between the quantity of such "comments" and one lecturer's informal assessments of the students' abilities in general, although the data are clearly too limited to go far with.

While the "comment" parts of the student notes are where, not surprisingly, most individual variation occurs, there is good agreement between students on what visuals to note down. The omission of slide 3 was at the prompting of the lecturer (" . . . you don't need to jot any of this down, the, this or the next slide, you won't need to refer to it at all henceforth . . . "); slide 4 was in fact not presented until after another transparency had been put up, and when the slides were switched, the lecturer's signal that the slide did not need to be incorporated in the notes was present, but less explicit (" . . . before I go any further perhaps I should deal with the next slide very briefly, just to reinforce the point about unit elasticity . . . "). Possibly as a result, it figures rather more in students' notes, though still abbreviated overall when compared to the majority of slides. On the other hand, there is no explicit prompting when slide 5 is presented.

To sum this up, students seem to be in general agreement about what visuals to note down. There is more variation in the extent to which they capture the verbal message, and it is possible that students who are regarded as better capture more of the message, as Table 2 seems to indicate.

Discussion

This analysis produces findings which are not always in agreement with the conclusions of previous researchers.

1. There seems to be a clear division of function between the verbal and visual aspects of these lectures. While evaluation features strongly as part of the verbal message, it is seldom given visually. One example of where it does occur as part of the visual presentation is in transparency 7 of lecture A1, which shows four methods of estimating elasticities, and contains comments for the first two: "no, unreliable", and "possible but expensive" respectively.
2. Students generally note down the visuals unless there are indications from the lecturer that they do not need to do so.
3. The students followed in this study all (to varying degrees) reformulated what was presented visually or verbally, and all (to varying degrees) captured some of the evaluations offered by the lecturer. The question of correlation

between the amount of the non-visual element which is captured and success on the course in general remains to be investigated further.

4. There seems to be a risk, which may be greater for L2 students, of mis-interpreting the verbal element – cf. the errors above in attribution of the evaluations "fast" and "slow" and the possibility that a "good correlation" may not be the same as one which is actually "possibly too good". The former signifies approbation; the latter counsels caution.

5. Murphy and Candlin (1979), noting that a satisfactory set of notes was what was recorded on the blackboard, were talking with reference to under-graduate lectures. The present research deals with postgraduate lectures, and here at least it is clear that lectures contain a complementary message which the lecturers, approached informally about this, regard as very important: while the facts (which are what is generally presented visually) represent the knowledge foundation necessary to become a qualified engineer, the ability to evaluate the facts (which corresponds approximately to what is going on in the verbal message) is what makes the difference between an engineer and a good engineer. There is an interesting parallel with a point raised in Houghton and King (1990) where a lecturer expresses the expectation that a good student would be able to make inferences from a table of data, while a lower order of skill consists in simply noting the values. This suggests an area of useful further research, not necessarily confined to notetaking.

6. The notetaking of these students does show some signs of use of symbols and abbreviations, but there is also evidence of students composing grammatical unabbreviated sentences which involve some reformulation of the wordings actually presented in the lecture. This is another area which would repay further investigation, in which it would be important on data such as these to distinguish between creative use of symbols and abbreviations by the students and simple copying of those used by the lecturer. While Janda (1985) notes the systematic use of symbols and abbreviations, Fisk (1982: 41) says of one of her students "most of what she wrote was a copy of what the instructor wrote on the board with the addition of a minimum number of function words, and a minimum number of definitions, explanations and examples that were not on the board". Dunkel (1988: 39) reports that more students identified abbreviation techniques as more especially helpful than any other technique (though only 15 out of 110); the next step would be to see how extensively in fact they do so, and in what circumstances. The students followed in the present research appear to have made less use of symbols and abbreviations than might have been expected. It is not known whether any of them, in fact, had received training in notetaking. There is an argument, however, against reducing redundancy in notetaking on the grounds that the test of successful notes may be whether they still make sense months later when students are revising for exams (see on this Chaudron et al., this volume, for a good example of difficulties in retrieval caused by overabbreviation and oversymbolisation).

Conclusions

The question of where we go from here can be looked at in respect of each of the two topic threads identified earlier. In the first place, further analysis of the existing data is necessary in order to arrive at a more detailed and differentiated statement of the relationship between spoken and visual elements in the lecture. The basic elements in this relationship are clear enough, but an analysis of the types of evaluation, beyond the distinction begun here into content evaluation and interactive evaluation, is called for. More investigation into lecturers' intentions, here scarcely touched on except as discernible in the discourse, would help to establish their view of the role of the visuals. It is clear that visuals play a central part in the culture of this particular course, which is unlikely to be distinct from similar ones in other universities or in adjacent disciplines.

In the second place, focusing on student notes themselves, there are a number of follow-up questions which can be asked. Firstly, the present research has not looked longitudinally at any possible changes in strategy or tactics on the part of the student subjects. Assuming that we can distinguish in some way "better" notes from less good notes, do students individually show any change over time towards better practice? Another important area where more work needs to be done is in establishing a relation between quantitative measures of notes and qualitative ones, which might investigate student success on the course against the *nature* of the propositions contained in the notes, and perhaps on how directly the information was retrievable from the lecture. In addition, it would be desirable to complement this research with an investigation along the lines of Dunkel's (1988), looking at the notes of a greater number of students (perhaps including L1 students) over a few lectures, and relating notes to outcomes in a naturalistic setting – an extension of Benson's (1989) approach.

At this stage, the research does not offer detailed guidance to the producers of materials for notetaking courses. What it does suggest strongly is that we need to know more about the cultures of departments before we can make generalisations. In this particular case, the questions to ask are: if evaluation is important and is systematically under-represented in the notes of L2 students, (a) is this also true of other disciplines (with or without visuals); (b) does this correlate with quality of performance; and (c) what are the implications for the EAP teacher? If students fail to capture evaluation in their notes, is this because they do not know it is going on, or because they do, but fail to realise its significance? A knowledge of the variety of approaches which L2 students face and the expectations which departments have of them is necessary for properly-rooted EAP work to flourish; this research is intended to heighten such awareness.

References

Benson, M. J. 1989. The academic listening task: a case study. *TESOL Quarterly* 23 (3): 421–445.

Brown, G. K., and D. Tomlinson. 1979. How to improve lecturing. *Medical Teacher* 1: 128–135.

Coulthard, M., and M. Montgomery. 1981. The structure of monologue. In *Studies in Discourse Analysis*, M. Coulthard, and M. Montgomery (Eds.), 31–39. London: Routledge and Kegan Paul.

Dunkel, P. 1988. The content of L1 and L2 students' lecture notes and its relation to test performance. *TESOL Quarterly* 22 (2): 259–282.

Dunkel, P., and S. Davy. 1989. The heuristic of lecture notetaking: perceptions of American and international students regarding the value and practice of notetaking. *English for Specific Purposes* 8 (1): 33–50.

Fisk, E. C. 1982. A sociolinguistic study of notetaking in a college lecture classroom. Ph.D. thesis, Arizona State University.

Gibbs, G. 1981. Teaching students to learn. Milton Keynes: Open University Press.

Hamp-Lyons, L. 1983. Survey of materials for teaching advanced listening and note-taking. *TESOL Quarterly* 17 (1): 109–122.

Hartley, J., and I. K. Davies. 1978. Note-taking: a critical review. *Programmed Learning and Educational Technology* 15 (3): 207–224.

Hartley, J., and H. Fuller. 1971. The use of slides in lectures: an exploratory study. *Visual Education* August/September: 39–41.

Hoey, M. P. 1983. *On the Surface of Discourse*. London: George Allen and Unwin.

Holes, C. 1972. An investigation into some aspects of the English language problems of two groups of overseas postgraduate students at Birmingham University, unpublished M.A. dissertation.

Houghton, D., and P. King. 1990. What it makes sense to ask: students' and lecturers' questions in English for development economics. In *The Language of Economics: the Analysis of Economics Discourse*, T. Dudley-Evans, and W. Henderson (Eds.), ELT Documents 134. Modern English Publications in association with the British Council.

Hutchinson, T. 1978. The practical demonstration: an analysis of the effect on discourse structure of a visual display. *Practical Papers in English Language Education* 1: 1–42, University of Lancaster.

Janda, R. D. 1985. Note-taking English as a simplified register. *Discourse Processes* 8: 437–454.

Johns, T. F., and A. Dudley-Evans. 1980. An experiment in team-teaching of overseas postgraduate students of transportation and plant biology. *ELT Documents* 106 – Team teaching in ESP. British Council.

Main, A. 1980. Encouraging effective learning. Edinburgh: Scottish Academic Press.

McDonald, R. J., and E. G. Taylor. 1980. Student notetaking and lecture handouts. In Veterinary Medical Education in *Journal of Veterinary Medical Education* 7: 157–161.

Montgomery, M. 1977. Some aspects of discourse structure and cohesion in selected science lectures. Unpublished M.A. thesis, University of Birmingham.

Murphy, D. F., and C. N. Candlin. 1979. Engineering lecture discourse and listening comprehension. *Practical Papers in English Language Education* 2: 1–79. Institute for English Language Education, University of Lancaster.

Olsen, L. A., and T. N. Huckin. 1990. Point-driven understanding in engineering lecture comprehension. *English for Specific Purposes* 9 (1): 33–47.

PART V:
PEDAGOGIC APPLICATIONS

Editor's introduction to Part V

The two chapters in this section differ from those in the rest of the collection in so far as their main focus is not research in itself, but the application of research findings to pedagogical issues.

Hansen and Jensen's paper describes the development of an academic listening test (the T–LAP, or Test of Listening for Academic Purposes), designed to screen L2 entrants to a North American University, and how the test is built upon state-of-the-art academic listening theory. After reviewing the relevant literature on listening comprehension and lecture discourse, the authors describe the theoretical considerations which guided the development of the test and the format of the test itself. The main feature of the T–Lap is that it is a "direct" test, i.e., it attempts to replicate the real-life lecture listening task as accurately as possible. In this it differs from the listening component of other currently used tests, such as the Michigan Test and TOEFL, which are "indirect" tests, not involving authentic tasks based on authentic lecture discourse.

In accordance with its aim of authenticity of task, the situational context is set for the T–Lap testees beforehand; videoed segments of actual lectures are used as the stimulus; short answer question formats that require the testees' own words rather than the words of test writers are employed; and both detail and global question formats are used.

Having described the salient features of the T–LAP, Hansen and Jensen's chapter goes on to describe research which was conducted to evaluate the test. This research is first focussed on reliability and validity criteria, but then moves on to investigate wider issues to which the use of a direct test of academic listening such as the T–Lap gives rise. These include the issues of technical vs. non-technical lectures as stimuli, performance across proficiency levels of different question types, and the effect of prior knowledge of topic on test performance. The paper is thus a rich mine of information for those concerned with academic listening testing.

If Hansen and Jensen's chapter, although not a true research report, nevertheless addresses a number of research, as well as pedagogic, issues, the chapter by Lynch contains no original research, but is, rather, a position chapter. The justification for including this chapter in the collection is two-fold. On the one hand, the question Lynch addresses, the training of content lecturers who lecture to non-natives, is an important one, but one which is too often neglected by both researchers and practitioners. On the other hand, Lynch reviews and synthesises, from a particular perspective, a considerable amount of research that is relevant to the theme of the collection as a whole; his chapter is thus a useful additional review to that provided by Flowerdew, in Part 1, of significant research in the academic listening and related fields.

In much of the literature on academic listening emphasis is put on the need for learners to improve their listening proficiency to a level adequate enough for them to be able to cope with authentic L1 lectures. It is the role of the language teacher to develop such a level of proficiency. It is rarely, if ever, suggested that a more fruitful approach might be that rather than all the responsibility being thrust upon the learners and their language teachers, at least some of the responsibility for adequate comprehension might be passed over to the content lecturers. In terms of cost effectiveness, it might well be that a higher level of understanding would be achieved by the lecturers' modifying their lecturing style, so as to enhance comprehension optimally, than by the learners and their language teachers struggling to improve their level of listening proficiency. If such was the objective, then the question would arise as to what, if anything, could language professionals tell content lecturers about making their lectures more effective for L2 listeners. This is the purpose of Lynch's chapter.

Lynch briefly reviews research on listening comprehension in general, lecture discourse analysis, native/non-native classroom interaction, L2 lecture discourse, L2 lecture comprehension, and lecturing methodology. Some of these areas are dealt with also in the first chapter in this collection, but most of the references Lynch provides are new. The review of the literature leads Lynch to his recommendations for the training of lecturers who lecture to international audiences. Particular features of such training which Lynch considers might be useful include sociocultural issues (in particular the use of analogies), the use of visual materials as support for the spoken word, and the use of questions in lectures. As the last chapter in the collection, Lynch's chapter rounds the collection off nicely in reviewing research of relevance to L2 listening and showing how it might be applied in one important area, that of subject lecturer training.

12 Evaluating lecture comprehension

Christa Hansen and Christine Jensen

Abstract

This chapter focuses on the development of a listening test that will be used for placing students in intensive English classes or exempting them from further English language coursework. The test uses excerpts from actual university lectures and a short answer format to test more directly the listening skills students need to navigate in a U.S. university classroom. The chapter has three main sections: listening comprehension and lecture discourse theoretical considerations, a description of the format of the test based on such considerations, and statistical analysis of the performance of the test. Included in the statistics is the investigation of such issues as the effect of using both technical and non-technical lectures as listening stimuli, the effect of prior knowledge of topic on test performance, and performance of different proficiency levels on different types of questions. Recommendations are made for teaching and testing based on the findings.

Introduction

There have been two competing traditions in language testing, indirect and direct testing. Indirect tests "tap 'true' language performance obliquely or indirectly" (Henning 1987), predicting performance in language use situations. The discourse and tasks are designed to be generally accessible with a greater emphasis on skills and microskills. The tests are less natural, more contrived and are what many people call tests of general language proficiency. The emphasis is on reliability, getting the same results with different forms, different administrations, and being able to test any population. It is important to be able to say how one individual's performance compares to that of all the other individuals throughout the world who have taken the test. Examples of indirect tests of listening would be the Michigan Test of Aural Comprehension and Section A of the listening section of the TOEFL test.

Direct tests, on the other hand, measure language use in what Henning (1987) calls "real and uncontrived communicative situations." They emphasize attaining the proficiency to perform the particular tasks needed in real world situations. These tasks are specific to the language need or performance area. Direct tests emphasize macroskills or tasks rather than the skills or microskills emphasized in indirect testing. There is a great concern about content validity and positive washback; the test reinforces the principle that both teaching and learning should focus on what students really need to know. It is important to know how a particular individual will perform in the specific situation that will follow.

The question we wanted to address with our research was whether the comprehension of academic lectures can be measured directly using authentic discourse as stimuli. In order to do this we needed to study the literature, develop a test that would directly test the comprehension of academic lectures, evaluate the performance of this test, and investigate research questions related to using this type of test.

In the first third of this chapter, we look at a number of theoretical issues, including what listening comprehension is, the roles of short-term and long-term memory in decoding information, and how scripts and schemas are used to help interpret information that listeners take in. The discussion of theoretical considerations then turns to the features of lecture discourse.

The second major portion of the chapter describes theoretical considerations which guided decisions made about the format of the test we developed. That test, called the T–LAP for the Test of Listening for Academic Purposes, is described in detail.

At this point the chapter turns to a discussion of the research conducted on the performance of the test. The first phase of the research is designed to see whether the T–LAP satisfies reliability and validity criteria critical to fair and consistent testing. In the second phase of the research, issues are raised that might concern educators looking at using this type of test. These issues include what content areas should be used for lectures, whether a single test can be used to place students with a broad range of proficiency levels, and whether prior knowledge of a lecture topic will give some test takers an unfair advantage. We will discuss the implications of our findings for teaching listening comprehension.

Listening comprehension

When we look at listening comprehension from the perspective of what listeners do, we find that listening comprehension is not *a* process but the result of a series of processes. These processes include, but are not limited to, phoneme recognition, morpheme chunking, lexical selection, and creation of a referential meaning for words. It has been a matter of debate for those studying first language listening comprehension as to whether these processes are ordered in a serial fashion in which higher level decisions (i.e., clause or sentence level decisions) do not affect lower level decisions (phonemic or word level decisions), or whether there are interactions among the higher level and lower level processing decisions. (Carroll and Bever 1976; Fodor, Bever, and Garrett 1974; Forster 1979; Garrett 1978; Levelt 1978; Marlsen-Wilson 1976; Marlsen-Wilson and Tyler 1980) Evidence from first language research on listening comprehension (Marlsen-Wilson and Tyler 1980) and from error analysis of first and second language listening comprehension (Voss 1984) indicates that there is indeed interaction among the different processing levels. In fact, Voss concluded from the evidence he gathered in his error analysis work that the stretch governed by a single decoding decision could not be the segment, word, or even the tone group alone, nor is speech primarily processed through a sequential identification of segments and units of increasing size (1984: 119).

van Dijk and Kintsch (1983) have expanded upon the theme of interaction among the different listening processes in their development of a model of discourse comprehension in general, and listening comprehension specifically. They theorize that the stream of sound is held very shortly in the short-term memory where phoneme recognition and morpheme chunking is begun. It is there that listeners call on their knowledge of syntactic structure to organize the chunks into clauses. These clausal units are matched with information from the long-term memory to elaborate and verify the interpretation of the input.

As listeners process input, they develop a semantic representation of the text of the discourse in the long-term memory which van Dijk and Kintsch have labeled as the *textbase* (1983). The textbase is organized into semantic propositions with referential meaning. At the same time that they are creating a textbase, listeners create a unique *situational model* of the input, i.e., a cognitive representation of events, actions, and the people a situation is about, to make inferences from their knowledge structures to the referential propositions of the textbase. They do this by collecting information from the *scripts* or *schemas* from their knowledge base in the long-term memory. Scripts and schemas are knowledge organized around "predetermined stereotypical sequences of action that define well-known situations" (Schank and Abelson 1977: 41). In addition to stereotypical sequences of action, there are textual schemas, that is, knowledge of discourse-level conventions of a text; pragmatic schemas, knowledge of speech acts; contextual schemas, knowledge of the discourse situation; and rhetorical schemas, knowledge of the organizing conventions of a type of discourse. This configuration of listening comprehension takes into account the effect of a listener's real world knowledge and experience on a listening situation. Once semantic propositions are developed, the element of the proposition that connects it with the previous propositions is held in the short-term memory to aid in connecting clauses together for an interpretation of the whole text. As the textbase is expanded, propositions are fitted into the macrostructure, or overall structure, of the discourse in the long-term memory in an approximation of a coherent whole.

Listeners use two major coherence strategies in the listening comprehension process, *global* and *local coherence strategies* (van Dijk and Kintsch 1983). Local strategies are used to connect a clause to the preceding clause and to make sense of the discourse at the sentential level. Rather than connecting one sentence to the next, global strategies are used to define the macrostructure of the discourse. Global strategies are used to recognize the discourse theme or topic, to recognize the relationships among the major ideas of the discourse, and to recognize the overall structure of the discourse. The interplay of information between the global level and the local level is used in the local strategies to predict and to verify sentence connections. However, local strategies need the support of information from the global level to be able to interpret consecutive sentences within a discourse passage. Otherwise, language users build a textbase without reference to all the information relevant to an adequate understanding of the text. Interpretations created through local strategies are used to verify the validity of the global guesses. All of this guessing, interpreting and interaction at the global and local level happens without waiting for a clause to be completely interpreted or even stored in the short-term memory space.

The use of global coherence strategies is referred to as *top-down processing* of information by Voss (1984), van Dijk and Kintsch (1983), and Shohamy and Inbar (1988). Top-down processing allows the language user to set up expectations about structures, meanings of sentences and the whole text. The use of local coherence strategies is characterized as the main *bottom-up processing* strategy. In contrast to top-down processing, bottom-up processing consists of interpreting the sound stream word by word to build a representation of the discourse. Proficient language users use both strategies to understand a text. They begin to process the sound stream by using bottom-up strategies to identify words and build clauses; at the same time they build a global macrostructure to be used as a top-down device to interpret subsequent sentences (van Dijk and Kintsch 1983). Voss's (1984) research demonstrates that relying solely on bottom-up processing rather than using it in combination with top-down processing is a less effective listening comprehension strategy for native speakers and second language speakers. In fact, he concluded that "successful speech perception . . . depends on the application – as a final step – of top-down procedures assigning ultimate values to segments and other lower order units on the basis of hypotheses about longer stretches of speech" (1984: 119). Gary Buck's work on second language listening comprehension also supports van Dijk and Kintsch's model of discourse comprehension (1990). When he used introspective reporting techniques with second language listeners, he found that listeners have a different cognitive environment for listening to the same passage a second time. Cognitively, they are not listening to the same thing twice. This is certainly understandable in the light of what van Dijk and Kintsch have postulated about discourse processing. After listening to a passage for the first time, a listener's understanding of the discourse would be stored in the long-term memory in a propositional format rather than being stored verbatim in the memory. These propositions can be accessed to help create a situational model of the text for elaborating on the textbase that is being developed as they listen. This would allow listeners to use the propositions identified from the first time they listened to a passage to set up predictions and expectations of the direction of the text.

Lectures

Lectures are extended pieces of discourse that are delivered by one person to a group of people. They may range from an extemporaneous expostulation on a topic, to speaking from an outline or from detailed notes, to delivering memorized scripts or reading written scripts. Because academic lectures are rarely memorized and delivered or written and read, they contain features that have been labeled by Tannen (1982) as *oral* features, in contrast to features that predominate in written discourse. These features include the pauses, hesitancies, misspeaks, and disfluencies that reflect the spontaneity, fast pace and temporary nature of spoken discourse.

Spoken discourse is produced in spurts of language (Chafe 1979; Brown and Yule 1983), labeled as *idea units* by Chafe (1979). He defines an idea unit as having a single intonation contour followed by a pause. The idea units in lectures have a mean word count of 11 words, whereas the mean word count for idea units in conversations is 7 words (Chafe 1979). Idea units in lectures are expanded through the use of a number of different syntactic devices such as nominalizations, attributive adjectives, indirect questions, complement and restrictive relative clauses, adverbial phrases and prepositional phrases. Thus, lectures exhibit a greater degree of syntactic complexity and more literary vocabulary than is found in informal speech situations. These features are reflective of the planned nature of a lecture and the formality of the speaking occasion (Tannen 1982).

In a lecture situation, the communicative focus of speakers is on disseminating information to the audience. To facilitate the audience's understanding, speakers present the information in a structured fashion that follows a logical sequential argument structure. They use thematic redundancies, not only to emphasize important points in the lecture, but also to help the audience deal with the pace of the flow of information and as an aid to their memories. More information is encoded in an idea unit in a lecture than in conversational discourse, but less than in such written and read discourse as news broadcasts (Shohamy and Inbar 1988). Propositional density, the amount of information encoded in an idea unit, is a feature that is affected by the degree of planning by speakers and their attention to and awareness of the audience's ability to cope with the flow of information.

In most lecture situations, speakers do not have the opportunity to negotiate meaning and verify the communicative effectiveness of the discourse with the audience. In our survey of university classes (Jensen and Hansen, in progress), we found that the number of students in the class and the format of the class directly influences the amount of listener–speaker interaction. Only in small (20 students maximum) discussion-type classes are students encouraged to interact with the speaker and the material in an active manner. In classes with up to 50 students, the speakers often make time for students to ask clarifying questions during the lecture presentation. They also tailor their presentation to maintain the attention of their audience by relating the information that they are disseminating to popular topics of the day. In very large classes (more than 100 students) speakers field questions before and after the lecture, but they rarely include a question period during their presentation. To compensate for the lack of interaction between speaker and audience, speakers often use the pronouns *we* and *you* in their presentation of information in order to develop and enhance the audience's awareness of a shared context.

Speakers also compensate for the lack of interaction with the audience by using *meta-talk* and other discourse markers to signal topic changes in a lecture (Hansen 1991). Meta-talk is defined by Schiffrin (1980) as "talk about the talk." Meta-talk has referents that point to items in the text and verbs that name acts of speech. These expressions are used to indicate something that will be done to a piece of talk, for example: "I want to say a little bit about each of these allotropes in turn . . . " (Hansen 1991: 65). Meta-talk also includes the use of expressions which have an evaluative or directional function such as *I mean, for example* or *in fact*. Topic change is also signaled with pauses, change in viewpoint, change in time or place, topic titles, and such discourse markers as *on the other hand*.

To recap, lectures can be characterized as planned, message-oriented discourse delivered by one person to a group of people. There is a minimal amount of interaction between speakers and listeners. Lectures are syntactically complex and have a literary rather than a colloquial vocabulary. But they also contain the following *oral* features: redundancies, pauses, disfluencies, misspeaks and repetition of information. Gary Buck (1990) found that the normal speaking rates, pause structure and disfluencies of authentic oral discourse, i.e., Tannen's oral features, are what distinguish the listening trait from the reading trait in testing. This means that in order to separate statistically test takers' listening comprehension skill from their reading comprehension skill on a language proficiency test, the listening stimulus must have the features of oral discourse listed above. To present a lecture that has been scripted and read aloud in a listening comprehension teaching or testing situation does a disservice to the students. This is not the type of material that they will have to grapple with when they attend a lecture.

Question types

To help in the decision as to the most appropriate types of questions to use to evaluate students' comprehension of lectures, we studied the results of Powers's 1986 survey (see also Flowerdew, this volume), in which university lecturers gave their opinions as to the importance of various listening skills to students' successful academic achievement, and Richards's 1983 list of micro-skills needed for academic listening. Richards's taxonomy includes, among others, such skills as the ability to identify the purpose and scope of a lecture, the ability to recognize key lexical items related to a topic, and familiarity with different styles of lecturing. Not all of the micro-skills listed by Richards can be assessed by the use of questions. Some can only be taken into account by ensuring that students are exposed to different accents, speeds, registers, and lecture styles. It would not be appropriate to base an assessment of students' skills in lecture comprehension in the following areas even if these skills do affect their classroom performance: knowledge of classroom conventions, ability to follow different modes of lecturing and recognition of instructional/learner tasks. Other tasks like recognizing markers of cohesion and signals of discourse markers are micro-skills that listeners use to help them recognize ideas, themes, and relationships among ideas. These skills do not have to be directly assessed in proficiency testing, but may be appropriate for diagnostic testing or achievement testing.

The nine most important listening activities as identified by university lecturers in the Powers survey (1986) were:

1. identifying major themes or ideas of lectures
2. identifying relationships among major ideas in a lecture

3. identifying the topic of the lecture
4. retaining information through notetaking
5. retrieving information from notes
6. inferring relationships between information supplied in the lecture
7. comprehending key information presented in the lecture
8. following the spoken mode of the lecture
9. identifying supporting ideas and examples in the lecture.

The micro-skills from Richards's taxonomy that the lecturers rated as important for academic success were those that address a listener's understanding of the main points and supporting details of a lecture.

We wanted to ensure that the questions we developed would actually assess students' abilities to understand academic lectures. After studying the most important activities listed in Powers's survey and studying Richards's academic listening micro-skills, we incorporated what we know about the process of listening comprehension to make decisions about the most appropriate ways to assess comprehension of lectures. We decided that there are two major task areas, *global comprehension* and *local comprehension*, that would be appropriate for evaluating listeners' understanding of lectures. Global comprehension calls for understanding the major themes and topics of the lecture, whereas local comprehension focuses on understanding specific items within the lecture, such as identifying key terms or extracting information from key clauses.

The questions that we developed for use on this test have two objectives: to evaluate test takers' understanding of the lecture content and to assess their use of listening skills. We have developed two types of questions to assess students' abilities in these task areas, *global questions* and *detail questions*. From a lecture comprehension perspective, global questions are used to evaluate listeners' understanding of the major points in a lecture. Some of the skills listed in Powers and Richards that could be subsumed under this question type are identifying major themes or ideas, identifying purpose and scope of lecture, identifying topic of lecture and following topic development, identifying relationships among units within the discourse, and inferring relationships. The listening skills a test taker needs to answer these questions include the ability to synthesize information across clauses (or idea units as defined by Chafe 1979) in the lecture and the ability to identify the macrostructural items of the lecture.

In contrast to global questions, the comprehension focus of detail questions is on the listeners' ability to extract important details from the lecture. Listeners need to recognize key lexical items in regard to subject/topic, to deduce meaning of words from context, to identify supporting ideas and examples, and to comprehend key information. For this type of question listeners need to be able to extract information from within a clause (i.e., idea unit); detail questions do not call for synthesizing information across clauses. The detail questions that we have created do not include numerical details and names that are not directly related to the main topic because questions of this type were found by Shohamy and Inbar "to be unstable and serve no meaningful purpose as evaluation tools" (1988: 21).

Evaluating the comprehension of academic lectures

We believed that the comprehension of academic lectures should be measured directly. To evaluate better whether this was possible and how to do this in a testing situation, we taped introductory level university lectures and compared them to the audio-taped lectures used on the TOEFL (*Listening to TOEFL* 1989). We felt this study would also tell us whether we could use a commercial test for our purposes. Although the university lecturers we taped had different lecture styles, we found certain features to be common in their lectures. Lecturers restated or paraphrased key ideas two or three different times. They used pauses to give themselves or to give listeners time to organize material. Pauses were also used to indicate topic shifts (Hansen 1991). Hesitation words, disfluencies, and misspeaks typical of natural, conversational speech were features found in all of these lectures. Speakers used restatement, paraphrasing, pauses, pacing and a decreased syntactic complexity to control the density of propositions, as work by Shohamy and Inbar (1988) and Chafe (1982) would predict. When we examined examples of lectures that were used on TOEFL tests, we found that these lectures had been scripted and recorded. They lacked repetition and paraphrase; had the syntax of written discourse; and certainly lacked the pauses, misspeaks, and disfluencies which Buck (1990) identified as distinguishing the listening trait.

After comparing university lectures with scripted lectures and finding such distinct differences in the discourse, we decided it was essential not only to use a direct test but to use authentic lectures. We audiotaped class sessions in a variety of introductory level university classes in order to identify suitable topics. The lecture segments we chose to use in the T–LAP had certain features. These lectures were no longer than 10–15 minutes and could be condensed to 5 minutes by leaving out lengthy digressions or extra examples. They did not require prior knowledge of content or vocabulary and were not dependent on visual material. These segments were coherent as segments, exhibiting clear logic structures. Finally, there was an adequate amount of testable information in the pieces selected.

Once we had chosen lecture segments, we went back to the lecturers whose lectures we had taped and asked them to deliver the lecture in a recording session in a sound studio as they would in a class. We wanted the speaker to self-edit to retain the organization, types of examples, and discourse and delivery styles of the original lectures. In order to keep the discourse natural, we asked the lecturers not to use scripts or to memorize the material. We offered to serve as the student audience for any lecturers who seemed to want an audience to react to. We compared the original recorded material to the studio recorded material to see if they could maintain their original styles. We had to abandon recordings if they could not maintain their classroom intonation, pacing, relative level of formality, and use of examples to support explanation of new concepts.

In addition, we recognized the importance of providing context to enable listeners to activate the schemas they have available including situational, rhetorical, knowledge-based, experiential, and linguistic. We provide a situational context where the listeners are told, orally and in writing, that they are students attending a lecture in, for example, a chemistry class. We also tell them what lecture topic they will be listening to. This allows the listeners to set up expectations and to make predictions about the content and structure of the information they will hear based on their prior knowledge of the topic and experience with the structure of this type of discourse.

After listeners are given the situational context, they are given time to preview the questions that are written in the test booklets. This is done to replicate the experience students have coming into class with expectations about what will be important from what they have read in textbooks, and predictions about what they will hear based on what they have heard in earlier lectures. By setting the context and allowing listeners to preview questions, we also hope to facilitate top-down processing. This allows listeners to set up expectations about structures, meaning of sentences, and the whole lecture, a strategy that has been identified as being critical to final assignment of meaning in successful speech perception (Voss 1984).

What should listeners be asked to do to show they comprehend lectures? The TOEFL, for example, asks listeners to listen first to a mini-lecture and then hear single-sentence questions and select the correct multiple-choice answer from four written responses. However, to answer such multiple-choice items successfully, listeners must

1. recognize and store any important information from a mini-lecture as it is read
2. listen to a question
3. read four responses
4. refer back to the information stored in long-term memory to find the propositional information that answers the question

5. select the response that most closely matches the stored proposition
6. repeat the whole process for each question.

It is easy to see that the cognitive load involved in answering such questions within a matter of seconds is heavy; clearly, listeners who have good memories, are fast readers, or are strong in grammar would enjoy an advantage on this type of test. Additionally, this type of test does not allow listeners to give their understanding of the information in their own propositional formats.

Those who favor using multiple-choice style listening tests might point out that university content classes still use multiple-choice tests especially in large introductory lecture classes. However, students taking such tests have had a chance to (1) read the material, (2) hear the lecture, (3) take notes, and (4) study both text and notes. In that case, students are being tested on their ability to assimilate and store written and oral material and on their ability to retrieve information from memory. They need to rely heavily on reading skills both in preparing for the test and in taking the test itself. Such tests certainly do not test listening.

On the T–LAP, we decided to use short answer responses because this type of task would be more appropriate to their own real-life situation, a criterion set forth by Weir (1990: 24). Students answer the questions in real time, meaning they write their answers as they hear the information. Using real time prevents the test from being a memory test: listeners can answer either with the information as stated in the lecture or they can use their own propositional formats if the information has already been transferred to the long-term memory. Since the questions are answered in real time, the questions follow the chronology of the lecture.

In order to focus on the listeners' comprehension of the lecture, we use two types of questions, detail and global. These question types cover the two major task areas, local and global comprehension. We have listeners answer detail questions the first time they listen to a lecture; we reserve synthesizing questions for a second play through of the same lecture. Since work by Shohamy and Inbar (1988) shows that less proficient listeners will not be able to answer global questions unless they have extracted the answers to detail questions appropriately, it seems fairer to allow second language listeners to extract details before they are asked to answer global questions in an evaluative instrument used to test learners with a broad range of proficiency levels.

In addition, Buck's research shows that the first play through adds information to a listener's cognitive environment to set up more accurate prediction and interpretation on the second play through. However, this is not to suggest that local and global strategies are used separately. To answer a synthesizing question, listeners might first need to use local strategies to identify words and build clauses in order to start building a global macrostructure. A continuing interplay of information from the global and local levels is used to recognize details, set up predictions about the topic, and validate those predictions. The information cannot be obtained by simply pulling out transitions and cohesive markers. Nor will using sentential markers to combine the ideas in two consecutive sentences be enough. The interplay is more complex. Recognizing the topic will make recognition of detail level information more accurate, while the addition of specific details to the textbase will make further predictions of the structure and direction and relationships of global structure more accurate.

The T–LAP test

The Test of Listening for Academic Purposes (T–LAP), which we have developed, has two parts: an academic and a non-academic part. The first part, the non-academic section, is a series of 3–4 dialogues ranging from 0.5–1.5 minutes in length; each series is based on a central theme such as buying something, renting an apartment, or planning a trip. The responses are information transfer or short answer.

The academic part of the test, which we are focusing on in this chapter, has two 3–5 minute lectures, one from a technical discipline and one from a non-technical discipline. Before the listeners hear each lecture, the context is set orally and in writing; they are told the field of study and the topic of the lecture. Then, time is allowed for them to preview the questions before they hear the lecture. The first time through the lecture, the test takers answer detail questions; on the second time through, they answer global questions. They respond with short answers written in real time. These answers are scored by trained raters using an extensive answer key, one that essentially lists the possible answers or types of answers and assigns 0, 1, or 2 points of credit.

The population

The T–LAP is being developed for a population of students preparing for university course work in the United States. The T–LAP will be part of a battery of tests – reading, composition, grammar paraphrase, and listening – used to exempt students from language study or to place them in appropriate levels of language classes in an intensive English program. This test was developed to replace the Michigan-style test currently being used since that test is really a test of oral grammar, and since it does not distinguish well among listeners at the upper end. Students who are able

TABLE 1. TEST POPULATION IN GROUPS BY MICHIGAN-STYLE TEST AND
APPROXIMATE TOEFL RANGES

Group	n	Michigan style test score range	Approximate TOEFL score range
Group 0	12	0–100	33–43
Group 1	14	101–119	43–46
Group 2	31	120–139	45–50
Group 3	86	140–166	50–56
Group 4	92	167–200	55–60

to pass that Michigan-style test are often not able to understand class-room directions or to follow academic lectures.

This population includes students from about 65 countries. These students are undergraduates and graduates as well as students admitted for language study only. The range of listening proficiency levels represented in the population of students used for this research project is shown in Table 1. The table shows the number of students in each proficiency level, the score ranges on the Michigan-style test currently used to place students, and approximate TOEFL ranges.

The placement in the groups is based on the Michigan-style test scores. Since the Michigan and the TOEFL do not separate listeners into the same groups, the TOEFL score ranges overlap. The TOEFL ranges were provided to give some idea of what the group levels represent.

Research questions

The research we conducted had two major phases. The first phase focused on whether a listening test using authentic discourse could satisfy reliability and validity requirements.

1. Will test takers get consistent scores no matter when they take the test?
2. Will this type of test discriminate well among proficiency levels?

The second phase was designed to look at specific concerns related to using a content-based test.

3. Will there be a significant difference in the difficulty level of the technical and non-technical lectures for our population?
4. Will this test work to separate out upper level listeners? Can a single test be used to test students with such a broad range of proficiencies?
5. Will prior knowledge of a topic give some test takers an unfair advantage?

TABLE 2. DESCRIPTIVE STATISTICS FOR THE T–LAP TEST

	Mean % correct scores	S.D.	Reliability
Total test	79.83	19.13	.92
Non-academic	76.34	16.18	.88
Total academic	49.55	19.10	.87
History	52.13	23.69	.79
Chemistry	47.82	19.60	.81

Methods

We administered the T–LAP to a population of 235 students enrolled in the intensive English program at the end of the spring semester in 1991. The test was administered within two weeks of the end-of-semester proficiency test so that we could compare results to those on the Michigan-style test.

Results: Phase 1

The test was analyzed using an SPSS program. The descriptive statistics for the test are given in Table 2. Results are given for the whole test, the non-academic and the academic sections, and the non-technical (history) and technical (chemistry) lectures which make up the academic section.

Reliability

We needed to know whether this test would rank students consistently; i.e., whether students with high proficiency levels would receive high scores. The Cronbach's alpha for the whole test (63 items) was .92, well above the .80 often used to demonstrate strong reliability. This indicates that the test is performing extremely well. The alphas are lower for the individual subtests, which is not surprising since alphas decrease as the number of items decreases. The lecture portion alone (25 items) had an alpha of .87. Even the lowest coefficient, .79 for the history lecture, is more than satisfactory for a subtest with 10 items.

Validity

The use of authentic lectures with response tasks that match those that successful students need to use gives the T–LAP strong content validity (i.e., it tests directly what students need to be able to do). However, tests must also satisfy the requirement of construct validity. The test should

TABLE 3. STANDARDIZED DISCRIMINANT
FUNCTION COEFFICIENTS FOR ACADEMIC
AND NON-ACADEMIC SUBTESTS

Subtest	Function coefficient
Non-academic	.51971
Academic:	
History	.39248
Chemistry	.43573

Note: One significant discriminant function
$U = 42$, x^2 (18) = 223.23, $p = .0000$ was
obtained.

TABLE 4. STRUCTURE COEFFICIENTS OF
NON-ACADEMIC AND ACADEMIC SUBTESTS

Subtest	Structure coefficient
Non-academic	.78165
Academic:	
History	.72149
Chemistry	.71282

assign scores consistent with language proficiency, separating out the
different language levels.

We ran a discriminant analysis to look at how the non-academic
subtest, the history lecture, and the chemistry lecture separated out
listeners. To do this, the listening proficiency groups were defined as
described in Table 1. Discriminant analysis was used to determine
whether the T–LAP subtests predict group membership; in other words,
would listeners from group 1 be assigned to that group based on scores
on the new test. The discriminant function coefficients showed that each
of the subtests contributes significantly to separating out the groups
(Table 3). This is indicated by the positive signs and the fact that the
coefficients are relatively closely grouped.

Structure coefficients were run (Table 4). These coefficients are
meaningful if they are positive and greater than or equal to .30, showing
that there is a strong correlation between the scores on the individual
subtests and the composite which is the score which best assigns
membership to the correct level. The non-academic subtest contributes
the most to separating out the groups while the chemistry lecture

TABLE 5. MEAN DISCRIMINANT FUNCTION
SCORES BY LANGUAGE PROFICIENCY GROUP

Group	Mean discriminant function score
0	−2.92
1	−1.97
2	−1.22
3	−0.09
4	1.18

contributes the least as the descending order of structure coefficients indicates. There is not a great difference in their relative contributions; these magnitudes may reflect no more than the difference in the number of items in the subtests.

Finally, when group centroids were run, they showed that groups were being separated out magnificently. The group centroids should increase as the proficiency level goes up, and there should be approximately the same distance between each of the neighboring centroids. Not only is the directionality correct (Table 5), but there is maximum separation between levels.

The T–LAP satisfied reliability and validity requirements at a very high level. We are satisfied that we can measure listening comprehension directly using authentic discourse as the stimulus.

Results: Phase 2

There are other questions raised by having a content-based test with authentic discourse. In general terms, these questions address these areas: What content areas should be used? Will this type of test better separate out upper level listeners? Will a test with detail and global questions be useable for a population with such a broad range of abilities or will low level listeners be disadvantaged? Will the specific content of lectures give students with prior knowledge an unfair advantage on the test.

Technical vs. non-technical lectures

Since our students represent around 50 different majors every semester, it was, of course, not possible to develop tests for each discipline. Instead, each T–LAP test form will have two lectures. We elected to use a technical and a non-technical lecture in each T–LAP as a result of a survey of our population which showed that of the students with

TABLE 6. MEAN PERCENTAGE CORRECT SCORES ON HISTORY AND
CHEMISTRY LECTURES FOR PROFICIENCY GROUPS

	History		*Chemistry*	
	Mean	*S.D.*	*Mean*	*S.D.*
Low proficiency[1]	38	21	38	17
$n = 119$				
High proficiency[1]	66	16	58	16
$n = 114$				
Total group	52	24	48	20
$n = 233$[2]				

Note:
[1]Groups divided by Michigan-style test scores. Low proficiency = below 50th
percentile, High proficiency = above 50th percentile.
[2]2 cases rejected because of missing data.

declared majors, 53% were in technical fields and 47% in non-technical
fields.

As we piloted the tests, we wanted to see whether there would be a
significant difference in the way our population would score on the non-
technical and technical sections. This particular test form had a history
and a chemistry lecture. In addition, we wanted to see whether there
would be a difference in the way high and low proficiency students
would perform on the two lectures since some believe that technical
material will be less accessible. To compare the two sections, we translated the mean scores for the subtests to percentages. When the mean
scores for the total group are translated to percentages, the total group
scored 52% on the history lecture and only 48% on the chemistry
lecture, a difference of 4% (Table 6). This was a significant difference
(.001). The history lecture was easier than the chemistry lecture for the
group as a whole.

After looking at how the whole group performed on the two lectures,
we divided the test takers into high and low proficiency groups by their
scores on the Michigan-style test. As Table 6 shows, the low group
had a mean percentage correct of 38 for both lectures while the high
proficiency group went from a mean of 66 on the history lecture to one
of 58 on the chemistry lecture. The low group finds the two lectures
equally difficult while the upper group finds the history lecture easier.
The sharp contrast in the performance of the two groups can be seen
graphically in Figure 1.

To test whether this difference in the change for the two proficiency
groups was significant, we ran a MANOVA (Table 7). The results

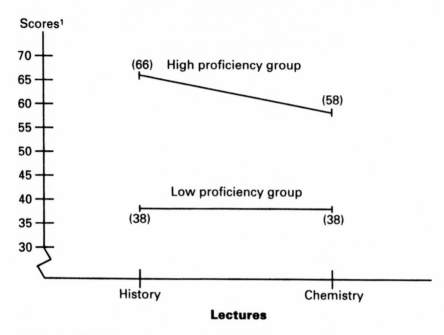

Figure 1   *Graphic representation of change in performance on history and chemistry lectures for low and high proficiency groups*

(p = .002) show that there is less than .2% probability that this difference would happen by chance.

Since the means for the two lectures are the same for the low group, it is important to ask whether a floor effect is involved. In other words, since the same test is being administered to persons with a broad range of proficiency levels, are the questions on the academic lectures so difficult that the low group could not answer them? One way to determine whether this is the case is to look at the range of scores, represented in the standard deviations shown in Table 6, for the low and high proficiency groups. The standard deviations for the low group for the two lectures (21 and 17) are larger than those for the high group (16 and 16). These large standard deviations for the low groups for both lectures indicate that these lectures do elicit a range of performance across the low group; it is safe to assume that there was not a floor effect.

The drop in scores on the chemistry test by the high proficiency group needs to be investigated further since other factors could have been involved. The chemistry subtest is the last on the test, and while the whole test takes less than 35 minutes, fatigue could have been a factor.

[1] Mean percentage scores from Table 6.

TABLE 7. TEST OF SIGNIFICANCE ON CHANGE IN PERFORMANCE ON
HISTORY AND CHEMISTRY LECTURES FOR LOW AND HIGH PROFICIENCY
GROUPS

	SS	*DF*	*MS*	*F*	*p*
Subtest	2007.71	1	2007.71	11.26	.001
Proficiency × subtest	1708.29	1	1708.29	9.58	.002
Error	41190.97	231	178.32		

TABLE 8. SYNTACTIC ANALYSIS OF CHEMISTRY AND HISTORY LECTURES
(HANSEN, IN PROGRESS)

	History lecture	*Chemistry lecture*
Words	377	400
Syllables	580	598
T-units	26	23
Sentence nodes	55	49
Prepositional phrases	51	50
Modals	7	1
Present tense	15	31
Present progressive tense	5	2
Past tense	25	2
Future tense	1	0
Present passive tense	1	0

However, if that were the case it would be logical to assume that
the lower proficiency group would also be affected by fatigue. One of the
areas we are looking at more closely is that of relative syntactical
complexity of the text for the two lectures. As Table 8 shows, the
lectures are relatively equivalent in overall length – 377 words to 400
words, T-units, sentence nodes and prepositional phrases, indicating
that syntactic complexity of the text is not a factor in the difference in
performance for the two groups. Interestingly enough, the main area of
deviation in regard to syntax shows up in the verb tenses; the history
lecture has a more sophisticated verb tense system. This certainly does
not explain why the chemistry lecture is more difficult for the proficient
listeners.

Once the element of syntactical differences had been eliminated from
consideration, we looked more closely at the vocabulary content of the
two lecture texts and found that the chemistry lecture featured a more
field-specific vocabulary than the history lecture. This may be the feature
that distinguishes the two lectures.

TABLE 9. MEAN PERCENTAGE CORRECT SCORES ON DETAIL AND GLOBAL
QUESTIONS FOR PROFICIENCY GROUPS

	Detail questions		Global questions	
	Mean	S.D.	Mean	S.D.
Low proficiency[1] $n = 119$	41	17	33	21
High proficiency[1] $n = 114$	63	15	60	18
Total group $n = 233$[2]	52	19	46	24

Note:
[1]Groups divided by Michigan-style test scores. Low proficiency = below 50th
 percentile, High proficiency = above 50th percentile.
[2]2 cases rejected because of missing data.

TABLE 10. TEST OF SIGNIFICANCE ON CHANGE IN PERFORMANCE ON
DETAIL AND GLOBAL QUESTIONS FOR LOW AND HIGH PROFICIENCY
GROUPS

	SS	DF	MS	F	p
Subtest	2949.05	1	2949.05	17.01	.000
Proficiency × subtest	721.15	1	721.15	4.16	.043
Error	40039.10	231	173.33		

Detail vs. global questions

In light of Voss's (1984) and van Dijk and Kintsch's (1983) work
showing that proficient language users employ top-down processing
skills, it would be reasonable to expect more proficient language users to
perform better than less proficient language users on global questions,
which would mean listeners with high proficiency would be separated
out better.

To look at whether our data bore this out, we again divided the test
takers into high and low proficiency groups by scores on the Michigan-
style test. We compared the performance of the two proficiency groups
on the detail and global questions by examining mean percentage correct
scores. Not surprisingly, the high group outscored the low group by 60
to 33 on global questions (Table 9).

But did this really mean that global questions are functioning to
separate out the high level listeners? Or, will there be a parallel difference on detail questions? The performance of the high group is quite

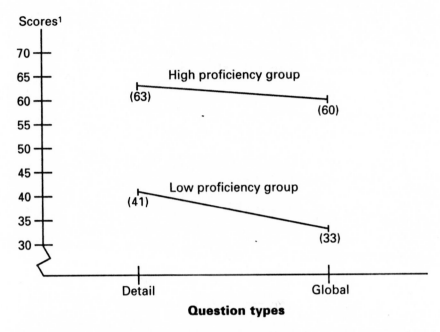

Figure 2   Graphic representation of change in performance on detail and global questions for low and high proficiency groups

stable on detail and global questions, decreasing only 3 percentage points, from 63 to 60. This comparison is displayed graphically in Figure 2. The change in performance for the low proficiency group is much sharper, dropping from 41 on detail questions to 33 on global.

The graphic representation makes it clear that the performance of the two groups does not remain parallel from detail to global questions. It appears that the global questions do in fact separate out the high group; that difference in the change of performance was significant at the 0.43 level (Table 10).

In summary, high proficiency listeners do better than low proficiency listeners on global questions. This is also true for detail questions, but the relative difference is greater on global questions. This would suggest that there is a difference in the processing strategies for high and low proficiency listeners.

In the next phase of our research, we are looking at the processing strategies used by the five different proficiency levels to extract information from lectures. Preliminary evidence from that research shows that low level listeners rely much more heavily on verbatim response

---

[1] Mean percentage scores from Table 9.

patterns, meaning they answer with the exact words used in the lecture. Global questions, however, call for synthesizing information across clauses, and, therefore, verbatim response patterns are less successful on those questions. In order to synthesize information successfully, listeners need to give propositional answers; in other words, these answers are in the listener's own words. This is a task that the high group is much more successful at. Interestingly enough, high proficiency listeners are also able to use propositional answers successfully in response to detail questions.

A second concern we had was whether this type of test could be used for the broad range of listening proficiencies represented in our population. Since it separated out the upper level listeners, would that mean it was not accessible to the low level listeners? A review of the group centroids given in Table 5 shows that, in fact, the separation of the lowest two groups is exactly what we would hope for: it is similar to the separation between other groups and certainly not a larger separation. The test was not relatively more difficult for these low groups.

Prior knowledge

One of the chief concerns that people have about content-based tests is whether the test will be biased in favor of listeners with prior knowledge. To test the effect of prior knowledge of a lecture topic on the performance of a test taker, we asked all the test takers to indicate whether or not they had studied the lecture topics before. Of the 235 test takers, 30 reported prior knowledge of the history lecture. In contrast, only 8 reported they had studied the chemistry topic.

To test the effect of prior knowledge of the history topic (Coronado's exploration of the New World), we ran multiple linear regressions which used the part of the test not being examined as a measure of listening comprehension proficiency. To determine whether prior knowledge helped to predict scores on the history subtest, the first step was to covary or control for the amount of variance that is accounted for by the performance on the remainder of the test. The performance on the rest of the test accounts for 48% of the variance (see R^2 in Table 11). When prior knowledge is added in as a predictor of performance on the history subtest, the R^2 does not change, indicating that prior knowledge does not have a predictive value. The finding that prior knowledge of the history topic did not improve listening scores was reassuring especially since we have a fairly large representation of Spanish speakers.

The same procedure was followed for the chemistry lecture. Again the measure of listening comprehension predicted the chemistry subtest scores. However, for the eight listeners reporting prior knowledge of

TABLE 11. MULTIPLE REGRESSION ANALYSIS OF PRIOR KNOWLEDGE ON HISTORY LECTURE

Step	Variable(s) entered	b	Beta	R	R^2	R^2 change
I	Total test minus history	.1992**	.6945**	.69	.48**	
II	Total test minus history	.1996**	.6960**			
	Prior knowledge of history	−0.0488	−0.0052	.69	.48**	.00

*$p \leq .05$, **$p \leq .01$

TABLE 12. MULTIPLE REGRESSION ANALYSIS OF PRIOR KNOWLEDGE ON CHEMISTRY LECTURE

Step	Variable(s) entered	b	Beta	R	R^2	R^2 change
I	Total test minus chemistry	.2443**	.6544**	.65	.43	
II	Total test minus chemistry	.2343**	.6283**			
	Prior knowledge of chemistry	2.5087**	.1557**	.67	.45**	.02

*$p \leq .05$, **$p \leq .01$

the chemistry lecture (allotropes of carbon), prior knowledge was a significant factor in their performance of the section. The R^2 change of .02 indicates that prior knowledge added 2% to the prediction of the performance on that subtest (Table 12). Somewhat surprisingly, that amount of change is significant.

However, the fact that there were only eight cases, and of those eight listeners seven were speakers of Arabic, makes the finding difficult to interpret. To know whether this finding is significant, we will need to collect a larger number of cases with prior knowledge of that topic. This will allow us to see if the particular language grouping is a factor and to find out why in this case there were so few self-reported cases of prior knowledge of a relatively basic chemistry topic. We should also find out whether test takers have studied the topic in English.

Our strongest evidence on the influence of prior knowledge, a group of 30 out of the total of 235 test takers with prior knowledge of the history topic, suggests that prior knowledge is not a factor in performance on the subtest involved. However, the fact that the evidence is mixed at least suggests to us that the exact underlying factors haven't been pinpointed.

Conclusions

The T–LAP was developed for the purpose of placing non-native speakers of English into listening courses in a college preparatory intensive English program. The final outcome of the listening course-work is that students will be operating in English-only university classrooms. The design problem we grappled with as test constructors was creating an instrument that would directly measure listening comprehension in replicated real world situations and would also reliably place students across the spectrum of language proficiency in the appropriate intensive English coursework. In the secondary phase of our research on this project we looked at such issues as performance on technical and non-technical lectures, performance across proficiency levels on different question types and the effect of prior knowledge of topic on test performance.

In order to measure listening comprehension directly in lecture situations, we used segments from actual university lectures for the listening stimuli, we set the situational context for the students before they listened to the lectures to replicate the classroom experience, and we used a short answer format to allow students to provide answers in their own words rather than recognizing answers developed by the test makers. Detail and global questions were used to assess students' understanding of the lecture. Detail questions focus on the important supporting information in a lecture and require listeners to extract information from within clauses; global questions focus on the main ideas and relationship of ideas·in the lecture and require listeners to synthesize information across clauses. All of these considerations and decisions indicate that the test has high *content validity*; it directly measures students' listening comprehension proficiency in regard to academic lectures.

However, as Henning pointed out, content validity, which requires a diversity of items and comprehensive coverage of the content, often conflicts with the reliability of internal consistency of an instrument because this form of reliability depends upon the homogeneity of items (1987). The first question we addressed in our assessment of the test is whether the T–LAP is a reliable testing instrument. Does it rank students with high listening proficiency skills high and students with low skills as low? The statistical evidence (Tables 2, 3 and 5) has borne this out. It is reliable, parts and whole. This indicates that we have found a balance between content validity and internal reliability.

After looking at the reliability of the instrument as a whole, we investigated a number of questions about the test content. We had elected to use lectures from technical disciplines and non-technical disciplines on the T–LAP because our population almost equally divided between these two general areas. This would ensure that the test would not give preference to students in non-technical fields over students in technical fields, or vice versa. The different statistics that we ran on the lecture sections of the test gave us a mixed picture as to the performance of the technical (chemistry) lecture and the non-technical (history) lecture. The Cronbach alphas for the subsections of the test show the chemistry lecture (.81) as more reliable than the history lecture (.79), but the structure coefficients identify the history lecture (.72) as more important for identifying group membership than the chemistry lecture (.71). Nevertheless, the lack of magnitude of these differences indicates that the two lectures are equivalent. Interestingly enough, the chemistry lecture proved to be harder than the history lecture with the performance of the high proficiency group marking that difference between the two lectures. The source of the difference in performance across the high proficiency group has not been identified yet. Because the two lectures have comparable syntactic complexity except for the amount of variety of verb tenses, syntax does not seem to be the source of difference between the two lectures. Although the lectures have similar syntactic complexity, the chemistry lecture features more field-specific vocabulary than the history lecture. This may even be a factor in the effect of prior knowledge of topic on performance on the lectures.

The other major area that we looked at in regard to the test is students' performance on detail and global questions. This area of research directly addresses the theories behind the construction of this type of test. Our assumption, based on previous work by Voss (1984) and Shohamy and Inbar (1988), was that high proficiency students would perform better on the global questions than low proficiency students, and this assumption was validated. High proficiency students performed well on both types of questions, while low proficiency students' performance dropped dramatically from the detail to the global questions. They did not maintain the same level of performance in relation to the high group on the two types of questions. We submit this as evidence that global questions are effective in spreading out test takers at the high end of the proficiency scale, a design problem that we needed to address with the new test. We also feel that it is indirect evidence that low proficiency students rely heavily on bottom-up processing skills and do not yet know how to process across clauses. We found that low proficiency students generally rely on extracting information from the text and recording it verbatim rather than formulating a response in their own words. This appears to be a factor in their performance on the test. When we looked at students' responses, we found that they can successfully use propositional responses for both detail and global questions, but verbatim responses are generally not a successful strategy for answering global questions, that is, questions that call for synthesizing information across clauses. In contrast to low proficiency students, high proficiency students can synthesize information across clauses, indirect evidence that high proficiency students use top-down processing strategies in listening.

What are the implications of our findings for testing and teaching listening comprehension, specifically of lecture material? The first thing we can conclude is that it is possible and even efficacious to use authentic lecture material as the listening stimuli. The information we have about the performance of the test, and therefore the performance of the test takers, gives credence to the validity constructs and the psychological theories that we used in the construction of the test. Lecture comprehension requires much more from a listener than just to recognize phonemes and to understand information at the essential level. Listeners also need to be able to recognize the macrostructural items in a text, synthesize information across clauses and be able to put lecture information into their own words. Teachers and testers of listening comprehension must be willing to expand the scope of the amount of information and the type of information that students will be exposed to and tested on. Buck's 1990 finding about natural speech, making listening a trait clearly separable from reading, reinforces the need to provide students with material that features natural speech, not contrived written and read discourse. Test takers' performances on this test indicate that they can handle natural speech, extended discourse and technical and non-technical lectures, even at the lowest level of proficiency. What this means for teaching listening comprehension is that students from all proficiency levels should be exposed to natural speech and to extended discourse as a regular part of their listening curriculum. The curriculum should work on developing listeners' strategies to comprehend extended discourse. In order for listeners to comprehend extended discourse effectively, they need to use global and local coherence strategies, and both top-down and bottom-up processing strategies. Teaching students to integrate information culled from global strategies with the detail information from local strategies should be an integral part of a listening comprehension curriculum.

Acknowledgements

We would like to acknowledge the efforts of Dr. Glasnapp's EPR 921 class from Fall, 1991 in helping us with the statistical analyses for our research. We are grateful for the extra work of Monica Castator, Sandy Gahn and Jeff Townsend. We would especially like to express our appreciation to Jeff Townsend for his work on this project. His help on the interpretation of the results of the analyses was invaluable.

References

Brown, G., and G. Yule. 1983. *Discourse Analysis*. New York: Cambridge University Press.

Buck, G. 1990. The testing of second language listening comprehension. Ph.D. dissertation, University of Lancaster, England.

Carroll, J. M., and T. G. Bever. 1976. Sentence comprehension: a study in the relation of knowledge to perception. In *The Handbook of Perception, Vol. 5, Language and Speech*, E. C. Carterette and M. P. Friedman (Eds.). New York: Academic Press.

Chafe, W. L. 1979. The flow of thought and the flow of language. In *Syntax and Semantics* 12, T. Given (Ed.), 159–83. New York: Academic Press.

1982. Integration and involvement in speaking, writing and oral literature. In *Spoken and Written Language: Exploring Orality and Literacy*, D. Tannen (Ed.), 35–53. Norwood, N.J.: Ablex.

Dijk, T. A. van, and W. Kintsch. 1983. *Strategies of Discourse Comprehension*. New York: Academic Press.

Fodor, J. A., T. G. Bever, and M. F. Garrett. 1974. *The Psychology of Language*. New York: McGraw-Hill.

Forster, K. 1979. Levels of processing and the structure of the language processor. In *Sentence Processing: Psycholinguistic Studies Presented to Merrill Garrett*, W. E. Cooper, and E. C. T. Walker (Eds.). Hillsdale, N.J.: LEA.

Garrett, M. F. 1978. Word and sentence perception. In *Handbook of Sensory Physiology, Vol. VIII, Perception*, R. Held, H. W. Leibowity, and H.-L. Teuber (Eds.). Berlin: Springer Verlag.

Hansen, C. 1991. Topics in a lecture: how does a linguistic analysis compare to the professor's and students' notes? Unpublished Master's thesis, University of Kansas, Lawrence, Kansas.

In progress. Syntactic analysis of T–LAP lectures.

Henning, G. 1987. *A Guide to Language Testing*. Cambridge: Newbury House.

Jensen C., and C. Hansen. In progress. Survey of university classes.

Levelt, W. J. M. 1978. A survey of studies in sentence perception: 1970–1976. In *Studies in the Perception of Language*, W. J. M. Levelt and G. B. Flores D'Arcais (Eds.). New York: Wiley.

Listening to TOEFL. 1989. 45–60. Princeton, N.J.: Educational Testing Service.

Marlsen-Wilson, W. D. 1976. Linguistic descriptions and psychological assumptions in the study of sentence perception. In *New Approaches to the Study of Language*, R. J. Wales, and E. C. T. Walker (Eds.). Amsterdam: North-Holland.

Marlsen-Wilson, W. D., and L. K. Tyler. 1980. The temporal structure of spoken language understanding. *Cognition* 8: 1–71.

Powers, D. E. 1986. Academic demands related to listening skills. *Language Testing* 3 (1): 1–38.

Richards, J. C. 1983. Listening comprehension: approach, design, procedure. *TESOL Quarterly* 17 (2): 219–240.

Schank, R. C., and R. P. Abelson. 1977. *Scripts, Plans, Goals and Understanding*. Hillsdale, N.J.: Erlbaum.

Schiffrin, D. 1980. Meta-talk: organizational and evaluative brackets in discourse. *Sociological Inquiry* 50: 199–236.

Shohamy, E., and O. Inbar. 1988. Construct validation of listening comprehension tests: the effect of text and question type. ERIC Doc. No.
ED296594.

Tannen, D. 1982. The oral literate continuum in discourse. In *Spoken and
Written Language: Exploring Orality*, E. Tannen (Ed.), 1–16.

Voss, B. 1984. *Slips of the Ear. Investigations into the Speech Perception
Behavior of German Speakers of English*. Tubingen: Narr.

Weir, C. 1990. *Communicative Language Testing*. Great Britain: Prentice Hall
International.

13 Training lecturers for international audiences

Tony Lynch

Abstract

The growing number of non-native students at English-medium universities and colleges raises the issue of how such institutions can adjust to the needs of an international clientele. This chapter explores the implications of research for the (re)training of subject lecturers at institutions now catering for an ethnically and linguistically more diverse population. It discusses findings from listening comprehension research, lecture discourse analysis in general and second language lecture studies in particular, and argues that much of the available research has focussed on spoken discourse as input. *Drawing on research into native/non-native classroom communication and on the lecturing methodology literature, the chapter suggests that programmes to train lecturers for international audiences should also raise awareness of the need to make clear the sociocultural rules of the host academic context and of the benefits of adjusting lecture presentation to increase the degree of interaction* between *speaker and audience. The importance for international classes of two particular aspects of lecturer performance is discussed: the selection of culturally accessible examples when giving explanations and the management of audience questions. The chapter concludes that methodological programmes of the sort illustrated here would bring benefits for international and home students alike.*

Introduction

Over the last two decades political, educational and economic circumstances have led to an increase in the number of international students attending L2-medium courses in tertiary education institutions, not only in the principal English-speaking countries (Australia, Britain, Canada, New Zealand and the United States) but also, for example, in the European countries participating in the ERASMUS and TEMPUS exchange schemes. In Britain, a combination of demographic and economic factors – a fall in the native university-age population and the raising of overseas student fees to a level several times those for home

269

students – has meant that universities and colleges are keen to attract students from other countries. While provision is generally made to help international students adjust to novel demands on their language and study skills, little attention appears to have been paid to ways of (re)training lecturers to take into account the particular needs of non-native listeners. The purpose of this chapter is to make practical suggestions for such training, based on a range of applied linguistic and educational studies: listening comprehension research, lecture discourse analysis, work on native/non-native interaction modifications, L2 lecture comprehension and lecturing methodology.

Listening comprehension research

The salient feature of research into listening comprehension processes over the last 15 years or so (for reviews see, for example, Flores d'Arcais and Jarvella 1983; Brown and Yule 1983; Garrod 1986; Dunkel 1991) has been an increasing awareness of the importance of elements beyond the text in determining the listener's degree of success in understanding the speaker's meaning. As in the case of native language comprehension research, L2 listening research surveys draw on a wide range of scientific fields; to take two representative examples, Nagle and Sanders (1986) refer to work in second language acquisition, memory and information processing, and Rost (1990) additionally reviews findings from reading education, L1 speech education, L1 acquisition, cognitive science, language pathology and artificial intelligence. In short, work on listening is now multi-disciplinary. A second common element is the rejection of linear characterisations of the listening process. Rost (1990) criticises the step-by-step comprehension models proposed by Clark and Clark (1977) and Demyankov (1983); Nagle and Sanders emphasise the need for any model of listening to allow for the reprocessing of information, for the various components of the model to "talk together" (Schlesinger 1977: 176). This interconnectedness is a point underlined by a number of contributors to this volume.

Figure 1 below sketches these two aspects of current views of listening comprehension. Firstly, it highlights the fact that the listening process draws on multiple sources of information – schematic knowledge and context having at least as important a role as knowledge of the L2 system. Secondly, the direction of the arrows leading to "comprehension" underlines the potential co-occurrence of top-down, expectation-driven processing and bottom-up, data-driven processing.

In this perspective "context" – including physical setting, speaker(s), listener(s) and co-text – has important implications for research into listening. "Any model of how people come to understand instances of spoken language will have to take into account the definable features

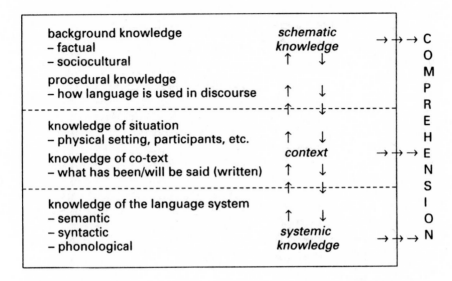

Figure 1   Information sources in comprehension (Anderson and Lynch 1988: 13)

of the events and the participants where language is used" (Rost 1990: 7). One of the points I will be making in this chapter is that research into L2 lectures may have concentrated too narrowly on the language dimension and given too little weight to the contributions of background knowledge and context to the comprehension process.

Lecture discourse analysis

The empirical data on which assumptions about "typical" features of lectures are based have been restricted, in three senses. Firstly, as Flowerdew (this volume) comments, the sources cited with great regularity – e.g., Cook 1975 and Murphy and Candlin 1979 – rely to some degree on the approach and terminology of Sinclair and Coulthard's (1975) study of British secondary school classroom discourse. Secondly, as Olsen and Huckin (1990) point out, many of the current lecture discourse analytical studies are unpublished dissertations, making them relatively inaccessible to non-British readers in particular. Thirdly, they are based on a small number of lectures and, therefore, illustrate a limited range of content areas. Even in a recent paper critical of such narrowness, Strodt-Lopez (1991) bases an alternative analysis on just nine lectures – the equivalent of two or three mornings in a typical undergraduate timetable.

More generally, Strodt-Lopez (1991) criticises the prescriptive nature of applied linguistic studies of lectures, arguing that they are primarily concerned with tallying discourse markers and depict an essentially uniform thematic structure (lecture–exposition–episode–move). She claims that there is much less homogeneity in real-life lectures than appears to be the case on the evidence of the regularly cited sources. On the other hand, the more diffuse style of lecturing found in Strodt-Lopez's data – in particular, the asides, digressions and regular "annotations" – might be more typical of the humanities and social sciences sampled in her study than of the fields investigated by, for example, Murphy and Candlin (engineering) and Cook (soil science) and taken as canonical in the subsequent literature.[1] Strodt-Lopez makes two valuable points: (1) that analysts should be willing to see each lecture on its own merits, rather than assuming it will fit a theoretical mould, and (2) that it is essential to familiarise the "uninitiated" non-native listener with the interpretive strategies that lecturers assume and that native students may use. I will come back to the issue of "initiation" in my final section.

Native/non-native classroom interaction

Although the lecture theatre and the language classroom are superficially distinct communicative settings, their common didactic purpose makes it worth examining the literature on native-speaker/non-native-speaker (NS/NNS) classroom interaction for potentially helpful insights into how lecturers can improve their chances of being understood. For our present discussion, it is important to recall that the focus of research into NS/NNS modifications made in the interest of comprehensibility has shifted from linguistic *input* ("Foreigner Talk", Ferguson 1975) to *interaction* of conversational structure ("Foreigner Talk Discourse", Hatch 1978); for a comprehensive review, see Chaudron (1988). This has been accompanied by a second type of change, a move from a preoccupation with description and quantification of NS/NNS modifications, with comprehension *assumed* (e.g., Arthur et al. 1980; Chaudron 1983a) towards experimental studies controlled to illuminate the extent to which comprehension *achieved* might result from specific modifications (e.g., Cervantes 1983; Kelch 1985).

Two aspects of current views on speaker/listener adjustment are of special relevance to the issue of lecturer training. Firstly, in studies of performances of communicative tasks, modifications of interaction (e.g., comprehension checks, confirmation checks, clarification requests)

---

[1] Dudley-Evans (this volume) and King (this volume) have also taken up the question of interdisciplinary variation in lecture theatre discourse.

have proved to be more frequent and more consistent than input adjustments (Long 1981) and also more helpful to NNS learners of English completing classroom tasks (Pica, Young, and Doughty 1987). Secondly, it has been argued that it would be beneficial to L2 learners' linguistic progress for there to be a realignment of discourse roles, so that it is not only the teacher that exerts control over the timing, nature and extent of participation (e.g., Pica 1987; van Lier 1988; Lynch 1991). Without such a realignment of roles, it is likely that

given the unequal relationships of teacher and student established by the design and organisation of classroom activities, students may begin to feel that their clarification requests and confirmation checks will be perceived as challenges to the knowledge and professional experience of the teacher. (Pica 1987: 12)

These two points – the superiority of the comprehension-enhancing effect of interaction modifications over adjustments of input, and the need to find ways of encouraging NNS students to take the initiative in resolving comprehension difficulties – are germane not only to the general ESL classroom but also to the advice we might offer academic staff lecturing to NNS listeners. Later I will be exploring ways in which lecturers might make their lectures more interactive in order to communicate more effectively with international audiences.

L2 lecture discourse

The frequent criticisms of a lack of rigour in NS/NNS interaction research in general (e.g., Gaies 1982; Chaudron 1985) also apply to studies of NNS-addressed lectures: low comparability both within and across studies; a frequent lack of baseline data in the form of parallel samples of NS/NNS discourse against which to measure NS/NNS versions; poor generalisability, due to marked variation in individual speakers' patterns of adjustment, and so on. This last weakness – the high level of individual variability in listener-oriented modifications – was particularly criticised in a series of papers (Griffiths 1990, 1991; Griffiths and Beretta 1991) focussing on the role of speech rate adjustment in NS/NNS modification. In a scathing critique, Griffiths attacked the vague and impressionistic nature of previous research, which, he argued, renders cross-study comparison impossible: "The result is that on a fundamental issue such as recommending rates of delivery to language teachers, L2 research prior to 1989 had nothing to say. There was no evidence upon which a reply might even have been attempted" (Griffiths 1991: 359–60).

Griffiths' own empirical work on L2 lectures (Griffiths and Beretta 1991 – also reported in Flowerdew, this volume) suggested that substantial variation in speech rate between speakers, which had been submerged in others' results by the use of overall mean figures, is an inherent characteristic of NS/NNS modification. Griffiths and Beretta found "not so much a spread of rates according to addressees' English language proficiency, but a clustering of rates on an individual basis" (Griffiths and Beretta 1991: 9).

Of twelve temporal variables investigated in the study, only two reached statistical significance: the number and total duration of filled pauses. However, they did so in the opposite direction to that hypothesised: the lecturers produced fewer filled pauses and with shorter overall duration to the low-proficiency L2 group than to the high-proficiency L2 group and the native listeners. Even if it were possible to decide whether the filled pauses were indications of *on-line planning* or of *repair*, the potential lessons to be drawn for lecturer training from this most rigorous of investigations remain unclear. The implications that Griffiths and Beretta draw for staff training relate to the short term (to the ESL classroom, to the selection and training of ESL teachers and to materials design), rather than to longer-term recommendations for the training of subject-matter staff lecturing to international students.[2]

An investigation of L2 lecture discourse offering further insights into lecturers' communicative behaviour is that of Wesche and Ready (1985). As in the case of Griffiths and Beretta (1991), Wesche and Ready found variations in individual lecturers' patterns of language and (inter)action. Since they analysed lectures by just two speakers, there was in any case no intention of identifying possible "constellations" of modification across lecturers; however, what their research may lack in quantitative terms, it more than compensates for in two particular qualitative respects. Firstly, it involved lectures delivered as part of an ongoing academic programme, and not set up for the ulterior purposes of the lecture analyst. The two lecturers in question were each teaching courses in their L1 (English in one case, French in the other) to two groups of students at the University of Ottawa: one group of native listeners and one group of high-intermediate proficiency non-native listeners. Given what we have read in this volume of the importance, for lecture listeners' comprehension, of context – both the immediate linguistic context and the wider cultural context – the in-course setting of the lectures investigated in Wesche and Ready (1985) provides an additional dimension to their study. Secondly, not only were the lecturers teaching the same course (in introductory psychology) but also on the same topic, "shaping" or "*le façonnement*", which allowed Wesche and Ready to

---

[2] Flowerdew (personal communication) has pointed out that the Omani research described in Griffiths and Beretta (1991) was originally intended to lead to the development of a lecturer training course, although this was never initiated.

make direct comparisons within and across speakers, given the fully parallel relationship between all four lectures to the two sets of NS and NNS audiences. As far as I am aware, this configuration is unique in published NS/NNS research.

Wesche and Ready analysed differences in the characteristics of the speakers' linguistic and non-linguistic input and found no consistent pattern. On some parameters, such as speech rate and a number of syntactic measures, the English-speaking lecturer made a statistically significant number of NNS adjustments, while the French speaker did not. On another parameter, the position was reversed; the French-speaking lecturer produced significantly more filled pauses (contrary to Griffiths and Beretta 1991) to the NNS group. The statistically most robust feature to emerge was content redundancy, in the form of exact replication or exact repetition plus reformulation; both lecturers used this device with significantly higher frequency when addressing their NNS group. Wesche and Ready also comment on the greater use of non-verbal redundancy by both speakers, in the form of gestural cues and visual support on the blackboard in their non-native lecture. As well as using more marked gestures to the NNS audience, the lecturers wrote in more detail and more clearly on the board. In the light of Olsen and Huckin's (1990) findings, to be discussed in the next section, clear blackboard work is one element of lecturer repertoire that should be emphasised in lecturer training.

Wesche and Ready's research offers invaluable qualitative insight into lecture-theatre behaviour in a regular university course, into what lecturers actually do when their attention is focussed on the job in hand (namely, giving one of *their* lectures), rather than showing us what speakers may do when simulating a lecture to an unfamiliar audience in a tightly controlled language experiment. From the quantitative point of view, their study has obvious limitations of sample size and possible "contamination" by differences due to the different languages used in the lectures. Although they mention in a footnote their intention to carry out a further study dealing with the effects on comprehensibility of the parallel L1 and L2 presentations, I am not aware of that work yet being published. But one of their concluding comments is an intriguing one: "Of course, native speakers will also vary in their underlying sensitivity to – and even interest in – the comprehensibility of their input to non-natives" (1985: 108). If true, this would suggest a need for awareness-raising such as that discussed in my final section.

L2 lecture comprehension

We turn next to the issue of which features of NS/NNS modification have been shown to make a difference to listeners' comprehension. An inherent problem with much of the experimental research into the possible influence of discourse adjustments on NNSs' success in understanding lectures is that it has centred on the controlled manipulation of adjustments in *scripted* recordings. This has been done in the interests of experimental control, but has to be set against the fact that it is widely agreed (cf. Dudley-Evans and Johns 1981 and various authors in this volume – Flowerdew, Mason, and Hansen and Jensen) that the informal, note-based lecture is far more common than the formal, scripted presentation.

I will briefly consider studies that have investigated specific types of modification, rather than those that have focussed on the effect of global modifications (e.g., Long 1985) or have been based on texts recorded in a way that has rendered them even less like lectures (e.g., the dictation studies of Cervantes 1983 and Kelch 1985).

Chaudron (1983b) measured the relative effect of various topic reinstatement devices inserted to increase redundancy: immediate repetition of the noun; noun alone; rhetorical questions; if-clause and synonym. The texts were five short lectures on a range of themes; NNS subjects were grouped in three bands of ESL proficiency. Chaudron found that, although the repeated noun was the most effective of the reinstatement devices overall and for low- and middle-proficiency groups, it had no greater facilitating effect for the more advanced, suggesting that the greater degree of redundancy becomes unnecessary at higher levels of target language competence. He concluded that what actually contributes to "simplified speech" will vary for learners at different levels of ESL proficiency – which, in our context, means that lecturers addressing an audience of mixed ESL levels will contend with particular difficulties in getting their message across.

Chaudron and Richards (1986), discussed elsewhere in this volume by Flowerdew, and Dunkel and Davis, found that the greatest effect on listeners' comprehension came from the version of their lecture scripted to contain "macro-markers" – metastatements about major propositions of the lecture and important transition points. Chaudron and Richards speculated that the reason for the Macro version's measured superiority over Macro–Micro (the version they had hypothesised would help listeners most) is that the latter increased the attention requirements on listeners without adding any substantial information, thereby detracting from the assistance available from Macro alone.

As the original lecture on which Chaudron and Richard constructed their four experimental versions dealt with the subject of U.S. history, nine of the 25 macro-markers inserted into versions (3) and (4) were markers of *narrative sequence* (e.g., "What happened next was that . . . ", "our story doesn't end there . . . "). It could be argued that such sequential markers are more salient than comparable discourse markers in a lecture where the speaker's aim is, say, to develop an *argument* or explain a *complex interrelationship*.

However, the findings of their study contrast with those of Dunkel and Davis (this volume), whose investigation of possible differential comprehension effects of elaborated and non-elaborated lecture texts found no measurable significant enhancement from the insertion of discourse structure cues. The difference in results between the two studies may lie, as Dunkel and Davis suggest, in the differences in text type and comprehension measures, but it might also be that the influential variables affecting the reception of lecture discourse are so numerous and their interactions so complex that no amount of experimental manipulation and control will enable us to establish a primary influence on comprehension.[3]

Some light has been shed on the extent of the difficulties faced by many listeners in dealing with the complexity of arguments and relationships in lecture comprehension by Olsen and Huckin (1990) – discussed earlier in this volume by Tauroza and Allison and Dudley-Evans; Olsen and Huckin argue that the successful lecture listener achieves "point-driven", rather than "information-driven", understanding – in other words, that full lecture-theatre competence requires the ability to follow overall development as well as to recognise the detail:

We have observed many students who, even though they understand the lecturer's use of discourse markers, still do not fully grasp the gist of a lecture. They understand how utterances "stick together" and they can anticipate various "moves", yet they do not understand the speaker's main points or the logical structure of his argument. (Olsen and Huckin 1990: 34)

Of particular interest for my present discussion of lecturer training is Olsen and Huckin's conclusion that some NNS listeners failed despite adequate English. The authors hypothesise that the reason for this failure may lie partly in the NNS students' *expectations about lectures* and not solely in their aural decoding ability:

many nonnative students are used to having professors in their home countries write the main points and the rhetorical structure in one corner of the board, each new point being added as it appears in the lecture . . . Unfortunately for the nonnative speakers, few American professors have such obvious signposts for their lectures, even though their lectures may be well organised and carefully delivered. (Olsen and Huckin 1990: 41)

They also refer to the disciplinary "cultural" conditioning that comes with experience: their non-native subjects may have been currently too

---

[3] As I recently heard an IBM scientist say in a radio programme, "The main problem is that the world isn't binary."

inexperienced in the less straightforward intellectual problem-solving typical of graduate work to recognise the schema underlying a lecture.[4] Their call for the need to help (NS and NNS) students "to see the larger goals, agendas, and contexts, in their fields, as well as the organization of their discourse" (p. 44) will be taken up in my final two sections.

Lecturing methodology

In the United Kingdom, at least, it is only relatively recently that it has come to be thought necessary to train lecturers to teach their subject, and there is no British equivalent of the North American programmes for international teaching assistants (discussed in the next section). The notion that the change from successful doctoral researcher to university teacher might require instruction and guidance is based on what has been tactfully described as the "common experience that scholarly ability (or scholarly achievement) and ability to teach are imperfectly related" (Startup 1979: 22). In addressing the issue of possible failures of communication between speaker and listener, the British University Grants Committee (1964) was perhaps overoptimistic in believing that

The lecturer knows, or should know, when he has lost contact with his audience, and where the audience is not too large *he can give opportunities for questions* which will show if he has failed to make himself clear. He can then go back and *try another explanation* in different words, whereas the student who has to go back in his book will only be able to read the words over which he has stumbled. (University Grants Committee 1964: 53, my italics)

I will shortly return to the two discourse elements highlighted in the latter extract – questions and explanation – but first I would like to comment briefly on the concept of the lecture as "problem" rather than opportunity. The dissatisfaction expressed and felt by students with lectures can stem from what they perceive to be a lack of consistency in standards of presentation and clarity of structure. There can certainly be marked differences between lecturers' and students' perceptions of lectures: 91% of the lecturers responding to Brown and Bakhtar's (1983) questionnaire regarded their lectures as successful, while Hartley and Cameron (1967) found as much as 80% disagreement between lecturers' and students' identification of the main points in a lecture. Given current views of comprehension as a process of complex interaction rather than

---

[4] There is the additional issue of the probable beneficial effect of relevant topic knowledge on comprehension, which remains largely unaddressed in L2 lecture studies, although widely discussed in other areas of L2 research: for example, Johnson (1982) and Carrell (1983) on reading comprehension; Crookes and Rulon (1988) and Zuengler and Bent (1991) in relation to speaking; Reid (1990) and Tedick (1990) for writing.

simple reception, some degree of discrepancy should not come as a surprise. However, since the primary purpose of lectures is to present information, the fact that failure rates can be so high is a cause for concern. Against this background one finds a growing number of training courses and publications giving guidance on lecturing – much of it familiar to trained language teachers, but helpful and reassuring for new lecturers. The following is my summary of a set of recommendations widely cited in the U.K. lecture methodology literature:

1. Speak loudly, and clearly . . . don't go too fast.
2. Plan, prepare, structure every lecture.
3. Make it understandable – explain, emphasise, recap, repeat and summarise main points and relate to current examples and applications.
4. Watch out for reaction and feedback, invite questions and ask questions, encourage participation, involve your audience.
5. Be adequate, do not try to cover everything.
6. Know your subject.
7. Keep time.
8. Look at your audience.
9. Assemble . . . materials to which the students won't have easy access.
10. Don't read from your notes.
11. Be interesting and humorous but not too much.
12. Prepare handouts.
   (abridged from Brown and Bakhtar 1983)

Questions

That apparently uncontroversial and commonsense list conceals a potentially radical agenda. For example, what would be the effect of item 4 – the suggestion that the lecturer should invite questions from the audience? For some, this could create "tension between the teacher's authority (expressed in his control over content) and his aim of making himself receptive to feedback" (Startup 1979: 29) – or, as Jay puts it, "The power of questions to help a presentation is less than their power to damage it" (Jay 1971: 67).

Here, then, lies a real difficulty for the lecturer who wishes to encourage questions and clarifications from the audience in the course of a lecture: that a point raised by a student may sidetrack the speaker to the extent that the lecture loses its intended coherence and transparency. What is required is some way of reconciling lecturers' willingness to deal with questions and their need to present the planned package of information. In the final section I suggest one way of achieving that balance: the "question pause".

Questions also pose difficulties from the student's point of view, since those who raise a query find themselves in an exposed, public position. "Asking a question requires such an effort that, having got it out, the questioner is too emotionally drained to pay attention to the answer" (Shaw and Bailey 1990: 325). Question askers also run the risk of being considered (in the British student culture) "stupid, attention seekers or creeps" (Gibbs, Habeshaw, and Habeshaw 1987: 155), and so it is understandable that "the ubiquitous 'Are there any questions?' at the end of a lecture is so routinely ineffective that it has come to mean 'That's all for today'" (loc. cit.).

It is revealing that in much of the literature on lecture methodology (e.g., Costin 1972; Bligh et al. 1975; University Teaching Methods Unit 1976; Curzon 1980), the word "question" is used exclusively to refer to questions asked of the audience by the lecturer, rather than vice versa, with all that implies about the relative statuses of "asker" and "asked". In NS/NNS research terms, "question" in this field means "comprehension check" rather than "clarification request". Those who do advocate encouraging listeners to raise queries offer some practical suggestions as to how this might work: Cannon (1988) says that stressful public performances can be avoided by getting students to jot down their questions on pieces of paper, which the lecturer then collects before selecting which ones to deal with; Gibbs et al. (1987) propose a variation on the "buzz group", in which students compare the points they would like further information on and then discuss how best to formulate the relevant clarification requests. This recalls the work of Dudley-Evans and Johns (1981) on team teaching, involving cooperation between subject lecturer and language instructor in assisting NNS listeners. One of the advantages of the teaching experiments they described was that the follow-up session after the lecture proper allowed students the chance to ask questions. Since, according to Dudley-Evans and Johns, the students themselves clearly benefited from that opportunity, it seems reasonable to propose that we seek ways of ensuring that, in a wider sense, "normal" lectures also provide a similar opportunity for student contributions.

Explanations

Item 3 in Brown and Bakhtar's list was "Make it understandable" and the first of their imperatives was "explain". In a number of his books (Brown 1978; Brown and Bakhtar 1983; Brown and Atkins 1988), Brown has argued that the skill of explaining is "at the heart of teaching in higher education just as its obverse, understanding, is at the heart of learning" (1978: 39). The basic communicative resources he lists for lecturers indicate an understandable overlap with points we have considered in the NS/NNS context: emphatic gestures, simple sentences, appropriate pauses, blackboard illustration, variation in speed of delivery, clear statement of the problem, eye contact, use of appropriate examples, illustrations and analogies. Again, all this seems sound enough advice, but as I will argue in the final section, some underlying assumptions – such as the appropriacy of examples and analogies – need to be teased out when training lecturers to assist their non-native learners.

Training lecturers for international audiences

The growing internationalisation of university populations, particularly in English-speaking countries, has led to the development of training initiatives of various sorts to tackle the communicative problems involved. The increasing number of *NNS teaching assistants* in the United States, for example, has resulted in programmes and publications addressing the "foreign T.A. problem" (e.g., Bailey, Pialorsi and Zukowski/Faust 1984; Rounds 1987; Shaw and Bailey 1990) and more recently in practical guides for use with NNS university instructors (Byrd, Constantinides, and Pennington 1989; Pica, Barnes, and Finger 1990).

However, the greater part of the effort has been invested in helping *NNS students* through language/study skills training, in the form of pre-session and in-session programmes, and an extensive range of published materials – in the specific case of interest here, discourse-oriented lecture comprehension courses such as Lynch (1983), Mason (1983), James, Jordan, Matthews and O'Brien (1990). Like all teaching materials, however, they have their limitations, one of which is a degree of idealisation in the recorded texts they feature:

as authentic as they sound, however, one has to recognise that special care has been given to the structure of the talks. They *have* a structure and it is clearly marked. Sadly this is not always the case with a real lecture. Perhaps we should start training the lecturers. (O'Brien 1984, original emphasis)

However, there seems to have been no published work on training programmes specifically designed to take up O'Brien's recommendation, i.e., to cater for NS lecturing staff faced for the first time with classes where a sizeable minority, or even a majority, are NNS students. In this final section I suggest which points might be highlighted in such a training programme, drawing on the literature reviewed in this chapter.

Research has isolated two areas of lecture presentation likely to provide some degree of assistance to NNS listeners: greater attention to the clarity of discourse "signposts" (showing overall aim and structure, main ideas, and transition between sections); and increased redundancy (both verbal and non-verbal). However, it might be argued that this boils down to little more than the advice already available in standard lecture methodology texts. Moreover, even adopting such apparently commonsense advice as speaking more slowly and clearly, using simpler language and building in more repetition than they would to a NS audience runs the risk of being perceived by the NNS listeners as patronising (cf. Wesche and Ready 1985; Lynch 1988).

An important first step will be to help lecturers appreciate the socio-cultural problems faced by students entering university. These are not, of course, unique to students attending courses in a foreign country, but feelings of dislocation are likely to be more severe for NNS students. Ballard (1984: 48) refers to the "double cultural shift" that the incoming NNS student faces: the transition from high school/secondary school to university (or from undergraduate to postgraduate course), and also the move into an alien culture, with different norms of authority, relevance, criticism, etc. (see the recent collection of papers edited by Adams, Heaton, and Howarth 1991). In particular, the basic issue of the statuses and rights of learners and teachers will affect whether and to what extent NNS students actually take up the available support in the host academic system; we might recall the words of a Vietnamese student quoted in Adamson (1990: 72) – "I feel I am here to learn, not for somebody to solve my problems".

This takes us back to the comments of Olsen and Huckin (1990) and Strodt-Lopez (1991) on the need to "initiate" NNS listeners into the local educational culture. In the specific case of lectures, teaching staff need to appreciate the additional adjustments necessary for international students, who are having to identify and meet local expectations of lecture-theatre performance (by lecturer and by students). Perhaps the most important contribution lecturers can make is to give an explicit and public statement of the "ground rules" for their particular lecture series. This point has been made about lectures in general (e.g., Gibbs et al. 1987; Ellington n.d.) but is even more important in the case of lectures to audiences including NNSs (Shaw and Bailey 1990). The fact that these rules can vary both between disciplines and also between individuals in the same discipline can lead to confusion and unease on the part of non-native students. Let us now consider how such training might address the two specific issues raised in the previous section – explanations and questions.

Explanations

As we have seen, Brown regards explanation as the very heart of the lecturing process. However, in an ESL classroom study Chaudron (1982) found that the need to explain unknown terms to L2 learners places a considerable burden on the teacher, who has both to signal reformulation unambiguously and also to avoid overelaborate content which low-proficiency listeners will simply "tune out". In the EAP context, a number of writers (e.g., Sturtridge, McAlpin and Harper 1977; Hutchison and Waters 1981) have stressed the role of cultural background knowledge in enabling the audience to draw on shared facts and fictions, in order to recognise what is intended to be a helpful explanation or reformulation. Attested examples from the British context that might well confuse NNS students include an engineering lecturer's references to Edward the Confessor (Hutchison and Waters 1981) and an economist's to Dickensian characters like Bob Cratchitt or Mr Micawber (Tadros 1980). Even apparently more straightforward physical comparisons involving cricket pitches or sixpenny bits may be less than helpful, and not only to L2 listeners; even within the native British student population, factors such as age, type of schooling and region of origin will affect whether a listener is able to follow a lecturer's allusions to cricket and pre-decimal coins.

Lecturers should be sensitised to the need to avoid unwarranted assumptions of shared knowledge and to the risk that the use of cultural "insider information" will exclude NNS students. I am not suggesting that lecturers should use no examples or analogies, but that they have to exercise care in choosing those that are likely to be accessible. Lecturers should be prepared – in two senses, i.e., *trained* and *willing* – to think through the background knowledge that their illustrations require. NNS-oriented explanation and analogy is of course a common feature of the L2 language classroom, but may need to be practised by subject lecturers unused to communicating with international audiences.

One further aspect of explanation that needs highlighting in lecturer training is awareness of the importance of visual support in a wide sense, including the use of blackboard or overhead projector as well as the provision of handouts. Wesche and Ready (1985) and Olsen and Huckin (1990) have underscored the benefits of clear board work, not only for setting out a "map" or overall structure plan for the lecture and orientating students to the current location in the discourse, but also for dealing with terms or concepts which students are finding hard to understand. Similarly, my own experience with students in ESL classes is that handout notes or summaries offer an additional or alternative route to the comprehension of points that weaker listeners in the group fail to identify or fully understand in spoken form.

Questions

Questions offer one way for students to clear up doubts and comprehension problems but, as we have seen, there can be complications. Lecturers may fear dislocation of the lecture. Students in general may be reluctant to venture questions; NNS listeners, in particular, may apply the home culture belief that "questioning" implies a slight on the teacher's authority. I recall giving what I felt was an unsuccessful explanation of a language point to an Indonesian group. The following exchange then took place between the oldest student, who usually acted as spokesman for the group, and myself:

T: Would you like to ask any questions about that?
S: (*immediately*) No questions.
T: What about the others?
S: They have no questions.
T: But how do you know the others don't have any questions?
S: Because you are a good teacher.

Clearly, the reasons why NNS listeners may avoid asking questions are not limited to imported norms of respect for authority; and they may be compounded by language difficulties (see Lynch and Anderson 1991). So, given the additional tensions discussed earlier relating to public questioning, it is worth exploring ways in which lecturers might increase the chances that their listeners will ask questions.

One possible approach would be to recommend to lecturers that when preparing material for lectures they should allow time for two or three "question pauses" – short breaks in their presentation during which students would be free to raise queries about what has been said up to that point. As Dudley-Evans and Johns (1981) point out in their analysis of lecturing styles, each style presents its own difficulties for the NNS listener with possible effects on comprehension of detail or gist. By clearly establishing "time for questions" (irrespective of the overall style of presentation adopted) the lecturer would provide an opportunity for doubts and queries to be raised.

The effects of this strategy would be firstly to allow listeners time to review what they have just heard and to formulate questions, and secondly to avoid the need to bid for a turn during the lecturer's flow, which is the difficulty that arises if lecturers simply say "if anything isn't clear, just ask" in a well-meant but vague way. Such question pauses, providing a clearly signalled space for clarification requests, might go a long way towards helping NNS students take the initiative in asking the questions that they know they need to ask.

A more general strategy would be for lecturers to spell out their preferred ground rules for questioning: whether questions from the audience are encouraged or expected, whether they can be asked during the lecture (and if so, whether as they arise or at signalled question pauses) or afterwards; if after the lecture, whether queries will be invited and discussed in plenary at the end, or whether it is up to the individual student to approach the lecturer either at the end of the lecture, or in a follow-up tutorial, or by making an individual appointment.

Such matters may appear commonsense, but the evidence from the methodological literature and students' comments suggests that such initial scene-setting is unusual; it is left to students to work out individual lecturers' varying preferences (Shaw and Bailey 1990).[5]

Lecturers need practice in negotiating the meaning of questions from the audience. It is not always easy to understand audience queries – whether at the level of intelligibility, comprehensibility or interpretability (Smith and Nelson 1985) – particularly if the student seeking clarification comes from a culture where questioning is made more polite by being framed in an oblique way. As in any form of public presentation, there is the risk that lecturers will answer the question they *believe* they have identified, rather than take up more time confirming the precise intent of the question. The habit of repeating or rephrasing audience questions – equivalent to the "confirmation check" discussed in the NS/NNS interaction literature – should also feature in a lecturer training programme. The sort of treatment such question negotiation is given in seminar skills courses for NNS students (e.g., Lynch and Anderson 1992) could also provide the basis for practice sessions for lecturers who will be teaching international classes.

Conclusion

Experimental research into L2 lecture discourse has highlighted certain areas in which lecturers might assist NNS listeners by adjusting the way they present information in lectures. Linguistically, this includes speaking at a slower pace with clearer articulation and with a greater degree of redundancy. Rhetorically, more explicit marking of overall lecture structure and of salient points should also enhance students' ability to understand. Other studies have drawn attention to the socio-cultural aspects of study in a foreign academic context and have shown, for example, that the key to successful explanation when addressing an international audience lies in the selection of culturally accessible illustrative material and not solely in the presentation of "simpler" input.

However, no amount of meticulous planning, careful delivery and explicit signalling can *guarantee* the comprehensibility of a lecture, and more needs to be done, through lecturer training programmes, to

---

[5] Unfortunately, even when lecturers do make an explicit statement of their particular "ground rules" at the start of a lecture series, these may not reflect their own behaviour. At a recent study skills workshop in Edinburgh, a Scottish undergraduate commented, "Oh yes, most of them *say* you can ask questions during their lecture, but you can see them getting annoyed when you actually do."

suggest ways of dealing with comprehension problems when they arise. The customary use of the term "lecture input" highlights an imbalance in the L2 research literature to date, which has concentrated on the lecture as presentation of input to an audience – its form, its comprehensibility and the relationship between the two. While this has brought valuable insights, there is surely a need to expand our horizons from a concern with what lecturers say and do, to ways of raising their awareness of the benefits of allowing *input from the students*, in the form of clarifying questions.

In a sense, I am arguing for attention to remedy as well as prevention; in addition to trying to "design out" likely causes of comprehension difficulty, we should "design in" mechanisms that will encourage students to seek remedies in the inevitable cases where communication fails or half-succeeds. Naturally we should continue to run study skills courses that develop NNS students' listening comprehension and note-taking skills, but we need also to assist lecturers to cope better with the demands of teaching international classes. Training which emphasises key points in NS/NNS communication, such as explanation and questioning, should pay dividends in making lectures more accessible – and not only for NNS listeners.

Acknowledgments

I am very grateful to three anonymous reviewers for a number of comments and suggested improvements, which I have incorporated into this final version.

References

Adams, P., B. Heaton, and P. Howarth. 1991. *Socio-Cultural Issues in English for Academic Purposes*. Review of English Language Teaching 1 (2): Modern English Publications/British Council.

Adamson, H. 1990. ESL students' use of academic skills in content courses. *English for Specific Purposes* 9: 67–87.

Anderson, A., and T. Lynch. 1988. *Listening*. Oxford: Oxford University Press.

Arthur, B., M. Weiner, J. Culver, L. Young, and D. Thomas. 1980. The register of impersonal discourse to foreigners: verbal adjustments to foreign accent. In *Discourse Analysis in Second Language Research*, D. Larsen-Freeman (Ed.), 111–124. Rowley, Mass.: Newbury House.

Bailey, B., J. Pialorsi, and J. Zukowski/Faust (Eds.). 1984. *Foreign Teaching Assistants in U.S. Universities*. Washington, D.C.: National Association for Student Affairs.

Ballard, B. 1984. Improving student writing: an integrated approach to cultural adjustment. In *Common Ground: Shared Interests in ESP and Communication Studies*, R. Williams, J. Swales, and J. Kirkman (Eds.). ELT Documents Special. Oxford: Pergamon.

Bligh, D., G. Ebrahim, D. Jaques, and D. Piper. 1975. *Teaching Students.* Exeter: Exeter University Teaching Services.

Brown, G., and G. Yule. 1983. *Discourse Analysis.* Cambridge: Cambridge University Press.

Brown, G. A. 1978. *Lecturing and Explaining.* London: Methuen.

Brown, G. A., and M. Atkins. 1988. *Effective Teaching in Higher Education.* London: Methuen.

Brown, G. A., and M. Bakhtar (Eds.). 1983. *Styles of Lecturing.* University of Loughborough: ASTD Publications.

Byrd, P., J. Constantinides, and M. Pennington. 1989. *The Foreign Teaching Assistant's Manual.* New York: Collier Macmillan.

Cannon, R. 1988. *Lecturing.* Kensington, N.S.W.: Higher Education Research and Development Society of Australia.

Carrell, P. J. 1983. Background knowledge in second language comprehension. *Language Learning and Communication* 2 (1): 25–34.

Cervantes, R. 1983. Say it again Sam: the effect of exact repetition on listening comprehension. Term paper, University of Hawaii at Manoa.

Chaudron, C. 1982. Vocabulary explanation in teachers' speech to L2 learners. *Studies in Second Language Acquisition* 4 (2): 170–80.

1983a. Foreigner talk in the classroom – an aid to learning? In *Classroom Oriented Research in Second Language Acquisition*, H. Seliger, and M. Long (Eds.). Rowley, Mass.: Newbury House.

1983b. Simplification of input: topic reinstatements and their effects on L2 learners' recognition and recall. *TESOL Quarterly* 17 (3): 437–458.

1985. Comprehension, comprehensibility and learning in the second language classroom. *Studies in Second Language Acquisition* 7 (1): 1–14.

1988. *Second Language Classrooms.* Cambridge: Cambridge University Press.

Chaudron, C., and J. Richards. 1986. The effect of discourse markers on the comprehension of lectures. *Applied Linguistics* 7 (2): 113–127.

Clark, H. H., and E. Clark. 1977. *Psychology and Language.* New York: Harcourt, Brace, Jovanovich.

Cook, J. 1975. A communicative approach to the analysis of extended monologue discourse and its relevance to the development of teaching materials for ESP. M.Litt. thesis, University of Edinburgh.

Costin, F. 1972. Lecturing versus other methods of teaching: a review of research. *British Journal of Educational Technology* 3: 1–31.

Crookes, G., and K. Rulon. 1988. Topic and feedback in native-speaker/nonnative-speaker conversation. *TESOL Quarterly* 22 (4): 675–680.

Curzon, L. 1980. *Teaching in Further Education.* London: Cassell.

Demyankov, V. 1983. Understanding as an interpreting activity. *Voprosy yazykoznaniya* 32: 58–67.

Dudley-Evans, T. A., and T. F. Johns. 1981. A team teaching approach to lecture comprehension for overseas students. In *The Teaching of Listening Comprehension.* London: British Council.

Dunkel, P. 1991. 'Listening in the native and second/foreign language: towards an integration of research and practice'. *TESOL Quarterly* 26 (3): 431–457.

Ellington, H. n.d. *Some Hints on How to be an Effective Lecturer.* Teaching and Learning in Higher Education 6: Scottish Central Institutions Committee for Education Development.

Ferguson. C. 1975. Towards a characterization of English foreigner talk. *Anthropological Linguistics* 17: 1–14.

Flores d'Arcais, G., and R. Jarvella (Eds.). 1983. *The Process of Language Understanding*. Chichester: John Wiley.

Gaies, S. 1982. Native speaker–nonnative speaker interaction among academic peers. *Studies in Second Language Acquisition* 5 (1): 74–81.

Garrod, S. 1986. Language comprehension in context: a psychological perspective. *Applied Linguistics* 7 (3): 226–38.

Gass, S., and C. Madden (Eds.). 1985. *Input in Second Language Acquisition*. Rowley, Mass.: Newbury House.

Gibbs, G., S. Habeshaw, and T. Habeshaw. 1987. *53 Interesting Things to do in your Lectures*. Bristol, England: Technical and Educational Services.

Griffiths, R. 1990. Speech rate and NNS comprehension: a preliminary study in time-benefit analysis. *Language Learning* 40 (3): 311–336.

     1991. Pausological research in an L2 context: a rationale and review of selected studied. *Applied Linguistics* 12 (4): 345–364.

Griffiths, R., and A. Beretta. 1991. A controlled study of temporal variables in NS–NNS lectures. *RELC Journal* 22 (1): 1–19.

Hartley, J., and A. Cameron. 1967. Some observations on the efficiency of lecturing. *Educational Review* 20 (1): 30–37.

Hatch, E. 1978. Discourse analysis in second language acquisition. In *Second Language Acquisition*, E. Hatch (Ed.). Rowley, Mass.: Newbury House.

Hutchinson, T., and A. Waters. 1981. Performance and competence in English for Specific Purposes. *Applied Linguistics* 2 (1): 56–69.

James, K., R. Jordan, A. Matthews, and J. O'Brien. 1990. *Listening Comprehension and Notetaking Course*. 2nd edition. London: Collins.

Jay, A. 1971. *Effective Presentation*. London: British Institute of Management Foundation.

Johnson, P. 1982. Effects on reading comprehension of building background knowledge. *TESOL Quarterly* 16 (4): 503–516.

Kelch, K. 1985. Modified input as an aid to comprehension. *Studies in Second Language Acquisition* 7: 81–90.

Lier, L. van. 1988. *The Classroom and the Language Learner*. London: Longman

Long, M. 1981. Input, interaction and second language acquisition. In *The Comprehension Approach to Foreign Language Instruction*, H. Winitz (Ed.). Rowley, Mass.: Newbury House.

     1985. Input and second language acquisition theory. In Gass and Madden (Eds.). 1985.

Lynch, T. 1983. *Study Listening*. Cambridge: Cambridge University Press.

     1988. Speaking up or talking down: learners' reactions to teacher talk. *English Language Teaching Journal* 42 (2): 109–116.

     1991. Questioning roles in the classroom. *English Language Teaching Journal* 45 (3): 201–210.

Lynch, T., and K. Anderson. 1991. Do you mind if I come in here? A comparison of real-life seminars and EAP materials. In Adams, Heaton and Howarth (Eds.). 1991.

     1992. *Study Speaking*. Cambridge: Cambridge University Press.

Mason, A. 1983. *Understanding Academic Lectures*. Englewood Cliffs, N.J.: Prentice Hall.

Murphy, D., and C. N. Candlin. 1979. Engineering lecture discourse and listening comprehension. *Practical Papers in Language Education* 2: 1–79. Lancaster: University of Lancaster.

Nagle, S., and S. Sanders. 1986. Comprehension theory and second language pedagogy. *TESOL Quarterly* 20 (1): 9–25.

O'Brien, T. 1984. Hearsay. (Review of Lynch 1983). *Times Educational Supplement.* June 22.

Olsen, L. A., and T. N. Huckin. 1990. Point-driven understanding in engineering lecture comprehension. *English for Specific Purposes* 9: 33–47.

Pica, T. 1987. Second-language acquisition, social interaction, and the classroom. *Applied Linguistics* 8 (1): 3–21.

Pica, T., G. Barnes, and A. Finger. 1990. *Teaching Matters: Skills and Strategies for International Teaching Assistants.* Rowley, Mass.: Newbury House.

Pica, T., R. Young, and C. Doughty. 1987. The impact of interaction on comprehension. *TESOL Quarterly* 21 (4): 737–758.

Reid, J. 1990. Responding to different topic types: a quantitative analysis from a contrastive rhetoric perspective. In *Second Language Writing*, B. Kroll (Ed.). Cambridge: Cambridge University Press.

Rost, M. 1990. *Listening in Language Learning.* London: Longman.

Rounds, P. 1987. Characterizing successful classroom discourse for NNS teaching assistant training, *TESOL Quarterly* 21 (4): 643–671.

Schlesinger, I. 1977. *Production and Comprehension of Utterances.* Hillsdale, N.J.: Erlbaum.

Shaw, P., and K. Bailey. 1990. Cultural differences in academic settings. In *Developing Communicative Competence in a Second Language*, R. Scarcella, E. Andersen, and S. Krashen (Eds.). Rowley, Mass.: Newbury House.

Sinclair, J. McH., and M. Coulthard. 1975. *Towards an Analysis of Discourse.* Oxford: Oxford University Press.

Smith, L., and C. Nelson. 1985. International intelligibility of English: directions and resources. *World Englishes* 4 (3): 333–342.

Startup, R. 1979. *The University Teacher and his World: a Sociological and Educational Study.* Aldershot: Gower.

Strodt-Lopez, B. 1991. Tying it all in: asides in university lectures. *Applied Linguistics* 12 (2): 117–140.

Sturtridge, G., J. McAlpin, and D. Harper. 1977. The British Council and the language problems of overseas students. In *English for Academic Purposes*, A. Cowie, and B. Heaton (Eds.). Reading: BAAL/SELMOUS.

Tadros, A. 1980. Prediction in economics text. *English Language Research Journal* 1: 42–59. University of Birmingham, England.

Tedick, D. 1990. ESL writing assessment: subject-matter knowledge and its impact on performance. *English for Specific Purposes* 9: 123–43.

University Grants Committee. 1964. *University Teaching Methods.* London: HMSO.

University Teaching Methods Unit. 1976. *Improving Teaching in Higher Education.* London: University of London.

Wesche, M., and D. Ready. 1985. Foreigner talk in the university classroom. In Gass and Madden (Eds.). 1985.

Zuengler, J., and B. Bent. 1991. Relative knowledge of content domain: an influence on native/nonnative conversations. *Applied Linguistics* 12 (4): 397–415.

Conclusion

John Flowerdew

The chapters in this book have taught us a lot about academic lectures and about the processes which are involved in their comprehension by L2 listeners. This final chapter has five objectives:

1. To summarise briefly what the individual chapters in the collection have taught us in terms of research findings;
2. To highlight the conclusions for pedagogy that the individual chapters provide for;
3. To highlight generalizations which can be made springing from the collection as a whole, both for research and pedagogy;
4. To examine the question of the generalizability of the findings of the individual chapters;
5. To highlight the most important areas where there is still a lot to be learned about L2 academic listening and where further research is thus most urgently needed.

What research findings have the individual contributions to the collection provided?

The chapters in this collection have individually provided a wide range of research findings. Very briefly, findings have been presented as follows:

About the L2 academic listening comprehension process
- the negative effect of an unfamiliar discourse structure on lecture comprehension (Tauroza and Allison);
- the role (or non-role) of discourse markers in facilitating comprehension (Dunkel and Davis);
- the role of note-keeping as an aid in the recall of information presented in lectures (Chaudron, Loschky and Cook);
- the listening comprehension strategies and problems of L2 students as manifested in elicited, "on-line" written summaries (Rost).

About the discourse of lectures
- how lectures can be analysed and student notes evaluated in terms of topic (Hansen);
- how discourse structure can vary across subject area (Dudley-Evans);

– how lectures, from whatever discipline, can be analysed in terms of the systemic concept of "phase" (Young).

About the ethnography of L2 lectures
– how the L2 lecture comprehension process can be viewed from a broad ethnographic perspective (Benson);
– how one group of graduate students and their lecturers view the lecture comprehension process (Mason);
– how the note-taking strategies of L2 students reflect their understanding of a lecture and the role of the visual element in this understanding (King).

About application to pedagogical questions
– how L2 listening comprehension theory can be applied in a principled way and the further theoretical questions which arise in the development of an academic listening test (Hansen and Jensen);
– how research findings in L2 listening comprehension and related fields can be applied in the training of content lecturers who lecture to international audiences (Lynch).

What conclusions do the individual chapters provide for pedagogical application?

The individual chapters in this collection provide information of value to pedagogic application in a number of ways. This information is of value to three main groups: learners, ESL professionals (teachers, course designers, testing specialists, materials writers) and content lecturers. In general terms, those chapters concerned with the comprehension process, in showing how effective (and less effective) comprehension takes place, indicate the problems learners can be faced with in comprehending L2 lectures and the skills which, therefore, need to be acquired and/or taught; at the same time research into the comprehension process can show content lecturers how they can present their lectures so as to ensure optimal comprehension. Those chapters concerned with lecture discourse, similarly, indicate what discourse structures and language need to be taught and learned by L2 learners, on the one hand, and how content lecturers can optimally structure their lectures, on the other. Finally, those chapters which study lecture listening from an ethnographic perspective show how listening activity is integrated within the wider context of the other activities and skills of learning and in so doing indicate to content lecturers and ESL professionals how this integration can help or hinder comprehension.

The two chapters in this collection directly oriented towards pedagogical application can be seen as models of how research findings can be applied in two areas: testing, on the one hand (Hansen and Jensen's chapter) and content lecturing, on the other (Lynch's chapter). But the other chapters also have things to say which are of immediate relevance to application. To list some of them for each chapter:

Tauroza and Allison

In their study of how an unexpected schematic structure of a lecture can lead to mis-comprehension, Tauroza and Allison consider and evaluate, in terms of their likely effectiveness, a number of possible ways of alleviating the problem. These are as follows: focussing on learners' expectations concerning discourse structure at a general level; raising awareness of formal schemata; activating task-relevant schemata through pre-listening tasks to familiarise students with various schematic structures; and training content lecturers to signal clearly any deviation from expected schematic structure.

Dunkel and Davis

In contrasting native speaker and non-native speaker performance on lecture recall tests, Dunkel and Davis conclude that although a score of 550 on the TOEFL test is accepted for entry to major research universities in the U.S., students with such a score are still at a significant disadvantage to native speakers in the area of listening. The authors argue for more training in academic listening for such students.

Chaudron, Loschky and Cook

Although this study was inconclusive in determining any overall positive effect of note-keeping on lecture recall, the results indicate that it is likely that over a longer period of time note-keeping would be useful. Certain information was found to be recalled better with the aid of notes, especially that needed for answering specific questions. With this type of notes – which often took the form of key-words or abbreviations and symbols – it was essential that information should be noted accurately.

Rost

In researching the value of on-line summaries as both a research and a teaching device, Rost makes a number of recommendations designed to help learners in L2 academic listening. Concrete strategies recommended are self-monitoring, questioning on the part of the lecturer, forming hierarchies (guided note-taking, building a lexical base), and the use of student and expert summaries to teach listening strategies.

Hansen

The framework Hansen provides for topic analysis, she claims, can be used as a measure of quality of student note-taking. In addition, her model would seem to have other applications, such as lecturer training, EAP materials development, etc.

Dudley-Evans

The aim of the study by Dudley-Evans is overtly pedagogic. The chapter shows the need for different lecture listening strategies for different subject areas. Dudley-Evans provides pedagogic materials which have been used to make overt the underlying discourse structure of the lectures he analysed and of which both students and lecturers were unaware. The author in this way provides support for the subject-specific, team-teaching approach to lecture comprehension employed in his institution.

Young

Young's model of schematic patterning provides teachers with a means of presenting students with the basic generic characteristics of lectures, whatever their discipline. Knowledge of this structure, it is posited, will allow for the application of schematic knowledge in lecture processing.

Benson

The conclusion that Benson draws from his ethnographic investigation of the L2 lecture comprehension phenomenon is that students need to be prepared by means of some sort of content-based instruction. Only by this means can they gain access to what he calls the "cultural grammar" of their putative discourse community and learn the necessary "interpretive strategies" of the language forms. Benson also makes the important point that ESL listening materials that focus on a single lecture or lecture segment are asking more of the listener than would be the case in a natural lecture situation where a single lecture would be part of a series and part of a total package involving other learning materials likely to help in the comprehension process.

Mason

Mason's ethnographic study carries a number of implications for pedagogy. Firstly, she notes the greater role for oral participation in lectures, something for which students are not traditionally prepared in preparatory ESL programmes. Secondly, in sympathy with Dunkel and Davis, she notes that a normally acceptable score on the TOEFL test for post-graduate university study does not ensure comprehension of lectures, such as those her subjects are exposed to, that deviate from the traditional talk and chalk style of lecture in standard academic speech. Thirdly, Mason observes the important role of student self-study in making up for inadequate lecture comprehension proficiency.

King

Although King, in his study of note-taking, makes no concrete suggestions for pedagogy, he shows the importance of a number of features: the need for students to capture visual information in their notes, the importance of evaluation in the narrative which accompanies visuals (but which is not present in the visuals themselves and is therefore often missed by students), and the importance for effective note-taking of knowledge of the culture of the discipline within which the students are studying. These are all issues that need to be taken on board by both ESL professionals engaged in preparing students for content lecture comprehension and the content lecturers themselves.

What has the collection taught us about academic listening comprehension research and pedagogy in general terms?

The conclusions to be drawn from the individual chapters listed above, both in terms of research and pedagogical application, are very wide-ranging. What, though, if any, are the general conclusions about research and pedagogy with regard to L2 academic listening comprehension that can be drawn from the collection as a whole?

A first generalization to be made is that the chapters in this collection unequivocally show that academic listening is a skill which can be clearly differentiated from both other types of listening skill and from other academic language skills such as reading or writing, and that it is a skill that thus merits its own place in the EAP curriculum and its own research agenda. The distinctive features of academic listening may be found at the level of discourse processing, discourse structure, or in the way listening inter-relates with other academic skills, as part of the culture of learning.

A second generalization that can be made from the collection as a whole is that there are many different conceptions of what a lecture is and the different contexts within which it takes place. The chapters in this collection together show us that a lecture may be interactive or non-interactive in style; it may be addressed to small or large groups; it may be presented to undergraduates or post-graduates; it may be given in an L1 context (e.g. the U.S. or U.K.) where non-native speakers are likely to be a minority of the audience or in an L2 context where the audience will be totally made up of non-native speakers; it may depend solely on the spoken word or it may make use of visual elements also.

Just as there is diversity as regards what a lecture is, so there is diversity in conceptions of the function of a lecture. The primary purpose of a lecture may be to convey facts or it may be to convey the attitudes and opinions of the lecturer. The role of a lecture can extend beyond the confines of the lecture hall; it can be viewed within the broader context of, on the one hand, the other lectures which make up the course, and on the other, the other study activities which are related to the lecture.

As regards research, the chapters in the collection show that the field of L2 academic listening comprehension is a very broad one, as indicated by the wide range of research questions addressed. Together with this, the range of research methodologies applied to these research questions is also very broad. Three main research methodologies are employed: psychometric (the chapters in Part II), discourse analysis (the chapters in Part III) and ethnography (the chapters in Part IV), but within these a range of different data collection and analysis techniques is used: multiple-choice comprehension, cloze-test and summary protocol analysis within the psychometric studies; topic analysis (Hansen), discourse community and problem-solution theory (Dudley-Evans), and functional/systemic analysis (Young) within the discourse analysis studies; and observation (Benson), interview (Mason, Benson), and examination of notes and visuals (King) within the ethnographic chapters. Researchers in the field of L2 academic listening comprehension have a wide range of research areas and methodologies/techniques at their disposal.

How generalizable are the findings of the individual chapters in the collection?

Given that the research presented in this collection was based on the many different conceptions, contexts and roles of a lecture referred to above, we need to ask the question, "To what extent can the research findings of the individual chapters presented in this collection be generalized?" The danger of over-generalization is something which is pointed out by the ethnographers. As Benson (this volume) observed:

The ethnographer quickly becomes aware that what is occurring in the class under observation would be unlikely to occur in any other context: should one factor change, everything would change. This lack of generalizability about education leads the ethnographer to distrust, at the research level, those findings which claim to have found general rules for specific teaching methods, texts, study habits, or indeed any other factor treated in isolation.

Does this mean, therefore, that the psychometric and discourse analysis studies in this collection are to be distrusted? It would certainly be sensible not to put too much faith in the findings of individual studies and to pay careful attention to the possible variables of the sort referred to above which may affect their generalizability. For example, in Rost's study, different subjects, at a higher proficiency level, from a different cultural background, or who had been taught English in a different way, might well not have exhibited the same comprehension problems as did those employed in the study. On the other hand, however, this warning about the generalizability of research findings could be interpreted as indicating a need for more concentrated research, with many studies investigating each individual question, both in the form of replications of previously conducted studies and with adjustment to the variables. This is a strength of Dunkel and Davis's research (this volume) on the effect of discourse markers on comprehension, which by changing some of the variables in a similar, well-known study by Chaudron and Richards (1986) achieved different results.

Dudley-Evans (this volume) refers to the distinction between "hard" and "soft" academic disciplines (depending upon the presence or absence of a research paradigm that underpins the discipline). In the so-called "hard" disciplines (medical research, for example), it is common for many controlled studies to be conducted before findings on any given question become widely accepted (consider, for example, the well-publicized research on the relation between cholesterol and heart disease, which is still controversial, in spite of hundreds of studies). In the field of applied linguistics (a "soft" discipline, if ever there was one), there is not much of a tradition of numbers of studies focussing on a single clearly defined issue. One useful function of ethnography is that it highlights important research issues which can be investigated more rigorously under controlled psychometric conditions. The field of applied linguistics in general and L2 lecture comprehension research in particular needs to put more emphasis on more rigorous controlled and replicated experimentation if findings are to have great value for pedagogy.

What is there still to learn?

The overview chapter in this collection made the point that there had been relatively little research into academic listening. The chapters in this volume therefore represent a considerable contribution to this field. These chapters, however, in spite of their undeniable value, still only scratch the surface of what is a very complex research area. Our knowledge is still seriously lacking in many respects. The following is a list of just some of the issues which still remain to be investigated.

- There are to my knowledge no longitudinal studies of a psychometric nature of the lecture comprehension process, i.e. of how comprehension ability develops over time.
- Although some of the ethnographic studies incorporate a longitudinal dimension (e.g. the Flowerdew and Miller (1992) study asked learners if and how their comprehension improved during a lecture course; the Benson (1989) case study focussed on a learner over a period of time), none of them make this the main research focus. There is thus a need, also, for ethnographic longitudinal studies.
- More studies are needed which contrast the very different contexts within which L2 lectures can take place e.g. interactive v. non-interactive styles, addressed to small or large groups; presented to undergraduates or post-graduates; in technical or non-technical fields, etc. What are the effects of such variables on lecturer styles, on discourse structures, and on learner strategies and levels of comprehension?
- Related to the previous point, more studies are needed of lecture comprehension in L2 contexts, where the audience is made up totally of non-native speakers. Most of the studies in this collection (with the exception of Tauroza and Allison and Rost) and indeed in the L2 lecture comprehension literature in general, focus on L1 contexts (North America or U.K.), where non-native speakers are likely to be a minority of the audience. However, as pointed out in my introduction, a lot of academic listening is going on in L2 contexts. It is

likely that lecturing styles will be quite different according to whether the audience is mostly native English speaking or not.
- Within L2 contexts, lecturing styles are likely to vary, again, where lecturers share the L1 of their audience. What is the role of code-switching, for example, in such contexts? What advantage, if any, are the shared cultural background and value system of lecturer and audience in such contexts? Research is badly needed in these areas.
- From the perspective of the listener, studies are needed which contrast the processing strategies and problems of learners at different levels of linguistic proficiency. Some of the speech rate studies reviewed in my overview chapter point the way here, by testing the effect of different delivery speeds on learners at different proficiency levels.
- Research needs to investigate the question as to what degree can/should students be taught academic listening and to what degree can they teach themselves. ESL professionals, materials writers, and publishers assume learners need to be taught. Mason, in her contribution to this volume, stresses that a lot of the learning that took place with her subjects was by dint of their own efforts. If students can indeed learn on their own, can research uncover ways in which this self-learning might be enhanced, by some sort of learner strategy training?

These are just some of the areas where research is badly needed. It is to be hoped that this collection of papers on academic listening will inspire others to take up some of these issues.

References

Benson, M. 1989. The academic listening task: a case study. *TESOL Quarterly* 23 (3): 421–445.
Chaudron, C., and J. C. Richards. 1986. The effect of discourse markers on the comprehension of lectures. *Applied Linguistics* 7 (2): 113–127.
Flowerdew, J., and L. Miller. 1992. Student perceptions, problems and strategies in L2 lectures. *RELC Journal* 23 (2).

Author index

Subject index

academic discourse community, 48
accent, 24–5, 205, 247
acculturation, 192
analogies, 283
anecdotes, 18
asides, 11, 18, 184, 272
attitude and opinions, conveyance of,
    18, 294
audience, relating to, 18
authentic lecture material, 266
authority, respect for, 284

back-channel cues, 21
background knowledge, 9, 11, 17,
    19, 283
blackboard, 137, 138, 221, 223, 225,
    275, 283
blackboard work, 221, 224, 228
bottom-up processing, 9, 56, 94, 244,
    265, 266, 270

clarification request, 272, 284
cognates, 10
coherence, 56, 96, 244
cohesion, 175
colloquial speech, 10
communicative competence, 7
comprehension
    in general, 8
    issues and strategies of, 205–207,
        210–213
    global, 248, 251
    local, 248, 251
    local and global, 266
comprehension check, 272
comprehension process, 8–10, 93–97,
    242–245, 270–271, 291
concentrate, ability to, 11

concentrating, difficulties in, 13
concepts, 13
conclusion phase, 165, 166, 167,
    170–171
confirmation check, 21, 272, 285
content-based language instruction,
    177, 196, 293
context, 162, 270, 274
conversational listening, 7
corpus, 39, 160
cultural aspects of study, 39, 271, 285
cultural comprehension, 207–209
cultural conditioning, 277
cultural differences, 223
cultural grammar, 195, 293
cultural knowledge, 195
cultural reference, 206
culture, 203, 206, 208, 285
    and language, 202
    of learning, 177, 178, 179, 181, 294

decoding, 9, 22, 37, 94, 277
definitions, 18
deixis, 136, 143
descriptive theory, 182
digressions, 11
disciplinary procedures, 130
disciplines, 17, 149, 167. 295, 296
discourse
    authentic, 242, 256
    evaluation in, 226, 231, 233
    extended, 266
    expository, 160
    influencing direction of, 214–215
    interactive 11
    main vs. subsidiary, 17, 193
    of L2 lectures, 14–20, 273–5
    style of, 204